ECONOMIC REFORMS NEED RADICAL CHANGES

ECONOMIC REFORMS NEED RADICAL CHANGES

B. Ramachandran

Publications

KALPAZ PUBLICATIONS

DELHI-110052

Economic Reforms Need Radical Changes

(*Economics*)

Rs. 875

ISBN: 81-7835-184-6

Published in 2003 in India by
Kalpaz Publications
C-30, Satyawati Nagar
Delhi-110052
E-mail : kalpaz@hotmail.com

Laser Typesetting at: Sharma Graphic, Delhi
Printed at: Mehra Offset Press, Delhi

Contents

Foreword

Is a critical analysis of Globalization and Liberalization Efforts undertaken by India Since 1991. Enormous amount of literature has been churned out on the subject since then during the last decade and more. Most of them are discouragingly repeat of the same arguments and practically all the present day economic ills of this country are attributed to these Economic Reforms.

In this context, the efforts of scholars like B. Ramchandran are quite exceptionally positive and critical and refreshingly offer alternative apporaches to this problem of Reforms.

It seems strange to me that while our academicians are by and large engaged in matters very mundane. Here we have a non-academician, a banker by profession, who has been able to supply solid material of a high standard to the Indian public.

To criticize and find fault is an easy exercise; but to critically analyze the Reforms from various angles and come out with workable solutions requires a masterly and scholarly mind. Mr. B. Ramchandran has done precisely this in his work. I consider that this book is a very good reference work to economic research scholars and presents an easy reading material to the general public.

I am particularly interested in and impressed by the Epilogue, which purports to answer problems raised. I understand from the discussion that the author is of the same view as mine that is, if the Reforms are to be a success, first and foremost condition is that the millions of the poor should be provided the Basic Needs and Employment; once these needs and employment of the people are met, they will acquire the power of Self Respect and not be a slave to anyone including the politicians; and finally they will enabled to exercise real Freedom and not be forced to sell it to the highest bidder.

These thoughts are interspersed in different chapters of the book.

This book is indeed a good worthwhile volume to possess.

Dr. (Fr.) M. Sebastian, S.J.
Chairman
Association of Economists of Tamil Nadu,
(Former Principal of St. Joseph's College, Tiruchirappalli.)

Preface

I am neither an economist nor an authority in any particular fileld but only a Banker by profession.

The credit goes to who has motivated me to to write the book on 'Economic Reforms Need Radical Changes".

Realising the importance of this subject and regarding it a great honour to have been permitted by a renowned publisher of academic books. I have accepted the offer, and started writing.

In writing the book. I have made sincere efforts to focus the multi-dimensional trend of our economy inter-alia analysed many critical sectors and areas from different angles, esp., Banking, Agriculture, Industry, Foreign Trade, Un-employment, Health, Water Management and Legal Sphere wherein radical changes are required to be made on a war-footing basis in the wake of Globalisation. Besides I have covered the ethos of governance, safety net, falling rupee, poverty syndrome, energy crisis, disinvestment, food security, Nehrus contribution, WTO and India, population explosion. New economic policy and several other economic issues.

Moreover, in conceptualizing and writing. I have studied quite a number of "Bibliographical" works which have helped me to a great extent in understanting the intricate problems connected with the Indian economic reforms which were introduced by the end of 1991.

I am beholden to all the enlightened souls throughout my long career in the sphere of Banking spanning over a period of 35 years for having shown me the kindly light and the spirit of wisdom in writing this book.

I am grateful to Dr. Rev. Fr. M. Sebastain. s.j., who is an economist by profession, and former Principal of St. Joseph's College, Tiruchirapalli who readily consented to take-off time from his busy schedule to write a "Foreword" to this book.

I shall always remain indebted to Ms. Kalpaz Publications, Delhi 110052 for having undertaken the printing, and publication of the book in a most elegant and satisfactory manner.

I am dedicating this book to my respectful parents who attained the Lotus Feet of Lord and their Divine Blessings will come to my rescue at all times.

I hope this book will be of immense use to the students belonging to economics, commerce, management faculties, research scholars, experts in the field of Private, sector undertakings, and the general public.

B. Ramachandran

1
Prologue

We believe that India has much to learn from what is happening elsewhere in the world. Many countries are bringing in far-reaching changes. We find major economic transformation sweeping large countries like the Soviet Union and China, as well as small countries in Eastern Europe. There is a change in outlook, a change in mind-set everywhere. India too cannot lag behind if she has to survive, as she must, in the new environment.

The Economic Reforms were introduced in India by the end of 1991. While the reforms have not moved as fast as was anticipated, there have been serious attempts in that general direction, and a promise of furtherance as and when circumstances permit.

There is scope for serious debate about many aspects of economic reforms that are currently being introduced in India, and specific arguments have been presented in different directions. Both the exact content of reforms and the policy approach in which they are embedded, call for much scrutiny. India has paid a heavy price for its over-regulated and dysfunctional rules of economic governance, and there is a case for removing that handicap.

The absence of any real commitment to social reform fits into that general pattern. The persistence of extraordinary gender inequalities in India, for example, is a major obstacle to social progress. There has been no decisive attempt on the part of the Government of India before or after the reforms to change these inequalities.

The Economic and Political Weekly Foundation has rightly pointed out the following flaws of the reforms :

1. absence of a broader development strategy,
2. hasty pace of reforms,
3. prerequisites of reforms ignored,
4. wrong sequencing of reforms, and
5. absence of human development goals as an integral part of strategy.

Recent policy developments in India, including those since the reforms, have continued the tradition of neglecting the fundamental importance of basic- capabilities in economic development, and of the positive role of the state in promoting these capabilities.

Judged in that perspective the current reorientation of economic policy is much less of a radical departure from the past than it is considered to be, and perpetuates some of the most debilitating biases, of earlier regimes. Correcting these biases, not just in political rhetoric but in practical action, calls for a major shift of emphasis in policy-making. Policy debates in India have to be taken beyond the over-whelming concentration on issues on liberalisation.

"Financial and trade liberalisation, with borrowing and lending at substantial real rates of interest made possible by stable price level, is not easy and is full of potential pitfalls. Nevertheless, it remains the only game in town as far as economic development is concerned".

Mc. Kinnon, 1989

The post-liberalisation evidence for the Indian economy suggests that, rather than following the optimal sequence, the external real sector seems to be liberalising the fastest, followed by the domestic and external financial sectors, with the domestic real sector lagging behind considerably. What is rather alarming is the very slow pace at which domestic real liberalisation is proceeding, considering the fact that it should have been the vanguard of the liberalisation process. This does not auger well for the long-run success of the liberalisation programme launched in 1991, and urgent remedial measures must be undertaken to speed up the pace of reforms in this sectors, esp., the external financial sector, because of the very grave dangers associated with liberalising this sector prior to the domestic sectors.

The issue of financial liberalisation is now seen as much more complex than what was originally envisaged. Because the needs of the real economy can be met only through liberalisation, the literature still holds as its ultimate goal the full liberalisation of the economy.

The basic purpose of economic reforms of stabilization has not been achieved. Today the urgency for the radical changes to be done in our economic reforms has increased manifold.

It has indeed become linked to the vital issue of survival of our nation as we have known it to be.

The Govt. has recently come out with a first-ever mid-year review. But with the few macro indicators selectively chosen do not by themselves paint a rosy picture.

In the wider national interest, the process of building a viable national consensus on major economic reforms needs to be further widened and deepened.

The last ten years are rich in negative lessons that help chalk out a positive course. Hence, what is required now is that the Government should speed up a common concrete political agenda for reforms.

The issues involved on various aspects of the Indian economy esp. issues of current and long-standing are dealt with in a broad perspective without going into excessive detail or technical specifics in umpteen chapters of this book.

2
Savings and Investment

It is the dramatic decline in the overall rate of domestic saving, which as per figures of the CSO in Feb., declined from 23.7 per cent of the GDP, in 1990-91 to 20 per cent in 1992-93 and 20.2 per cent in 1993-94. Savings as a percentage of the GDP, have declined by as much as 3.5 percentage points under the SAP, regime.

Even as the GDP, has seen growing at a satisfactory rate as per official statements, gross investment in India again as per CSO, data has seen an ever steeper decline than savings.

Perhaps the seriousness of this matter is ignored in the current euphoria about the inflow of significant volumes of external capital over the last ten years. This indicates a drastically altered approach to the problem of development which can be disastrous for the future of the Indian economy.

Be it emphasized here that the countries we should try to emulate, Japan and Sourth Korea, have each a domestic savings rate exceeding 33 per cent of the GDP. China, which is now attracting large volumes of external capital on its own terms has an even higher rate of domestic saving.

There has been a recovery in GDP, growth because of the increase in the output of the services sector. Official data on domestic saving and gross investment also show signs of revival and growth.

Though household savings have increased overall by a massive 28.4 per cent, the improvement in saving in financial assets has been lower by 22 per cent, and direct investment has increased by as much as 38 per cent. We must be a little circumspect in jumping to conclusions, especially in regard to the estimate of saving in physical assets.

The total estimate of household domestic saving, we have a large element of saving based on transfers by Indian workers abroad.

The Economic Survey indicates that private transfers increased from

$3595 million in 1993-94 to $6200 million in 1994-95, and further to $7480 million in 1995-96. We do not know how much of the amount was consumed by the Indian families of the workers abroad, and how much was saved.

Savings in the form of financial assets do have a firm mooring. A sharp increase therein reflects some definite trends and has certain policy implications.

The overall situation in regard to aggregate output, savings and investment, there is no doubt that output has recovered from the decline observed in 1991-92.

But a correct perspective in this context is important. Future fiscal and monetary policies need to be based on a precise assessment of past developments.

We are already up against capacity constraints in the major infrastructure sectors and these constraints can be overcome thro' higher investment rates. Additionally substantial investment will be needed to control environmental degradation in the years to come. For all these reasons, a significant increase in the rate of investment by about 5 per cent of GDP, is unavoidable.

The value of rupee has been fluctuating frequently in the range of 1 per cent of its median value which itself has been steadily falling. This has led to considerable uncertainty in the foreign trade sector and made both exporters and importers very nervous.

The cause behind the persistent uncertainty in the value of rupee could only be stock market fluctuations caused by the increasing role of foreign portfolio investment. The rest of the relevant economic factors such as exports and imports, inflation, FDI, and Govt. policy, have all been following predictable patterns. The effect of portfolio investment of Indian bourses is visible.

While the exposure of the Indian economy to the rest of the world has increased, the impact of the Indian economy fails to show signs of positive spin-off. Then, all these trends remain volatile, uncertain and loaded in favour of big players making FDI in India.

There does not seem to be anything in these trends that may add some cheers to the woeful existence of millions of poor unorganised and unemployed of the country.

Our liberalised external sector shows that the market in its pure unrestrained, unregulated modes of functions within the national boundaries bypass the poor.

Without a credible correction of fiscal imbalances, it will be rather difficult to create macro-economic conditions favourably to a high rate of investment, and low rate of inflation, a viable balance of payments position, and a reduction in real interest rates.

Control of Govt. consumption expenditure bristles with political difficulties. Subsidies continue to proliferate. Important economic services such as electricity, hydrocarbons, railway services and irrigation continue to be priced at unrealistically low levels. The political will to tackle the low profitability of a large number of public enterprises appears to be not in evidence.

The slide in savings and investment during 1998-2000 gives a negative verdict on the supply-side policies adopted for growth acceleration. Savings of the household sector, private corporate sector, and public sector are now lower than earlier levels.

The recent lowering of interest rates on small savings, PF, and term deposits too are unfriendly to the household sector savers who provide their savings to the net deficit corporate and public sector.

The overestimation of GDP, attributed to the tertiary sector also has to be taken into account to make sense of our very low rate of savings compared to the other 30 per cent rate of savings seen in the high voltage growth economies of East Asia.

Our country is large and diverse, but there is also enough administrative, political, and technical talent which can be used to initiate a change. It is necessary, not just for the sake of meeting requirements, but to preserve the political fabric and democratic principles of the country; to usher in dynamism within the system of governance, and to accommodate the aspirations of the local population in the decision-making process in a changing global environment.

All these factors suggest a change in the development paradigm and supporting institutional setup.

The basic requirements for such changes to be initiated are enumerated below:

(1) Good Governance; (2) De-centralisation of power and autonomy to local bodies, in itself means nothing unless some degree of financial independence is granted to those bodies; (3) Special institutions should accommodate a variety of conflicts emerging between the Centre and the States, between the rich and the poor, between different political formations and other conflicts.

And the challenge ahead is to develop a political consensus, uniting our people in a common national endeavour supportive of high rates of saving, investment and growth as part of a grand design to get rid of chronic poverty and to make India a major global power in the world economy.

An alert opinion and the strong support of the civil society alone can ensure that political processes move in the right direction.

3
Ethos of Governance

Good governance and decentralization seems to be the guiding light of our Indian Constitution.

The objective of good goverance in India was set up by Pandit Jawaharlal Nehru in his heart-throbbing speech delivered in the mid-night of August 14, and 15, 1947. It was "ending of poverty and ignorance, Mahatma Gandhi prescribed a set of yardstick for judging the efficiency of public policies in a system of good governance, to achieve the objectives of good governance." We have the Directive Principles of State Policy in the Constitution which are justiceable but nonetheless are fundamental to the governance of our country.

In a multinational society like us, good governance can only be achieved if decentralization down to the grassroot level becomes its style of functioning.

Today all modern states strive to attain good governance and revitalise all the channels leading towards good governance.

Paradoxically, decentralization can both be a offshoot as well as facilitator of good governance.

Though the Growth Stage Theory may be lacking in analytical power, its purpose is to distinguish the situations in which an economy may find itself.

While the concept of stage may be quibbled with and the theory dismissed as a blueprint for development, Rostow offers valuable insights into the development process.

Today, enough countries have followed consistent development policy over a sufficiently long period to make possible a comparison of the results of different economic and social policies and their impact of growth, employment, poverty, and income distribution.

In the 1990s the movement towards development ethics has gained momentum slowly but steadily in most countries. Development ethicists made a strong plea for just development that is comprehensive as opposed to being selective; people entered; and sustainable, not myopic. Just development should bring within its scope all sections of the community, especially, the poor and the marginalised, given them access to resources and goods. It is total in the sense that it should improve not only the material but also cultural, spiritual, and aesthetic conditions of human life.

The agenda of development ethics is through an interdisciplinary and cross cultural dialogue that deepens and widens the current consensus to apply ethical wisdom to enhance human well-being and international development.

The rising tide of the global economy will create many winners, but it will not lift all boats" (Global Trends 2015 Report, U.S. Intelligence Community).

To counter the hidden agenda syndrome of globalization, the perspective components are:

1. Prioritising social policy in favour of more social sector dynamics;
2. Education;
3. Health Care;
4. Sanitation;
5. Water Supply and environmental improvement;
6. Exhorting the State Govt. to enlarge the pro-poor safety-net programmes;
7. Reasserting an affirmative role of the state;
8. Filtering the transnational capital into national areas; and
9. Revising the strategic trade initiatives and imperatives of WTO, etc. with a more human face.

There should be positive people participatory development well-integrated with the country's problems and potential.

When we find that the process of globalization is hurting our economy, it is prudent to think about ways to equipping ourselves to stand upto the challenge and it is quite possible. The wayout is to give priority to the social sector wherein lies the scope for growth with equity.

In 'sum', with the march of the world towards globalization mania, where market-led development finds its place with a slim but vibrant state, emphasizing on physical and human infrastructure, the "ETHOS OF GOVERNANCE" has to be necessarily altered to make the Government, more responsive.

"The task of the Government is to supplement the people's efforts, to mobilise and make available the resources; to provide a blueprint and a plan; and to ensure that the enterprise and efforts. and efforts of millions of people have a well-defined aim and that they bear fruit."

(Smt. Indira Gandhi: April 8, 1971).

4

Economic Decentralization

Change in the direction of market-friendly economy brings into sharper focus the changing role of the state. Liberalization began with "deregulation" which calls for "de-bureaucratisation."

In India, concern has been expressed from time to time regarding the excessive concentration of political, economic and financial powers in the hands of the Central government. The subject was last extensively reviewed by the Sakaria Commission.

Deregulation and decentralization is not the same thing. Economic de-regulation transfers economic decision-making from the State to the private entrepreneur. Democratic decentralization, on the other hand, transfers State power from the centre to the peripheries.

The States continue to complain about central government's interference in essentially state subjects such as agriculture, health and education thro' mechanism of Central Sector and centrally sponsored schemes. It has often been argued that the design of these schemes is much too rigid and they do not pay adequate attention to specific conditions and circumstances prevailing in different parts of India.

Very often, there is poor monitoring of these schemes. In the process, they lead to insufficient use of resources. Also, if the bulk of funding comes from the Centre, the State's incentive to ensure most efficient use of resources gets diluted. We see considerable merit in these arguments.

In the Interest of both greater efficiency and increased accountability, there is clearly need to reduce drastically the number of such schemes. The Central Government's role should be confined to issue of general guidelines which could be adapted to suit local conditions.

There is the question of socio-economic structure of our society and the ground realities. When we talk of change of system, whom should we look to ? We are sure, the destinies of the countries are not being changed by legislations, they have been changed only when people have come forward to change the destinies and when social forces have come forward to change the conditions in which they are living.

If that is true, then where should we look to? Should we look to the capitals or should we look to those institutions which are nearer the people? And, if people have to bring the change, then the institutions which are nearer the people are the correct vehicles for change rather than the ones which are distant.

Today, the biggest dichotomy that arises in the power structure is the dichotomy of the Government, and the people. The divide between the Government, and the people whether it be the industralised countries, the capitalist countries, the socialist countries, centralised economies or decentralized economies.

So, those who are supposed to rule, they become the rulers, and those who write themselves as public servants, they become the rulers. How to get out of it ? The only way to get out of it is to go nearer the people. As the real decision-making is nearer the people, this dichotomy is removed or minimised if not totally removed.

That is the essence of the approach to Panchayat Raj. And, where will the social and economic inequities and the inequities in the system of the society fought?

Unless it is not fought in the villages, unless the forces of change are not generated the so many legislations made cannot reach the people.

We talk of political will of the Government, but what is needed and what needs to be generated is the political will of the people. Political will of the people once generated, can even dominate governments, which history has shown. And, unless that political will is not generated in the village to fight the inequities in the system, in the society, any amount of political will of the Government, is not going to succeed.

The Xth Finance Commission has suggested that instead of sharing only income tax and excise duties with the States, all central taxes ought to be so shared to the extent of 29 per cent. Currently, the States' share in central taxes (including additional duties) is about 26.5 per cent.

Thus the acceptance of the 10th Finance Commission's proposal will impart a greater measure of buoyancy and stability to the resources base of the States and to that extent give them greater autonomy in the management of their finances.

Decentralization in the modern world was preceded by a through going process of centralization embodied in the absolutist State. The fedual system was a very decentralized one, where effective power and authority—social, economic and political devolved on the local chieftain.

The success of the medieval monarch depended on his ability to obtain the allegiance of these local authorities. The absolutist monarch in Europe undermined the all embracing power and authority of these local chieftains, concentrating these in the "Enlightened Despot" thro' a centralised bureaucracy. In due course, was tamed by the middle class thro' Parliamentary institutions. Democratic institutions continued their downward march by empowering local institutions.

The major part of central assistance should be earmarked for strengthening programmes of social development with large externalities, especially, health and education, and support for programmes specifically designed for the weaker sections such as S.C., and S.T. For the rest, any surplus central funds meant for state plans should be placed at the disposal of national development banks specialising in term lending to agriculture, industry, and infrastructure and should be project linked.

Inter-State and inter-sectoral allocations would continue to be determined by the Planning Commission. Commitments and disbursements would, however, follow the normal discipline of project lending. The implementation of this suggestion will promote both greater efficiency as well as accountability.

The best way to remove inequities (or) any socio-economic injustice is to bring forward those sections of the society who are victims of the system. Middlemen will not do. We have seen that people do come from rural side to the Assemblies and the Parliament, but they fail to deliver the goods. That is why, let the weaker sections have their share in decision making and in power. Power in that sense, in a broader sense, is the biggest catalyst to justice, and to development also.

Today, we talk of Right to work. Is it not true that in the social set up that we have, that crores of people for thousands and thousands of years have been condemned to only right to work ? They have no other right. To the lowest rung of the social strata, for thousands of years, and in the present system, the social system said, we have no other right except work.

It is time if we have to address ourselves, we have to address to these larger issues, whether the productive forces in the society are going to get justice, whether they are going to find a place in the country.

Development cannot be imported nor it conform to a given pattern. It has to come through our own determined efforts tailored to our peculiar conditions and ethos.

The very process of our development calls for and depends upon our increasing participation in the World Trade.

We need to ponder more carefully how the institutional transition is to be achieved in a heterogeneous, continental society like India, parts of which are at very different stages of economic, social, and political development.

5
Safety Net

Both the World Bank, and the Government, of India have emphasized the importance of a "Safety net" for the vulnerable sections of the population in the process of economic reform.

Unfortunately, while some funds have indeed been earmarked by both the "Safety net" umbrella, there is little clarity so far as to the nature and purpose of this umbrella.

As per 1991 Census—of a total workforce (primary workers)—some 260 millions workers are either on their own, or employed in the informal sector where there are no paid holidays, no medical benefits, not even the semblance of official minimum wages being paid. So, the question arises for whom is the Government, devising a "Safety net" ? What are the objectives of the economic reform policy ?

Social security does not mean only such permanent measures; Transitory social security schemes are also necessary. This is especially important during a period of structural adjustments, when temporary unemployment is a real possibility. This is what the National Renewal Fund is about.

If measures are not taken to provide safety nets, they are likely to suffer when the long run comes around.

Social justice is the most talked about ideal objective in India and ironically it is also the first to be sacrificed at the altar of growth. Social justice refers to attainment of the principle of equity in the context of economic growth.

The present economic reforms in India was intensified since July, 1991. The main goal is to improve efficiency and growth thro' free competition in an open market economy.

However, in similar moves initiated by many other developing economies their poor vulnerable sections are often seem to be adversely affected in the short run.

Few however are fortunate enough to avoid any significant social cost of adjustment explained primarily by their initial conditions before the reforms started and often by launching more prudent anti-poverty and human development programmes as social safety nets.

In India, the market intermediaries are exploiting the situation for their benefits. The speculaters are black marketers, are hoarding the essentials at the time of harvest and earn more thro' their operation of marketing mechanism of demand and supply.

The well-known example is the cultivators of paddy, who do not get a remunerative price for their produce.

In fact, the prices of paddy go down but the price of rice in the open market is increasing. This is a peculiar situation in our country.

There has to be effective regulation and controlling of market intermediaries so as to enable them to operate in the desired direction of India.

In the process of solving problems pertaining to social justice, peoples' participation plays a vital role. The only vehicle which would enable different segments of population to alleviate their grievances will be their participation.

The reengineering process of solving problems pertaining to social justice should first concentrate to alter the outdated, and redundant rules and regulations.

The problem strategy is ideal, especially, in the long run where systems viewpoint is taken into consideration.

As a result of solving problems pertaining to implementation of policies, there is a great concern for the very purpose of framing such new policies. Such an act would certainly result in fulfilling the social needs like social justice in a country.

Here, the question of having an ideology comes into the forum.

According to Martin and Lodge (1975) "an ideology" is a group of fundamental beliefs that define the good life."

Each individual has an ideology, because everyone believes that certain things are absolutely essential if life is to be good, and personally fulfilling. Most people agree that freedom and justice are very important components for living in today's high-tech world.

The process of social and economic change has nowhere been a smooth linear path. Sustained economic growth no doubt creates possibilities for everyone in the end being better off. However, this requires careful social engineering to empower the poor to improve their absorptive capacity for participation in mainstream national economic life.

In the short run, technology and market-driven changes can create problems for those unwilling or unable to adjust to the pace of change.

Hence, there is a dire need for credible social safety nets to protect the more vulnerable sections during the phases of transition to more dynamic economy.

Otherwise, uncertainty fear of the unknown can create formidable psychological barriers to the acceptance of change seriously erode the effectiveness of the process of governance.

The best way to cope with a fast changing world is to have a well educated labour force. In this context, the greatest importance is to be attached to universalisation of elementary education.

Contrary to popular perceptions, India's allocation to education is not only low in comparison to the developed countries but also in comparison to the developing countries which it is trying to emulate in industrial growth—South Korea and a poor nation like Thailand allocate seven times, Sri Lanka six times, and Malaysia ten times more to education than India.

During 1992, the World Bank offered a social safety net to the Government, of India to "offset the adverse impact of structural adjustments" on the social sector. Since then these scattered externally funded projects were put under a single umbrella of District. Primary Education Programme (DLEP) with a plan to cover 110 districts in the 8th Plan period. The major contributor amongst the funding agencies would be the World Bank.

Suddenly, there is a great deal of fervour and activity in the normally placid and cynical Departments, of School Education all over the country, who await appraisal missions with their District, and State Plans.

There is every possibility therefore that along with donor driven development strategies, donor driven social development will predominate and soon a World Bank model of education appropriate to developing countries may emerge.

In short, the education scenario of the country presents a picture in which privatisation and commercialisation will provide education from upward mobility to a few urban and rural rich and for the rest soft loans frm multilateral funding agencies are likely to sustain a token of educational process, with possibly increasing influence of its content and process for the donor agencies.

At the international level, two major developments took place in the area of higher education. One was the international conference on higher education that UNESCO organised in 1998 (UNESCO, 1998; World

Declaration of Higher Education for the Twenty-first century, Paris) having realised that in the context of global EFA, activities, higher education was getting neglected.

The second one was a report prepared by the Task Force on Higher Education and Society-Higher Education in Developing countries: Peril and Promise, Washington D.C. World Bank, 2000.

Both the international conference and the Task Force have highlighted the need to pay serious attention to higher education.

These developments and the Wold Bank's constructing knowledge societies: New Challenges for Tertiary Education; Washington D.C. Draft, 2001—recent strategy paper on tertiary education argued in a sense a serious U-turn in the policies of the World Bank and of the government, that the discouraged growth of higher education in developing countries. But they attracted little attention of Government, which are engulfed in a continuing education crisis.

If the economy does not have the potential to absorb skilled human resource, assuming that the present teach anyhow education does have the potential skill development, while de-skilling of the traditional skill that accompanies modern education goes on, future is fraught with immense dangers. Right to education is a must but so is right to a dignified life and employment.

One right cannot be undermined at the cost of the other. And education that ensures both the rights is the real need.

The splitting of the Department, of Education in the Ministry of Human Resource Department, into two: a Department, of Elementary Education and Literacy was carved out of the Department, of Secondary Education and Higher Education. While the objective of creating a separate Department, exclusively could be to accord high priority and special attention to elementary education and literacy, the bifurcation of the Department, of Education may not help in working out a holistic approach to the problems of education.

There is a danger that special focus on literacy and elementary education may mean total neglect of secondary and higher education.

With inadequate and unevenly provided public services, carrying unaffordable user charges, with regional inequalities of the proportions causing economic balkanisation the poor will be forced into unimaginably lower depths.

The official assessment of the entire post-reform performance has turned from robust to matter of serious concern.

What is not realised is that the World is in any case globalised; that what is essential is increasing competitiveness and output.

6
Capital Account Convertibility

Financial repression tends to induce disintermediation, which can take the form of the emergence of a domestic information credit market or financial intermediation thro' external financial markets.

The factors that induce governments, to adopt a policy of financial repression will lead them to preempt the latter thro' the imposition of capital controls, and indeed such controls, with varying degrees of effectiveness, having long been ubiquitous in the developing world.

On Capital Account direct foreign investment rose sharply from $ 97 million in 1990-91 to $ 2144 million in 1995-96 and further to $3557 million in 1997-98 but since then it has shown a declining trend and amounted to $. 2167 million in 1999-2000. FDI in India is only 1 per cent of the total world direct investment. This only shows that the country cannot rely on FDI to accelerate its growth rate.

If this is true then the entire thrust since the economic reforms began to rely on foreign capital as a pañacea for higher growth appears to have flawed. While foreign investment in 2001 was $ 2911 million only as per the Report of RBI—the external debt of the country rose to $97666 million at the end of March 1999 to $ 98435 million at the end of March, 2000.

Debt servicing on external debts amounted to $ 10732 in 1998-99 which rose to $ 10936 million in the following year.

The rise in foreign exchange has also been achieved not by surplus over imports, but mostly from foreign borrowings and other capital inflows.

Globalization will result in greater exploitation of our resources by foreigners.

Table: Trends in Balance of Payments

Million US $ (Dollar)

Item	*1990-91*	*1995-96*	*1999-2000*	*2000-2001*
1	2	3	4	5
A. Current Account:				
1. Merchandise	-9438	-11,359	-17,841	-14,370
2. Invisible of which	-242	5449	13,143	12,106
(i) Private transfer payment	-2069	8506	12,256	12,798
(ii) Investment Income	-3752	-3205	-3695	-3918
Total current A/c	-9680	-5910	-4698	-2264
B. Capital Account:				
1. Foreign Investment (a+b+c)	103	4615	5117	2911
(a) Direct	97	2144	2167	2342
(b) Portfolio	6	2661	3024	1083
(c) Abroad	-	-190	-74	-514
2. Loans	5533	2201	1601	4531
3. Banking capital	682	762	2727	180
4. Rupee Debt Service	-1193	-952	-711	-617
5. Other capital	1931	-2537	2060	482
Total Capital Account (1to 5)	7188	4689	10,794	7487
C. Erorrs and Ommission	132	600	306	633
D. Overall Balance (A+B+C)	-2492	-1221	6402	5856

Source: 1. *Economic Survey 2000-2001*

2. Annual Report of Reserve Bank of India 2000-2001.

It should be noted that the authorities in many developing countries, including India, are currently implementing de jure liberalization of the capital account of the Balance of Payments. (BOP).

Two reasons can be identified for this interest in financial openness. First, there has been increasing de facto opening of the capital account; the effectiveness of capital controls has declined due to growing trade integration, financial innovations and financial opening elsewhere; and nineteen years after the debt crisis, credit rationing by commercial banks is fading away while flight capital is being repatriated.

Second, there is a proposal from the IMF to amend the Articles of Agreement to incorporate Capital Account Convertibility —as one of the obligations of Fund membership.

In such a milieu, many of the advanced developing countries are increasingly finding themselves involved, albeit sometimes reluctantly, in debates which urge them to remove existing capital controls without further delay.

In the policy sphere, careful distinction has to be drawn between opening the capital account and openness. Opening requires fiscal consolidation as a sine qua non for macro-economic stability and the establishment of financial markets to provide instruments for cushioning the loss of monetary autonomy implied by opening.

On the other hand, openness requires policy instruments to avoid inflation and exchange rate appreciation, exchange rate and debt management policies backed by consistent monetary policy implementation, in part to foster interest rate convergence to world levels. Given our commitment towards CAC, the recommendations of the committee on Capital Account Convertibility (RBI, 1997) showed that complete financial opening would demand a highly flexible monetary policy a difficult task considering the monetary autonomy is considerably attenuated when the exchange rate is fixed and capital is mobile which would have to keep up with the rapid pace of integration of the domestic economy with the world economy; as well as a sustainable exchange rate policy where the usually managed floating rate has to keep pace with the rate at which the shadow floating rate is depreciating in order to prevent a speculative attack on the currency and a subsequent run on reserves.

The rapid financial opening is fraught with difficulties because it entails extreme policy discipline. It is certainly premature based upon the Korean experience to write off CAC,

Indian policy makers are entitled to ask advocates of CAC, notably the IMF, what went wrong. The answers from these quarters may not be very convincing because the IMF, considers the South Korean debacle to be a product of insufficient liberalization.

Whatever that might be, although as long as the Korean model was working, no one, atleast of all the IMF, challenged its credentials. Regardless of the answers, however, the current circumstances underline the urgent need the re-estimate the preconditions for CAC, before we end up as one more casualty of the currency crisis.

The latest relaxation of exchange control regulations only reinforce the gradualist stance. When it advents capital account convertibility will be for all.

To a large extent foreigners will have easy access to not just the capital market but to the property market. A company such as Microsoft can tap the Indian debt market.

A resident Indian can buy Government, securities/ debt instruments as well as equities trading on an international exchange.

Very often capital account convertibility is confused with full convertibility of the rupee. The rupee has always been convertible against major currencies. Even it was pegged to the dollar.

Our Hon'ble Finance Minister: Jaswant Singh's (Jan, 2002) ten package is hence, more in the nature of liberalizing exchange control rules, one more step may be but not a sweeping abandonment of the controls regime.

Incidentally even the most liberal exchange regimes admit of some controls. The transformation now taking place in India is significant that it signals a certain willingness to allow resident individuals to invest abroad to a greater extent than ever before.

Earlier corporates and mutuals funds were given the permission and now they get additional leeway. But it is the permission being given to individuals to buy equities that seemingly suggested the onset of capital account convertibility.

The other ingredients of Mr. Singh's package measures such as doing with the limits for remittance under ESOP (stock options), certain types of loans to exporters appear procedural but relaxation of overseas investment norms sounds exciting.

Two points are relevant here: The relaxation has come with caveats. Second, are the new proposals workable (or relevant at the current state of the economy? An individual resident in India can buy shares of a well-known company quoted on an approved stock exchange abroad but that company should have a certain presence through its subsidiary/associates in the Indian stock markets.

There could be other practical problems that may stand in the way of individual investments flowing freely towards overseas stock exchanges.

In fact, the nuances of investing abroad are different from investing in India. Besides, the present juncture is hardly propitious for such activities even by the more knowledgeable fund managers of mutual funds.

The equity markets abroad have not yet recovered from the crash by the bursting of the technology bubble. A spate of corporate scandals in America has considerably muted even the most optimistic investor interests.

Besides, interest rates are at record lows. Debt instruments, including bonds, yield very little.

To top it all will be a foreign exchange risk which will have to be adequately understood, and managed by the investors in India.

One key variable has been the movement of the rupee against the dollar. The rupee appreciation will have to be taken into account—in any investment decision.

The latest round of relaxation on the exchange front may have been prompted by the healthy and rising forex reserves (nearly $ 71 billion during the 2nd week of Jan., 2003).

However, it is highly unlikely that there will be sizeable dent on the reserves due to the operation of these measures. It will be useful to examine in greater detail the implications of the unprecedented accumulation of reserves that has been going on recently.

There has to be awareness on what constitutes an appropriate level of reserves. Then perhaps ways of relaxing the exchange controls further can be contemplated.

At no stage however the concerns of the macro economy be overlooked.

7

Financial Sector Reforms: (FSRs)

Broadly speaking, the financial sector reforms (FSRs) may be considered as a process of intergrating financial markets with global financial and capital flows as part of the stabilisation and structural adjustment programme of the IMF and the World Bank, and lately, the trade regime under the World Trade Organisation (WTO). Negotiations under the General Agreement on Trade in Services (GATS), of which financial services are a major part, were concluded finally only in Dec., 1997. Financial services under GATS consist of insurance services and banking sector and other financial services which include a wide range of services from Foreign Exchange to money- brokering and inter- mediation services.

Reforms in India's banking sector are largely based on the recommendations of Narasimham Committee Report (1991).

The hall- mark of globalisation is the integration of the domestic money market with the bourses of the world. India has travelled enough on this road except probably stopping short of the capital account convertibility, thanks to the fear evoked by the recent East Asian Crisis. Foreign institutional investors (FIIs) and pension funds have been permitted to enter the Indian stock-market from 1993 onwards. As on March, 9, 2000, the number of FIIs registered with the Securities and Exchange Board of India (SEBI) has increased to 509. All the big names like Morgan Stanley, Jardine Flemings, Fidelity, Taurus etc., are very much on the scene and have their Indian counterparts. Indian companies are now permitted to list their stocks in foreign bourses. The American Depository Receipts (ADRs) and Global Depository Receipts (GDRs) have become important instruments for raising resources. Now India has stepped into the markets of derivatives and options which essentially are speculative market instruments, although their advocates would say that they help risk management.

An important aspect of the globalizing world of today is the dangerous decoupling of the real and the financial sectors. The global foreign exchange and financial capital transactions of a working day are estimated to be around two trillion dollars or $600 trillion for a year of 300 working days in a world of $28 trillion GDP and international trade of around $ 11 trillion. FSRs have steadily carried out the ground work for making India part of this global casino. Yet India still remains a minor partner in the game. Even so, the growing reliance on potentiality volatile external finance can increase financial vulnerability as happened in East Asia in recent times.

The FIIs have emerged as significant players in the Indian stock exchange market. Their net investments in both equities and debt since 1993 had been very high and work out to around $11.06 billion by March, 2, 2000. Their net investment in Feb., alone was around $ 708.2 million, the largest monthly inflow since 1993. These days the FIIs call the tune in the stock exchanges. The Bombay Sensex pierced the 6000 watermark in Feb., although it nosedived since the budget. The high fancy growth in share prices is largely due to the skyrocketing of the prices of IT software scrips like that of WIPRO and Infosys. Individuals and companies become rich overnight and may also be bankrupt in a jiffy,the unique hallmark of capitalism. The strange logic of valuation of assets on the market value of the shares owned makes many companies look disproportionately big and efficient. While many fortune hunters are led to think that a new millennium has set in, the rest of the economy and the masses of the people move undisturbed.

Probably one of the important beneficiaries of the FSRs has been the transnational corporations (TNCs) and big businesses who have started on a game of Mergers and Acquisitions (M & As) which have become a worldwide phenomenon for sometime now. The FSRs facilitated FIIs to move funds across the borders and enabled many TNCs to acquire Indian firms with resources brought from abroad. Though full convertibility for domestic businesses is not permitted as yet, commercial banks, exporters, and mutual funds have been liberalised to facilitate the integration of the domestic money market with the foreign exchange market. (M & As) were a rare phenomenon before 1991. According to one study, as many as 2369 merger announcements have been made during 1991- 97. (Ref. Khanna 1999). TNCS are engaged in a game of oligopolistic control over the world's market of goods and the opening up of the Indian market has been a big bonanza.

And, it is important to refer to a sector of the financial market that is hard hit in the process of the reform, namely, the Development Financial Institutions (DFIs). The Narasimham Committee (1991) recommended that the DFIs should either become commercial banks or non- banking financial companies. India pioneered the establishment of DFIs like the Industrial Development Bank of India (IDBI), Industrial Credit and Investment Corporation of India (ICICI), Industrial Financial Corporation (IFC) and several others to provide long term finance to development projects with long gestation periods. Under the liberalisation dispensation, the Govt. of India has taken a policy of leaving them to the market forces with the commercial banks and RBI withdrawing their support.

They do not enjoy concessional funding and in a high interest regime they would find it difficult to raise resources.These institutions are advised by many to take to 'Universal Banking'. Is this the best way to treat them because they have acquired considerable expertise in project financial and the scheme of division of labour in bank financing has not proved to be a failure as they are claimed by the advocates of the economic reform? But universal banking is likely to be the fashion of the future as it serves well the market interest.

We may bring home the need for re-thinking the role of finance in development. For one, there is a mixing up of objectives and instruments. Except for the pathological cases of misers and wild speculators, finance is an instrument to facilitate output, employment and human well-being. There is need to redefine the ends and means of the FSRs in India.

Real and financial resources are complementary factors that should ensure the various balances in the economy. The decoupling of the real and the financial sectors has gone to such an extent as is well exemplified in the cross- border movement of capital that is far removed by the real needs of production and trade.

Second, financial intermediation definitely is important in bringing together savers and investors, lenders and borrowers. In this task, the division of labour which the RBI and the early planners in the country promoted as between commercial banks, co-operative societies, rural banks, and the large number of DFIs here etc., has been historic and still remains important.

Third, interalia the role of the RBI has been the institutionalisation of credit and helping the flow of credit to productive channels and reducing regional disparities in the allocation of credit. Today the RBI appears to choose the laissez faire monetarist approach of managing the money supply on the assumption that price rise is dependent on the quantity of money. This approach needs a re- examination.

Four, the branch banking effort of India was an unprecedented event in the history of banking anywhere in the world, which is now sought to be discouraged on grounds of poor profitability. We have advanced some evidence to disprove this. Private sector banks normally would never have undertaken this. Activisation of an idle resource, be that cash with a saver or promoting the enterprise of a farmer, artisan, trader or any small entrepreneur, is an economic activity whose opportunity cost otherwise would turn out to be near zero.

Hence, from the societal point of view the public sector banks that activate these resources are doing a socially relevant, and from a long term perspective, economically rewarding task. Actually reform should concentrate on innovative banking.

The country is going to rely heavily on foreign savings which means a red carpet reception for foreign capital. Even so, India may not be their best destination, given the weak human development index, poor infrastructure and so on. Moreover, it is important to address the question, growth for whom and at what social cost?

We must note that the Financial Sector reform now being pressed by the IMF, the World Bank, the WTO and the neo-liberal economic thinkers, on the developing countries of the world, is wholly inconsistent with the very idea of capital controls. Is there then no hope for mankind? Perhaps we need an understanding and appreciation among the bankers and the finance managers of the world and more importantly among the neo-liberal advocates of a warped economic theory of the essential validity of the Wicksellian/ Schumpeterian theory: "the rate of interest" simply cannot exceed the productivity gains arising from new investment and that savings can get a return only if they are properly invested. Speculation can lead to capital gains for a few; and the capital gains of one-person must be at the cost of a capital loss for another.

In the process of integrating with the globalised world, we must not allow the Indian heritage to be lost or disrupted. In other words, even as we globalise, we must not embrace the concepts of 'individualism' and the maximisation of each of individual's welfare which is the prime mover of capitalist growth. To be able to do so, we need to resist the pressures of IMF, the World Bank, the WTO- all of them instruments of the developed capitalist countries for pushing forward their agenda and interests. Indeed, as of today, the pursuit of the policies currently backed by these institutions is likely to lead the world to a worldwide Depression of the 1929-33 variety. India, at any rate, must avoid getting into the trap.

While the globalisation of the world is, in part, a reality; our own efforts should be to gradually integrate with the world in a manner calculated to benefit all.

WTO., talks can succeed only if trade was de-linked from extraneous issues. West could bring pressure on the countries which had slided with India at Seattle to fall in their line. Hence, India must pre-empt this possibility by taking the initiative to convert the WTO., into genuinely democratic organisation so that a cartel of countries were unable to push their agenda.

8

Restructuring International Financial Architecture

Increasingly, analysts are questioning the present international architecture which is not only unmonitored but is highly uncontrolled. The speed at which trillions of funds move across the border without any restrictions poses new challenges to policy-makers and regulatory bodies, esp., in the recipient-countries. Analysts are also questioning the desirability of global currency trading, which, in recent years, has gained a life of its own, and much of it is not related with real economy. In 1995, the daily global currency trading reached $ 1.2 trillion. Futures and option trading around the world alone accounted for $1 trillion in the first half of 1998. In comparative terms, the volume of global foreign exchange trading in 1996 exceeded $ 280 trillion, nearly 10 times world GDP ($29 trillion) and over 40 times world export to goods and services ($ 6.5 trillion).

As substantial amount of financial flows in the 1990s are now speculative and volatile, the rapid outflows on account of "herd instinct", rather than drastic deterioration of economic fundamentals, can cause serious damage to the financial markets. Before policy- makers can take corrective steps to address the problem, the damage is already done to the financial markets as well as the real economy. On the one hand, rapid inflows can lead to excessive lending and to bubbles in equity and property markets, while outflows which are rapid than inflows can put downward pressures on currency, stock markets and real assets.

Since the collapse of the Bretton Woods system of fixed exchange rates in the early 1970s, more than 100 financial crises have occurred in both developing and developed countries. Due to globalisation of financial markets, even other countries in the region or outside cannot remain immune form getting affected by the contagion effects of the financial crisis. Thus, there is an urgent need to restructure the present, international financial architecture otherwise we will continue to witness more financial turmoil in the world. However, a return to the types of regulations that existed in the 1960s and 1970s will prove futile in the present context. Similarly, the way in which financial globalisation is taking place, a particular country or an institution alone cannot address the problems. Hence, there is and need to evolve a combination of policy machanisms at various levels to address the issues emerging from rapid transborder capital mobility and deregulation of financial markets.

Quite often the argument is made that it is very difficult to monitor and regulate currency trade, as the volumes are very large. If the modern elecronic system can enable cross- boundary flow of foreign exchange in trillions, the very same technology can be used to trace and monitor these flows.

To enforce regulatory mechanisms, regular monitoring of global financial flows is needed in both source and recipient countries. Unfortunately, there are no uniform disclosure standards. At best, increased transparency and disclosure standards can seve as effective tools to regulators to implement appropriate kinds of capital controls. But, these are no substitutes to capital controls. We must remember that the 1987 global stock market crash occurred when there was plenty of information.

Capital controls on the inflows and outflows-for example-Chile and Malaysia at the recipient countries may not be sufficient. Adequate regulatory mechanisms are also needed at the source countries from where these flows originate. Certain types of global funds are almost unregulated in their source countries. The recent near collapse of Long-term Capital Management high light this problem. In the global financial markets, there are over 2000 hedge funds operating without adequate regulations. Although the IMF insists that there should be greater surveillance of recipient countries, what about the surveillance of developed countries from where such financial instruments originate?

Apart from national level, proper policy mechanisms are required at the regional levels because the financial flows are, by -and-large, regionally concentrated particularly in Southeast Asian and Latin American countries, and contagion effects of the currency crises are more disastrous for countries in the region. However, there are no regional institutional machanisms to address the financial issues except the European Union. At the Asian level, the Reserve Bank of Austria has been advocating for an Asian version of Bank of Inter-national Settlement (BIS). As the BIS continues to be an European centric institution, with 13 of its 17 board members form Europe, the proposal of Asian BIS is worth examining.

At the international level, the Tobin tax can serve as perhaps the best instrument to discourage short term flows. Although the idea needs to be updated, modified and debated in the present context, nevertheless, it offers an attractive proposition to deal with many issues related to the volatility and instability of global financial flows.

9
Foreign Trade

On March 31, 2001 India finally scrapped quantitive restrictions (QRs) on the last bath of 715 items, throwing its gates open to one and all. Announcing the new Exim Policy the Commerce Minister stressed that QRs had to go because of government commitments to WTO but 'life will not be miserable. It would continue to be as safe as before. We are in fact, in command of the situation'. The situation referred to above is that of the Balance of Payments. The Exim policy and the confidence of the Commerce Minister are also reflected in the pre-budget Economic Survey 2000-2001: "India's balance of payments in 1999-2000 remained comfortable. The current account deficit in 1999-2000 was contained to 0.9 per cent of GDP despite of an unfavourable international trade and financial backdrop including a near two third hike in India's oil import bill. This was made possible because of a strong recovery of exports and a surge in net inflow of invisibles". However, to understand the real situation we may consider the Table-I.

Since economic reforms 1990-91 our exports have increased from $18,477 million to $ 38, 285 in 1999-2000-a growth rate of nearly 219 percent in the above period, and our imports have increased from $27, 915 million to $55, 383 million in 1999-2000-growth rate of nearly 199 per cent in the captioned period-the trade account deficit which was $ 9, 438 million in 1991 has increased to $ 17,098 million in 1999-2000-growth rate of 181 per cent in the above period, and is almost equal to six months deficit in 2000-2001. We must remember that removal of QRs was started in 1997 and so the full impact of removal of QRs is not reflected in these statistics of imports. This indicates that India's imports have been increasing at nearly the same rate as exports but due to difference in the size of the base or the initial import surplus, trade deficit has widened. So, removal of restrictions in trade has not to reduction in trade deficit, rather, it has aggravated the situation.

Table-I
Foreign Capital Investment

(All figures in million $)

	1990-91	1993-94	1994-95	1995-96	1996-97	1997-98	1998-99	1999-2000	2000-2001 April' Sep.
1 Export	18477	22638	26855	32311	34133	35680	34298	38285	21742
2 Import	27915	26739	35904	43670	48948	51187	47544	55383	38976
3 Balance of Trade	-9438	-4056	-9049	-11359	-14815	15507	13246	17098	-9234
4 NRI Deposits	1537	1205	172	1103	3350	1125	1742	2140	-
5 Foreign Investment	103	4235	4807	4615	5963	5353	2312	5117	-
6 Private Transfers	2069	5265	8093	8506	12367	11830	10280	12256	-
7 Subtotal of 3, 4 & 5	3809	10705	12672	14224	21676	18308	14334	19513	-

This part of Table: I shows that between 1990-91 and 1999-2000 foreign capital investment has increased from $ 103 million to $5,117 million- around 5000 per cent. Similarly NRI deposits in the same period have grown from $ 1,537 million to 2, 140 million- around 139 per cent and net private transfers have grown from $ 2, 669 million to $. 12,256 million-around 590 per cent. Foreign currency is also coming through other sources such as external assistance which stood at $920 million in 1999-2000, commercial borrowings at $ 311 million in 1999-2000.

All the East Asian countries have had very comfortable foreign exchange reserves and in addition to this they had balance of current account surpluses to feed the reserves, but within no time they were plunged into such a big slump that it took them more than five years to limp back to normalcy.

India was declared by the WTO., to be a country having no problems in balance of payment and hence the demand for total removal of QRs.

The real phasing out of QRs 2714 items started in 1999. In the first phase, 1183 items were removed from QRs. The second phase took place on March, 31, 2000 when 714 items were further removed from QRs and finally on March, 31, 2001 QRS were scrapped on last batch of 715 items. Now imports in India are totally free except on 600 items, which are of strategic importance.

With displacement of labour and fall in income due to closure of industries the level of aggregate demand as also the average buying capacity of Indian consumers will be pushed down.

For safeguarding the interest of Indians the Govt. has created a panel to watch the imports of 300 items classified as sensitive items. the Commerce

Minister said, "The panel would function like a war room; if there is surge in imports, duty on them might be increased and other safeguards found". Last year also he had announced "Industry has nothing to fear as tariff protection will continue to be available on all items". However, in a few months industry and the Indian people saw Indian markets being flooded with foreign goods.

On the question of the impact of the removal of QRs, we may have to wait and watch. Those optimists who are basing their assessment of the impact on the ground of the existing share of imports in the affected commodity segments should remember that the short run will not reveal the real impact.

Within less than 20 days of the removal of the last instalment of QRs, the Indian rupee crossed Rs. 47 against the dollar and the rate of inflation has dipped to 4.7 per cent. So the impact of the removal will appear firstly in the trend of falling prices, the likely effect of the down scaling of output and displacing of labour in the concerned commodity segment. We know that we need dollars for imports whether or not QRs exist. On the one hand while we are seeking dollars form world bank for things like roads, drinking water, primary education etc., on the other hand we are leaving it to the free will of traders to use as much dollars as they wish to purchase foreign goods in the post- QR regime. Should we allow WTO conditions in the garb of commitment to international agreements to distort our socio-economic priorities?

Whatever permutation and combination of nations may be, the global trade competition has generated a new design of trade which is to be fought by synergetic force, and not by individual alone.

10
Falling Rupee

The external value of the Indian rupee continued its free fall during 2000-2001. This process has accelerated during the 1990s. Though our export lobby welcomes it, the fall in the rupee vis-a-vis the U.S. dollar is a matter of serious concern.

There was a loss of International confidence as reflected in an outflow of overseas funds held in NRI deposits by non-resient Indians who withdrew a total of US.$ 1.3 billion NRI deposits between October 1990 and April 1991.

India's exports to the advanced countries as a percentage of her total exports declined during the second half of the 20th century. It is alarming that India's export as a share in exports by all Third World countries is declining.

The rupee-dollar relative value was stable during the first three decades of India's development. It took more than thirty years for this relative value to reach 8:1 in 1980-1981. It took further ten years to reach 18:1 in 1990-91, but took less than five years to reach 33:1 in 1995-96 and further two years to become 40:1 in Jan., 1998.

ASEAN countries devalued their currencies relative to U.S. dollar during the recent past. However, the depreciation of India's currency relative to U.S. dollar may be seen as India's autonomous strategy to compete in the export markets. This path of attaining depreciation led competitive growth does not seem to have succeeded.

The Balance of Trade for the Indian economy remained adverse for the 1990s as it was during the first four decades of development and persists to remain so generally at an increasing absolute level.

The high degree of exchange rate volatility has resulted in considerable uncertainty in the foreign trade sector. It has made both exporters and importers more apprehensive.

Given the enormous size of India's external debt. the increase in the rupee value of our debt. is also worrisome result of the falling rupee.

On the external front, the unprecedented currency turmoil which covered in its sweep all the economics of the South East Asian Region has opened up a virtual Pandora's box for the policy planners as well as private investors—alike. The problems afflicting these economies which has been loosely labelled as 'Currency Crisis' has made amply clear the vulnerability of the domestic economy in exogenous shocks. The genesis of the crisis though found in the fiscal profligacy and speculative investment, does not fully explain the severity and the magnitude of the problem.

Prof. Joseph Stiglitz maintains that exogenous shocks to the economy even when the economic system there is good financial market regulation, may be amplified by the economic system and give rise to effects which persist long after the end of the shocks.

During November 27, 2002 the rupee declined sharply against the U.S. currency on fresh month-end dollar demand from corporates and importers in fairly hectice trade at the inter-bank foreign exchange market.

Closing at 48.2400/2450 a dollar a steep fall of three paise from Tuesday's finish of 48.2050/2150, the rupee traded in a fairly broad range between 48.2000 and 48.2450 driven down by month-end pressures. It opened on a steady note at 48.20/21 a dollar. Dealers said that usual month-end corporate dollar demand exerted considerable pressure on the rupee even as dollar supplies kept pouring in from export proceeds and inward remittances at regular intervals.

If it was not for the healthy flow of dollar supplies, the rupee's fall would have been larger. Moreover, many operators, were covering dollar positions ahead of the U.S.

(*Source: The Hindu:* November, 28, 2002).

In the present Indian political context, there is no telling other than by the market what is the number that is warranted by a country's macro-economic fundamentals. For instance, it is Rs. 37.50 ? or Rs. 38.50 ? or even Rs. 40.00 ?. There is no an ambiguous answer. The exchange rate almost touched Rs. 40 to the dollar on December, 2, 1997. Market too, welcome the rupee's fall as necessary medicine after the South East Asian currency melt-down.

It is not that we have to match the depreciation of South East Asian currencies. That is because the export benefit that a country gets from currency depreciation depends on the import content in production. The higher the import content the lower the benefit. Certainly the devaluation of rupee enhanced the cost of production. As the Indian currency has devalued by nearly 8 per cent in the recent time, for all those units whose projects are based on imported raw material and coal, the production cost will increase by the minimum of 5 per cent which would lead a tremendous pressure on domestic market.

Although the rupee reached the lowest so far, the fall was mild in relation to the collapse of SEA currencies or the drop in some major world currencies. For instance, the German DM, went down by 13 per cent, the French Franc 12 per cent, and the Japanese Yen by 8 per cent. That itself had made the rupee overvalued and a correction was necessary quite sometimes back. What is of immediate relevance is the catastrophic fall of the currencies of SEA countries. The average weighted fall is 31.6 per cent since the crisis began.

Hence, the corrective steps may be taken on the following lines:

(a) The Government, should go in for slow devaluation of the rupee alike China.

(b) The Reserve Bank of India may intervene to stabilize the rupee if need be and

(c) Inflation rate should be increased.

Without the benefit of substantial foreign investment flows, the current trends on exports and imports will have a direct impact on the Balance of Payments.

11
India's External Debt

In 1998, for the first time International working group defined external debt as "to include the amount of disbursed and outstanding contractual liabilities of the residents of a country to non-residents, to repay principal with or without interest."

It was in December, 1991, that the Government, of India for the first time, felt the need to establish a policy group of review the existing system of classification of India's external debt.

The Report was released by the Reserve Bank of India in November, 1992 and the chief aim of this report was to ensure uniformity and transparency in India's external debt management.

The report has proposed an eight category classification of external debt by type of credit, as stated below:

1. Multinational
2. Bilateral
3. International Monetary Fund.
4. Commercial Borrowings.
5. Non-Resident Deposits.
6. Non-Resident Bonds.
7. Short-term debt including Non-Resident deposits up to one year and,
8. Export Credits.

As per the Government., of India: Ministry of Finance, India's External Debt-A Status Report, December, 1995—the growth of India's external debt from 1990 to 1995 provides that in dollar terms, India's external debt rose from US $ 75.86 billion in 1990 to US $ 99.04 billion in 1995, indicating a growth rate of 5.5 per cent per annum.

But figures of external debt in dollar terms really conceal the burden of debt since the exchange rate between the US dollar and rupee had also deteriorated from Rs. 17.94 in 1990-91, to Rs. 34.06 in 1995-96.

Consequently, in rupee terms, India's external debt rose from

Rs. 130199 crores in 1990 to Rs. 311972 crores in 1995, indicating a growth rate of 19.1 per cent per annum. This wide difference between the growth rate of India's external debt in dollar and rupee terms highlights the actual burden of debt. Whereas India's external debt rose by 30.6 per cent in dollar terms between 1990-1995, it rose by 139.5 per cent in rupee terms during the same period.

While making international comparisons, the White Paper mentioned:

"India's external debt, as percentage of GDP, was 36.9 per cent in 1993-94. This is comparable with Thailand and Malaysia and is much lower than the figures— for Indonesia, Philippines, Turkey."

(Ibid).

Table I

Projected Debt Service Payments

US $ million

	Principal	*Interest*	*Total*
1999-2000	6327	2816	9140
2000-2001	6202	2512	8723
2001-2002	5910	2165	8075
2002-2003	6301	1895	8196
2003-2004	9512	2843	12,355

Source: Ministry of Finance, *India's External Debt—A Status Report*, June 1999.

The Ministry of Finance, India's External Debt, A Status Report, June, 1999 has given projections of debt-service payments in the above Table I.

While making projections, the Status Report mentions:

"The projections do not include future debt service obligations out of committed undisbursed balance (disbursement in pipeline) and fresh disbursements."

But as these future debt service obligations become a reality, the hump in the debt-service payments in 2003-2004 would become still steeper. Obviously, debt service projections are under-estimates. In view of the Kargil Conflict, India may have to incur more defence debt to recoup its military arsenal consumed during the Kargil war. This may further raise debt stock and hence escalate debt services obligations. The country, hence, should not be lulled into complacency, keeping only the present obligations in view.

Thirdly, presenting figures of debt only in US dollar terms conceals the real burden of India's external debt. This is due to the fact the rupee has been continuously depreciating as against the dollar and other major currencies.

Whereas in dollar terms, India's external rose from US $ 83.80 billion in 1991 to US $ 95.72 billion by Dec., 1998, indicating an increase by only 14.2 per cent, in rupee terms, the debt increased from Rs. 163001 crores in 1991 to Rs. 407 101 crores in December, 1998, indicating an increase by 149.8 per cent. This sharp increase is due to deterioration in the exchange rate vis-a-vis the US dollar from Rs. 17.91 per US dollar in 1991, to Rs. 42.98 per US dollar in December, 1998.

The Indian economy has, therefore, to depend more on direct foreign investment and such other forms of long-term capital inflows to insulate itself from external shocks.

The first cause of our debt crisis is the gap between imports and exports while this cause has long plaguedus, it was greatly aggravated over the past decade.

The second cause of our debt crisis is that even as trade deficit burgeoned we were increasingly unable to service them out of current receipt from invisible items such as Tourism, aid and work remittances.

But an important cause for the shortfall in net receipt from invisibles was the mounting burden of interest payments on India's mounting external debts.

Our debt crisis has began to look increasingly like a debt trap. The substantiality of the debt burden depends to a large extent on the terms of borrowings rather than on the level of debt or GNP ratio.

According to 1991 World Development Report some parameters were evolved to ascertain the event to which countries have gone down in the quagmire of debt burden.

The debt problem had not suddenly fallen on Third World countries. If compared with mid-50 the foreign debt of Third World countries had increased by more than 100 times to reach 1.3 trillion dollars. The debts of many Third World countries have reached 80 per cent from 60 per cent of their GNP.

In 1980s developing countries paid 6.5 billion dollars as interest to developed capitalist countries every month. They paid 12.5 billion dollars as capital and interest. This is equivalent to expenditure per month on education, and health in Third World countries.

Paul Walele wrote in "Independent" published from England that in 1982-90 developing countries paid 40 crore pounds per day as interest to developed nations.

India's external debt dips to $ 98.4 billion. India's external debt stock at the end of December, 2001 stood at $ 98.4 billion, up from $ 83.8 billion at the end of March, 1991. According to an official release, external debt increased by $ 1.6 billion annually on an average from $ 83.8 billion on the end of March 1991 to $ 99.7 billion at the end of March, 2001. However, the debt stock declined by 2.9 per cent at the end of December, 2001 as compared to the corresponding period of the previous year.

Despite increasing debt stock in recent years, there has been a substantial improvement in external debt indicators. For instance, debt service ratio declined from the peak of 35.3 per cent in 1990-91 to 15.4 per cent in 2000-01 and further to 13 per cent at the end of December, 2001. This implied that the country could meet its debt service obligations by less than one-seventh of the current receipts at the end of December, 2001 while more than one-third was required in 1990-91. Similarly, the debt to gross domestic product (GDP) ratio which signifies the extent of external debt in relation to domestic output declined from a high of 38.7 per cent in 1991-92 to 20.7 per cent at the end of December, 2001.

Also, from March-end 1991 to December, end 2001, short-term debt to total debt ratio declined from 10.2 per cent to 2.8 per cent, short-term debt to GDP ratio from 3 per cent to 0.6 per cent and short-term debt to foreign exchange assets ratio from high of 382.1 per cent to 6.1 per cent. Among the top 15 debtor countries of the World, India improved its rank from the third largest debtor after Brazil and Mexico in 1991, to the ninth position in 2000 after Brazil, the Russian Federation, Mexico, China, Argentina, Indonesia, Korea and Turkey.

In terms of indebtedness classification, the World Bank has categorised India as a less indebted country since 1999 whereas it was in the severely indebted catogory in 1991 and remained as a moderately indebted country till 1998.

(*Source: The Hindu:* August, 21, 2002).

If we compare India with other developing countries, we will have relied less on external aid, and after Third Five Year Plan, our reliance on funds from foreign has become marginal.

The per capita external debt in India is, therefore, small. But the burden of external debt on people can be measured in relation to current earnings.

In this connection, in the very recent period, the Government, of India and the Reserve Bank of India had taken a number of measures to check high interest debts and moderation of interest rates.

But the success of such a strategy will depend on the continuing process of our economic reforms.

In conclusion, we may add here that a sensational incident occurred while leaders of World's richest countries, G-8, were meeting on the 16th May, 1998 at Birmingham—converged on Birmingham laid seize to royal palace and organised a Human Chain. They had only one slogan: Liberate poor countries from decades-old strangle hold of heinous debt burden.

People of capital countries themselvses fighting with their own rulers for economic benefit of poor countries is a rare incident in history.

12
Industrial Sector

The economic reforms introduced since 1991 have a growing impact on the industrial private sector, management practices, expansion or creation of new enterprises, new industrial centres.

In 1980, India was one of the most advanced countries of the Third World with its wide range of locally made industrial goods. Nearly everything was "Made in India" from cosmetics to heavy equipment-Imported goods had been cut by very high tariff and non-tariff barriers. India had relied too heavily on import substitution, without being able to promote, at the same time, an export- oriented policy as South korea and Taiwan did with so much success.

As a result, after the early industrial expansion of both private and public sectors with large imports of equipment goods until the mid- 1960s, India did not benefit from large transfers of technology from outside.

Many factories had become obsolete in the 1980s, from steel mills to the textile industry. Many manufactured goods were not coompetitive on world markets. Typical was the car industry. Between 1955 and 1985, most cars were Fiat 1100 and Morris-Oxford, both vintage 1955, entirely manufactured in India without hardly any change over 30 years.

The lack of innovation was no less affected by the growing controls (since 1967) imposed by the govt., on the private sector; creation or expansion of factories, price controls, reservation of certain industries for the small scale sector, regualtions on monopolies, severe restrictions on foreign direct investments (FDI).

Another aspect of India's industry was the role of big families, each taking a large part of the market for certain items. Tatas were dominant in making lorries, Birlas the Ambassador car (Morris-Oxford), Bajaj- two - wheelers, Mahindras Jeeps. They were facing little competition. All these factors combined led to a considerable lack of efficiency in public and often also in private enterprises. Between 1950 and 1980, the rate of total investments doubled while the average growth of GDP remained around an average of 3.5 per cent per year. The growing awareness of these weaknesses led to first a limited number of reforms in the 1980s and then, from 1991 onwards, to much deeper changes.

We must, however, mention some more positive aspects. At the time of independence in 1947, India enjoyed already sizeable- elites of all kind; civil servants, economists engineers, doctors, business people leading important companies in industry, trade, banking. Such elites kept on increasing , being trained in India and/or abroad, so that foreign companies needed only few expatriates or even none, an advantage more prominent than ever nowadays,when comparing India to China, or the South-East Asian countries.

Although the BJP after coming to power at the Centre in 1998—in favour of further liberalisation of the economy as well as globalisation, some of its members and some other parties keep on fighting for a more "Swadeshi" outlook.

Within private industries, a number of major companies argued that they needed time to adjust to a more market- oriented economy, so that the opening of the economy should not be too fast. Other companies, often recently created, forged ahead, using all the new opportunities by the reforms. Such attitudes were typical of the new creative spirit of young business people widespread in a number of rich or poor countries. Successes are particularly remarkable in Information Technology (IT) but a number of industries have also expanded in a considerable manner.

"In the past eight years, India inc. has been transformed beyond recognition", writes “Business World” dt. 22nd Aug., 1998. A survey of the top 100 private companies in 1990 and 1998 shows that only 55 have remained in the list while 45 have been replaced by new comers. Several of them are in I.T., like Infosys created by N.R. Narayana Murthy-Computer Engineer who started in 1981 with six partners and a capital of $ 10, 000. In 1998 its market capital amounts to one billion dollars and it is number Three in the list of top 100 companies. Wipro (pharmaceuticals, soaps, oil, IT) was a small company in 1990. In 1998 they take the fifth rank with a market capital of $2.25 billion. Gujarat Ambuja (Cement), Hero- Honda (motor cycles), hardly known ten years ago appear as numbers 27 and 29. Other smaller companies do no less well, like Titan Watches in Bangalore (Karnataka State). The factory can compare with the best Swiss firms. Its range of watches keeps on getting wider, from low-cost items to high quality watches. On the other hand, several 'big ones', well- known companies, such as Century Enka (B.k. Birla) which was number 11 in

1990, Oswal Agro Mills, number 22, Bombay Dyeing (Nusli Wadia) number 41 have dropped out.

The new entrepreneurs are not so keen to follow the practice of many older companies, which for long have relied on relatives, sons, sons-in-law etc. in 1996. "Family businesses accounted for 70% of the total sales and profit of the biggest 250 private companies" (the Economist, dt. 5th Oct. 1996). It may lead to troubles, poor management, intra- family feuds.

Indian companies have fairly often suffered from lack of transparency and croney capitalism. Today there is a growing emphasis on 'good corporate governance' as elsewhere in the world. At the beginning of 2000, new regulations have been introduced which strengthen the rules concerning audit, shareholders' grievances and rights, remuneration committees headed by independent directors.. The Securities and Exchange Board of India (SEBI) regulating India's stock market has adopted " one of the toughest corporate governance codes of any emerging economy "(Financial Times Dt. 16th June, 2000). Companies have to increase their number of independent directors. The new rules reduce also the power of the founding family which, with often less than 20 per cent of the shares, would run the company like its private property. Such changes imply considerable restructuring of old major corporations which, at the same time, are facing increasing competition.

However, the new code will encourage a better use of private capital and it may also attract more FDI as well as portfolio investments.

Already now growing competition is being felt, but it will go several steps further when by 2001 non- tariff berriers should be lifted and tariffs substantially reduced. Then quality and price competitiveness between Indian goods and between Indian and foreign companies will become crucial. A number of corporations are improving their market analyses, and improving their efficiency. Others may be too slow to adjust and will suffer.

While the market is expanding and becomes more diversified, forecasts remain shaky in a number of cases because of excess of optimism or for lack of careful marketing studies. In 1990, such a study forecasted sales of 8,00,000 cars by 2000, while it actually amounted to 6,00,000 with an overcapacity of about 60 per cent for the whole car industry. As to Kellogg, it did not succeed in really pushing its sales, which did not correspond to Indian habits, unlike MacDonald, which successfully adapted its products to Indian tastes. Other foreign corporations of semi- durable goods like washing machines got disappointed, because the latter were not adapted to local habits.

As Swaminathan S. Anklesaria Aiyar points out: "One should not overstate the impact of computer software and the knowledge area on economic growth" as shown in the growth rate of Karnataka and Andhra (5 per cent each per year) which is below the Maharastra, Gujarat, and Tamil Nadu States'. (Economic Times : 31.05.2000).

However, all these aspects of a new India and new emerging markets should not make us disregard the other side of the coin.

First come the slow moving states mentioned above, and the serious fiscal deficit at the Centre and in the States. Then come more basic problems; during the last two decades agriculture has been suffering from a lack of public funds for operations and maintenance expenditures as well as investments. Yet agriculture contributes still 26.8 per cent of the GDP and employs about 55-60 per cent of the working population. Since 1987, India has no more suffered from a very bad monsoon, Such times may come back.

Reforms of Public enterprises are very slow and as many as "78 public sector enterprises (out of 240 central units) have been enduring huge losses for more than three years" ... and "not a single such unit has been closed" (Mid Term Appraisal of the Ninth Plan, 1997-2002).

In its just published Mid Term Appraisal, the Planning Commission presents a most comprehensive appraisal of the economy, its achievements and its future. It issues a clear warning.

"Although the 9th Plan Growth Target of 6.5 per cent per annum is likely to be achieved, the sustainability of a 7 per cent growth or more remains suspect. Furthermore, the non- economic objectives of the Plan relating to the quality of life are unlikely to be attained since these are driven primarily by State governments' expenditures".

In spite of these shortcomings and uncertainties, business oppportunities- with positive social consequences keep on increasing. Multinational corporations established since long in India remain confident and keep on expanding. Possible new comers, less familiar with India are, not infrequently, reluctant to step in, which in the long run could go against their interests.

13
Agricultural Sector

Agriculture in India is central to growth strategy for socio-economic development and in a bid to take effective steps for making Indian agricultural more competitive.

Both in the year 1995-96 and 1996-97, agricultural exports grew at over 40 per cent and agricultural prices increased at over 10 per cent annually, much faster than the rate of increase in manufactured prices and so on. If this line of analysis was correct, there should have been a marked impovement in agricultural performance in the last five years.

But the agricultural performance has been poor.

During the 1990s, the growth rate of agriculture has moved down and has been below a half of what was stipulated in the 9th FYP—4.5 per cent per annum. But today small increase in production and super abundance of foodgrain stocks indicate an excess of supply over demand. It is a riddle that actual supply falling short of the stipulated supply turns out to be oversupply at the end of the day. Its simple resolution is that distribution failed to reach the people who need extra food.

After 1996-97, agriculture as a whole as also most of the individual crops have grown at a lower rate than the rate of population growth.

Moreover, for all items, the expected production growth level in 2001-02 is not upto the mark which indeed blames both high procurement prices, and poor offtake by the State Government for public distribution. It has analysed correctly the subsequent part of the episode. While volumes of foodgrains stocked by private trade lead to higher market prices during lean season as it reduces the supply in market. On the other hand, the public stocks lie unutilised in Government godowns due to poor off take.

There are various reasons for the deceleration in the growth of agriculture in India.

(1) The vagaries of weather; but a trend lineover a long period would tend to smoothen the effect of weather borne changes.

On a secular basis, an important reason has been the sharp deceleration in total investment, and more in public sector investment in agriculture.

(2) A decline in research investment has had more serious consequences and seems to be main cause for stagnation, and deceleration of yields of major crops.

(3) The major reason for decline in public investment has been fiscal compression, which has mainly fallen on investment.

In 1993-94 agriculture contributed to 31.7 per cent to GDP down from 56.5 per cent in 1951. The decline in agriculture has been accompanied by the failure of nonfarm activities to absorb surplus labour from agriculture.

Table 1 will indicate the growth rate of Indian agriculture.

Table 1
Trend in Growth of Indian Agriculture

	1994-95	*1995-96*	*1996-97*	*1997-98*	*1998-99*
All Crops	4.9	-2.37	-9.3	-5.7	+7.9
Food Grains	3.77	-6.19	10.1	-3.2	+2.2
Non Food Grains	6.59	3.21	8.2	-9.5	10.5

(*Source*: RBI Annual Reports 1999-2K, 1996-97).

Economic reform measures have two objectives: Short-term measures, and long-term measures. The short term measures aimed at stablilization of the economy while the long term measures are designed for structural adjstment and reform, which is called as liberalization, privatisation, and globalisation of economy.

The terms of trade are against the low value added agricultural goods. Moreover, if such policies are adopted which could make agricultural goods as a major source of export earnings for the payment of exports and repayment of foreign debts, it needs great caution as under these policies our resource may adversely affect the food security position.

The growth in agriculture should however, should be seen over a large time span in order to even out annual seasonal effects on growth.

The countries performance in agriculture during the last two decades has been reasonably satisfactory. The average annual growth recorded in agriculture and allied sector during the post reform period from 1992-93 to 1999-2000 was 3.6 per cent compared to 3.9 per cent in the period 1980-81 to 1991-92.

However, institutional

There are many structural and issues which are to be taken up on a war-footing basis in order to step up agricultural growth.

A multinational reform agenda for agriculture should be drawn up for improving incentives to produce, reactionalizing subsidies and promoting investments, besides extending protective cover to the poor.

Contrary to the expectation that recent changes in cropping patterns in favour of cash crops will significantly increase the employment potential in the agriculture sector, the reality is discouraging.

The "Cost-of-Cultivation-Data" estimates reveal that the increased employment potential works out to 440 million man-days per year. The FAO, estimate of economically active population in the agricultural sector 26, 58, 16,000 in the year 2000 implies an annual increase of 1.66 mandays per worker. Such growth is incapable of taking care of the incidence of poverty, and unemployment in rural India.

Analysis of data from the Annual Survey of Industries shows that there has been an overall decline in employment opportunities per unit of agro-based industries compared to that observed during 1985-86. This decline is accompanied by a considerable increase in capital investment indicating a—substitution of capital by Labour.

The efficacy of market-led model of agricultural development is ensuring securtiy of employment to the millions of rural people/population in general, and to those engaged in the agricultural sector in particular is questionable. The security of a decent livelihood for those engaged in the agricultural sector in the country appears to be in jeopardy. Above all, we have removed quantitative restrictions on a number of commodities well ahead of the time schedule to be adhered to under the WTO obligations. A good number of them are products from the agricultural sector.

A number of changes are required in the legal framework to remove the current restrictions in movement and storing of foodgrains by private entities, and to realise economy of scale.

Intellectual property must be protected to encourage research development and extension in the farm sector. It appears that in the original conception of the existing reform in different countries induced by IMF and WB, there is a respondents-visit of the unqualified laissez-faire paradigm of classical economics.

Different countries have adopted different variants of the strategy of economic reforms and hence, the effects of the reforms would be country specific.

No general statements about the impact of economic reforms would be proper. Even in the European subcontinent, which has experienced such reforms for a long period, the effects of the reforms for different sectors in difficult countries are not uniform.

"The National Policy on Agriculture" seeks to actualise the vast untapped growth potential of Indian agriculture development, accelerate the growth of agro-business, create employment in rural areas and face the challenges arising out of economic liberalization, and globalisation.

Reform process emphasized the growth of manufacturing and service sectors and thus neglected agriculture.

Big drop in public investment in agriculture, including rural development and irrigation will adversely affect food production. NABARD accumulated Rs. 13500 crores under its Rural Infrastructure and Development Fund, but was able to utilise it to the level of only 30 per cent.

In spite of so much technology, institutional finance, and infrastructural development introduced into the rural sector, agriculture still remains the backbone of 75 per cent of India's population.

The Trade Related Patent Rights advocated by the MNCs, like Monsotto and global organisations like WTO should be selectively implemented by GOI, so that the interests of the poor, marginal and small farmers are not betrayed.

The New Agricultural Policy of the GOI for 2001-2002 toes the lines of WTO guidelines, which are detrimental to landless agricultural labourers, and those states which have to make a breakthrough in Agriculture. "Growth is based in efficient resource use, increased demand and maximisation of exports." (Jayant Patil: keynote address delivered in the National Consultation on Agricultural Development in the States, Organised by IDS, Jaipur).

There is a need to nullify the negative aspects on the agricultural workers. Hence, along with globalization and restructuring the economy, concerted efforts should be initiated to restructure the unorganised agricultural workers so that they would also benefit in that process on the one hand, and on the other, contribute towards the success of globalization.

Following the Marrakesh Agreement, India adhered to its commitments by introducing consistent and gradual liberalization in the agricultural sector. As part of this, the quantitative restrictions on (QRS) have been replaced with high import tariffs for restricting imports of commodities. But, unlike it was argued, there has neither been a tangible opening up of foreign markets for India's agricultural products, nor has FDI come to rescue the agricultural technology in India which is in dire straits.

However, it may be premature to assess the long-term impact of the AOA on the Indian agriculture, on this basis.

The foremost thing is that the nature and character of the State Policy on agriculture will have to undergo qualitative changes rather than quantitative changes in order not only to realise the opportunities for exports, and foreign investments, but also to cope up with the implications of our agriculture coming into alignment with the international market.

A sustained increase in agricultural production and productivity is vital for the ahievement of our social and economic objectives.

Research and extension support has to be so organised as to extend progressively the production frontiers of agriculture. Public investment in irrigation and power has to be encouraged to enable farmers to invest in new agricultural technologies with reduced uncertainty.

Economic growth must not be a top-down process. It must provide opportunities for all people to participate freely in deciding their future. The rural community must be built around economic activities.

Organising people into small interest groups for securing economic gains would be highly useful.

Besides stepping up public investment, concrete efforts should be directed at attracting private capital for agriculture by encouraging contact with corporate farming.

India has a fairly well developed system of support for agriculture. In the last ten years, support and procurement prices were adjusted so as to provide enhanced incentives to farmers to increase production. Changes in the rupee's exchange rate and reduction of import duties on industrial inputs further improved agriculture's terms of trade vis-a-vis other sectors. Restrictions on agricultural trade—both internal and external were also reduced. However, there are still many restrictions on a free movement of agricultural goods within the country as well as international trade. A phased programme has to be evolved to remove them. Simultaneously, special emphasis has to be laid on the development of an efficient and dynamic agro-processing industry in close proximity to rural areas, offering significant scope for off-farm employment and also acting as a catalyst of social and economic change. Only then will our agriculture fully benefit from the liberalised economic policies.

India can take legitimate pride in the contribution made by agricultural scientists in modernising our agriculture. We have an extensive agricultural research and extension system but it is over extended and under funded. We have to ensure that our scientists and technologists do operate on the frontiers of knowledge taking full advantage of the immense potential of bio-technology and new information technologies. Greater attention has to be paid to increase the productivity of dry land agriculture, reduce losses in storage and transportation, and to control the degradation of India's land, forest, and water resources. The orientation of research and extension services has to shift from crop specific activities to developing farming systems as part of sustainable livelihood strategies. State level Councils for science and technology can be of considerable assistance in promoting the use of modern science and technology for the empowerment of the rural poor.

India's overall public expenditure on agriculture as a proportion of agricultural GDP does not compare unfavourably with other developing countries.

It has to be understood that a market driven liberalisation process in agriculture is bound to be strongly biased towards rich farmers and prosperous regions. The peasant movement would have to intervene effectively and play a crucial role in assuring that the interests of small farmers and disadvantaged regions are also protected and they are also enabled to partake the benefits of trade liberalisation.

*Around 7 per cent of India's Labour force in agriculture is into cotton and they cannot be left high and dry in a highly imperfect global market.

*We have competitive advantages in the grains economy which can be strengthened with technologies like hybrid paddy.

*Export markets in the current phase are not for the weak. It is quite obvious that the potential some policy makers had promised in the early 90s from agricultural exports and used it to justify their policies of unilateral 'reform' has not been realised. A more strategic approach would have been better then and is absolutely necessary now.

*(Source : The New Indian Express: May 20, 2003).

14
Poverty Syndrome

Year after year, experts from Planning Commission, World Bank and other institutions, as well as individual researchers debate over the magnitude and the trend of poverty figures in the country. The debate has got particularly heated up during the 1990s, because the impact of liberalisation on the incidence of—poverty has become a matter of high concern.

The incidence of poverty is estimated by the Planning Commission on the basis of NSS surveys on household consumer expenditure conducted quinquennially. Since 1990, such surveys have also been conducted annually albeit with a smaller sample size. Official estimates of poverty are available only for 1993-94, based on the quin-quennial 50th round of NSS with large sample size. The Planning Commission does not estimate poverty on the basis of annual surveys - because of their small sample size. However, individual researchers have obtained poverty estimates from this data using the same methodolgy as the planning commission. (Table : I)

According to both sets of estimates, poverty ratio in rural India shows a rising trend. Given the slowdown in agricultural growth, rising food prices, a decline in rural infrastructure investment and reduced employment opportunities, a rise in rural poverty is not surprising.

A review of the 9th Plan projections indicates that they are too optimistic and hope to practically eliminate poverty by the year 2012 AD. This would require a transfer to consumption expenditure from the top 10 per cent to the bottom 19 per cent of the population. Although the 9th Plan has indicated the desirability of these transfers of consumption expenditure, it has not suggested the specific mechanism for the transfers. The best mechanism is to enlarge employment, more esp. by revitalising agriculture and small industries. It may be noted that these two sectors account for 80 per cent of total employment. These sectors suffer from low level employment, disguised unemployment and underemployment which is responsible for the low earnings of the people. Unless these sectors are revitalised reduction of poverty would be very difficult.

Table 1
Poverty Estimates for the 1990s

(NSS Round) Year	*Rural*		*Urban*	
	Gupta	*Tendulkar Sundaram*	*Gupta*	*Tendulkar Sundaram*
(46) July 1990-June 1991	35.0	37.5	35.3	35.0
(47) July 1991-Dec. 1991	-	40.1	-	34.8
(48) Jan.1992-Dec. 1992	41.7	46.1	37.8	36.4
(49) Jan. 1993-June 1993	-	44.2	-	38.9
(50) July 1993-June 1994	37.3	39.7	32.4	30.9
(51) July 1994-June 1995	38.0	43.6	34.2	34.1
(52) July 1995-June 1996	38.3	40.1	30.0	28.7
(53) Jan. 1997-Dec. 1997	38.5	38.3	33.9	31.0
(54) Jan. 1998-June 1998	45.3	44.9	34.6	31.5

Source: Gupta, S.P. (1999), 'Trickle Down Theory Revisited: The Role of Employment and Poverty; VB Singh Memorial Lecture, Indian Society of Labour Economics (November 18-20).
Sundaram, K & S. Tendulkar (2000), 'Poverty in India: An Assessment and Analysis', *mimeo*, Delhi School of Economics.

Secondly, the projections of poverty, more esp. from high poverty ratio States like Bihar, Orissa, Madhya Pradesh and Uttar Pradesh, seem to be very ambitious. For instance, to bring down the poverty ratio in Bihar from 44.1 per cent in 1996-97, to 6.5 per cent in a period of fifteen years appears to be highly improbable, if not impossible. In case poverty ratio is brought down to 4.4 per cent for the country as a whole, then India can certainly claim a miracle happening in the next decade and a half. The exercise has not taken note of the leakages and other socio-economic factors which have delayed the reduction of poverty in these States. These factors are still persisting and have to be taken into account.

Thirdly, there seems to be excessive faith in the trickle- down approach of economic growth. Under the new economic reforms, growth is being achieved by the substitution of capital intensive technology and this is resulting in displacement of labour in the organised sector. Unless the economy reaches an employment growth rate of 3 - 4 per cent per annum, the chances of making such a heavy dent on poverty, as contemplated in the 9th Plan Projections - do not appear to be bright.

Table 2

Projections of Statewise poverty Ratios in the Perspective Period

	State	*1996-97*	*2001-02*	*2006-07*	*2011-12*
1.	Punjab	8.0	3.0	0.9	0.2
2.	Gujarat	17.1	9.1	3.9	1.3
3.	Andhra Pradesh	17.4	11.1	5.4	2.4
4.	Haryana	18.4	10.2	5.0	2.6
5.	Rajasthan	20.3	10.9	4.7	1.5
6.	Kerala	21.2	11.4	4.8	1.4
7.	Himachal Pradesh	22.4	14.0	7.3	3.1
8.	West Bengal	25.1	13.5	6.3	2.9
9.	Assam	26.5	10.7	3.8	2.1
10	Karnataka	30.7	17.9	8.7	3.5
11.	Tamil Nadu	30.7	18.1	9.0	3.6
12.	Uttar Pradsh	32.5	21.9	12.9	6.9
13.	Maharashtra	32.7	20.7	11.4	5.4
14.	Madhya Pradesh	33.4	22.0	12.8	6.8
15.	Orissa	40.2	22.9	10.8	4.6
16.	Bihar	44.1	27.5	14.1	6.5
	All India	29.2	18.0	9.5	4.4

Note: 1. States have been arranged in ascending order of poverty ratios in 1996-97. 2. Figures have beenrounded off to one decimal point. *Source:* Planning Commission (1998), Ninth Five Year Plan (1997-2002), Vol. I., p.34.

Lastly, to assume a growth rate of 7-8 per cent to be available throughout the 15 year period may not get translated into reality. Already 1997-98 is expected to end up with a 5 per cent growth rate of GDP and barely 4.2 per cent growth in industrial production. The prospects for 1998-99 also do not seem to be bright, more so due to a setback to foreign capital inflow as a consequence of the sanctions imposed by the USA following the nuclear tests in May, 1998; in the circumstances the country may not be able to sustain the 7 per cent growth rate. Despite all this, it may be mentioned that the growth process, if it can be accelerated and maintained at the 7-8 per cent level for the next 15 years and is also accompanied by measures to take special care of the problems of lagard States like Bihar, Uttar Pradesh, Orissa, Karnataka, Madhya Pradesh, Maharastra and Tamil Nadu, then it may be possible to make a definite and perceptible dent on poverty during the 15 years period 1997-98 to 2011-12.

However, there is evidence to show that the extent of poverty is both severe and staggering the world over. Whether it is a question of the developing countries or of the industrialised economies, the various studies- Ahluwalia 1976; Fields, 1980; Midgley, 1988; Hardiman and Midgley, 1989; to name a few report that: (a) there exists an overlap between poverty and inequality, and that they are closely related; and (b) incidence of poverty correlates with low levels of health, education, and nutrition, inadequate shelter and other unsatisfactory social conditions. It is also an accepted fact (ILO) : 1993 that poverty in most of the developing countries, despite being urbanised, still remains overwhelmingly a rural phenomenon. It is baffling to see (Fields, 1980; Gazette Canada, 1993) that the poor are not only concentrated in countries with low rates of GNP and per capita GNP levels, but also in fast growing countries with relatively high rates of GNP.

There is also a consensus on the suggestions (Economic Times, 1994) that poverty tends to be concentrated in the areas with little or no access to health, education, and infrastructural sevices like transport and communications. Beyond that, research about specific characteristics of the poor (Ravallion, 1992) is limited only to bi- variate correlations, and not to joint interrelationships with other characteristics of poverty. To give a few examples (Van de Walle and Ravallion, 1992; House, 1989; Schofield, 1979; Lipton, 1983; Levinson, 1974; Bardhan, 1992; 1982; Das Gupta, 1987; Muhuwi and Preston, 1991; Van der Werff, 1995), it is shown that the larger household size is associated with greater incidence of poverty as measured in terms of household consumption or income per person; Child-adult ratios are larger in poor households; poor-households are larger and younger, and higher mortality, esp. of children, among the poor households, stimulates excess replacement births; there is a strong association between high fertility and poverty; there is widespread feminisation of poverty esp., in male-dominated societies- in the sense that young females are more exposed to poverty- induced nutritional and health risks; poor households depend heavily on unskilled labour income; poor households often over- exploit their immediate physical environment and the subsequent degradation intensifies poverty; poor households increasingly lose access to private and common resources; and poverty in urban areas is often associated with pollution due to the concentration of people, industry and traffic.

Poverty, gets concealed and the pattern of consumption distorted towards visible and conspicuous items to restore their self-esteem at least in an extremely short pariod not in a sustained way. Beyond that the fall outs of this dramatised behaviour are highly damaging both for the poor and for the economy as a whole in terms of reduced gross domestic savings, which exercise their adverse impact on investment and growth.

Beyond the post apartheid era, there might have been some improvement in the scenario possibly because of two basic macro- level strategies of the Govt., namely, Reconstruction and Development Programme, (1994) and Growth Employment, and Redistribution. A Macro Economic Strategy (1996), but , (1) a large number of people still live in abject poverty; and are subject to periodic malnutrition; (2) the Gini Coefficient is still as high as 0.54 and indicates alarming income inequalities; and (3) unemployment, no matter how it is measured, is still very high (ranging from 24per cent in urban areas to 41 per cent in rural areas), and none of the sectors are growing adequately to alleviate it (Kingdon and Knight, 1998). Conditions are worse in the backward regions of the country like the North-West Province where 57 per cent of its 3.3 million people live below the poverty line and the unemployment rate is not only high but has been rising over the years; in 1994 it was 34 per cent and in 1996 it rose to 36.4 per cent and in rural areas it has been more than 50 per cent.

This is one side of the story. The other side relates to the high cost of these severe conditions to individuals, esp. the poorer lot. They suffer not only from the lack of income, but are also marginalised by society. This eventually translates into a heavy burden on the social fabric in communities and is extremely damaging for the society as a whole. It gets distinctly exhibited in the loss of income and, therefore, of savings too, resulting eventually in personal debt-traps, and the involvement of the majority of the poor in crime and its related activities.

When poverty, including wide disparities and high unemployment rates, gets combined with a perception that the State, on the one hand, does not do much for the poor, and the poor get highly marginalised, isolated and excluded socially, on the other, there emerge very strong incentives that force the disadvantaged poor to crime and violence (Kramer, 2000). It is also true that the less social support there is in a community, the higher will be the crime rate (Cullen, 1994). There is, therefore, a critical link between poverty, inequality, unemployment, exclusion, and violence that stems from the pursuit of monetary success thro' effective, illegal means. In the South African context, (Morris, 1996); Cross et al, 1996; and Louw and Bekker, 1996; Louw, 1996 A, 1996B, 1996 C all this is very true to a large extent, but combined with it is also its long history of apartheid and multi-racial texture. Despite its relative wealth, solid economic growth in recent years, and won plaudits from the international financial community for its effective budgetary policies, the country faces the serious problems of crime, violence, and corruption of course with inter-province variations which are directly proportionate to the various social indices of poverty inequality and unemployment.

And the fact remains that India has failed to meet poverty and hunger reduction targets. It has 250 million people below the poverty line, the largest in the world. About 208 million of these are seriously undernourished. However, the percentage of under-nourished population has decreased from 38 per cent in 1979-81 to 26 per cent in 1990-02 and 21 per cent in 1996-98. The biggest constraint in poverty reduction is an addition of 16-17 million people to the total population every year (Singh, 2001).

On the employment front, according to the UNDP's Human Development Report (2000) employment in the formal sector has grown impressively in the past decade with the result that the rate of employment increased 2.4 per cent a year during 1987- 1996, outpacing labour force growth of 2.2 per cent. But, according to the results of the survey conducted by the National sample Survey Organisation (NSSO, 2000), employment has declined marginally in both urban and rural areas during 1999-2000. In urban areas, employment for females was lower by more than 1 per centage while it remained on the same level for males.

Despite all this, there still widespread poverty and income disparities in the country. It comes worse when we add Amartya Sen's contention to say that poverty is much more than lack of income. It is also lack of voice, it also lack of empowerment, and it is also lack of good governance. Promoting opportunities for poor is not sufficient.

They need to be empowered thro' elections, decentralisation to the grass roots, responsive administration, an effective judiciary and good governance in general. And, they also need a grater voice in managing their future, and greater inclusion in the decision- making process. India has failed in reducing poverty in such a wider connotation.

What has been stated above should not be a cause of being complacent. There is still a long way to go, and much more has to be done to ameliorate the lot of the proletariat keeping in view the wider connotation of poverty as enuciated by Amartya Sen. There is a need to have fresh programme to encourage self-esteem and community solidarity, to eliminate discrimination against poor, and to increase the empowerment of the underclass.

"The greatest of evils and the worst of crimes is poverty...All the other crimes are virtues beside it; all the other dishonors are chivalry itself by comparison. Poverty blights whole cities; spreads horrible pestilence; strikes at the soul of all of those who come within sight, sound or smell of it".

(George Bernard Shaw: 1856-1950: Irish dramatist, critic.)

15

Public Distribution System

The present Govt's as well as of the earlier Govts.' Liberalisation policies are also to be blamed for the sustained inflation in recent years. There has been unabated growth of monopolies as a result of removal of restrictions such as abolition of Monopolies and Restrictive Trade Practices (MRTP), assets limits etc. on them. Growth in monopoly power leads to increased profit margins and thereby to profit inflation.

Over the years, the structure of national income has been changing in favour of services and against goods. The share of services in the national income has been rising continuously. The share of the service factor in GDP increased from a level of 41 per cent in 1990-91 to around 49 percent in 2000-2001.Higher service incomes, however, create more demand for goods than for services resulting in demand-supply imbalances in the economy. These macro-economic imbalances cause price instability; if supply of goods does not keep pace with growing demand, prices will rise.

The adverse effects of high inflation are many. Volatility in prices creates uncertainty in decision-making. High inflation has negative effects on savings and makes speculative investment lucrative. It adversely affects the competitiveness of our exports. More usually however, it is accompanied by depreciation of the rupee often at a rate higher than the rate of inflation, thus making imports expensive. That further fuels inflation and depreciation. This cycle thus goes on. But more importantly, inflation increases disparity, it redistributes income in favour of the rich who control industry and business. Although pro- business and pro-rich policies of the Govt. are largely responsible for growing inequality in the country in recent years, high inflation has also contributed significantly to the phenomenon of iniquitous growth. This is evident from the abundance of high- priced consumer durables such as cars in the market. These goods are beyond the reach of the vast majority of people, and can be acquired only by the rich, whose purchasing power has increased phenomenally in recent years.

Although pro- business and pro- rich policies of the Govt. are largely responsible for growing economic inequality in the country in recent years, high inflation has also contributed significantly to the phenomenon of iniquitous growth.

The PDS. is supposed to insulate the poor from the impact of rising prices of essential commodities and maintain their minimum nutritional status. The PDS has however failed in providing food security to the poor. In the past few years the importance of the PDS as an outlet for foodgrains to at controlled prices followed by more than proportionate increase in the central issue prices of good grains. The Govt. has recently announced yet another increase in the procurement price of wheat. The minimum support price (MSP) of wheat for Rabi 2000-2001 has been raised from an already high level of Rs. 580 per quintal to Rs. 610 per quintal.

The real beneficiaries of the large increase in procurement prices have been the surplus farmers of wheat and rice in three or four states which account for nearly 90 per cent of the procurement. The huge outlay in the name of food subsidy which is misnomer for all the losses- incurred by the FCI., helps sustaining food prices at very high levels.

As a result of the hike in PDS prices of foodgrains, the difference between the free market and the PDS prices have narrowed significantly. In fact, market prices during 2000-2001 were lower than APL (Above Poverty Line) prices for wheat supplied thro' PDS. This is because of the massive inefficiencies in the FCI operations which have made "the FCI 's economic cost" -incurred for procurement, storage and transportation more than the open market price. The FCI's charges for handling and storage of wheat are high. Moreover, the hike in the PDS prices exerts upward pressure on the market prices of foodgrains also. The increased issue prices help to keep the open market prices above levels that the market would otherwise determine. The poor thus are not able to afford to purchase food in adequate quantities either from the PDS or the open market.

The off take of foodgrains under PDS has been declining for several years (Table:1). Whenever the offtake is less than procurement, these operations unwittingly reduce overall- market supply and push up prices. Procurement of food- grains, on the other hand, has been witnessing an increasing trend. As a result, stocks of foodgrains as on Jan., 1, 2001 were at 45.7 million tonnes. The country did not need a buffer stock of more than 16.8 million tonnes of foodgrains in the month of Jan to tide over any problem caused by unforeseen factors. Extra stocks are being maintained at an enormous cost to the nation. Even though the problem of malnutrition and semi-starvation is widespread in the country, food stocks at the FCI have been increasing primarily because the people's purchasing power has declined in recent years.

Table 1

Foodgrains Procurement, Offtake under PDS, and Central Stocks

(Million Tonnes)

Year	*Procurement (Central Pool)*	*Offtake (Under PDS)*	*Central Stocks*
1996-97	20.38	19.66	20.0
1997-98	23.63	16.98	18.2
1998-99	24.49	18.69	24.2
1999-2000	31.41	15.45	31.4
2000-2001*	27.78	8.47	46.7

Note: * Procurement as on January 11, 2001; Offtake (Under PDS) up to December 2000; Central Stocks as on January 1, 2001.

The controller and Auditor General of India (CAG) has been critical of the government's procurement and distribution policy. CAG's paper "Food Security and Nutritional Support" published in Dec., 2000, states that, "This policy of procurement, without regard to requirement, has had several deleterious consequence. First it has deprived consumers of more free access to grain. Had the foodgrains not been procured, to that extent a larger quantity would have been available in the market. Second, it is not the case that this additional procurement was in the interest of expanding the buffer stock. The stock of foodgrains has generally been significantly higher than buffer stock norms and this extra stocking has led to extra costs estimated at about Rs. 1200 crores between 1993-94 and 1997-98. Third, the procurement beyond requirement adversely affected prices. Had the additional supplies been available in the market it would have had a sobering effect on prices. Lastly, it is common knowledge that losses during storage are, other things being equal, a function of duration of strorage, the longer the storage the higher the losses":

In recent years, annual increases in MSP have been substantial and unrelated to actual cost of production,. This has led to serious misadjustment between MSP, the consequent acquisition cost of FCI., and the PDS issue price. The annual increases in MSP since 1995-96 have been much above the inflation rate.

The Govt. on Dec. 25, 2000 launched a scheme, the Antyodaya Anna Yojana, with the aim to provide 25 kg of foodgrains each month to one crore poorest of the poor families at subsidised rates of Rs. 2 per kg. of wheat and Rs.3 per kg. of rice. The scheme is however, too limited in scope to make any dent on poverty. Its coverage includes only a small fraction of the poor in the country. In addition, identification of the beneficiaries is proving to be a major problem. This scheme has become operational only in five states so far where 36 lakhs families have been identified.

Secondly, given that a typical family's foodgrain requirement is above 60 kg per month., 25 kg does not meet even half of the monthly requirement. The Antyodaya scheme is also unlikely to result in any significant reduction in foodgrains stocks as it could result in an outflow of 3 million tonnes at most from the stock of over 47 million tonnes.

The Govt. in the budget for 2001-2002 has proposed a significant change in management of the food economy. It is proposed that the centre plays a considerably reduced role in future. Instead of providing subsidised foodgrains, financial assistance is to be provided to the state Govts., to enable them to procure and distribute foodgrains to BPL families at subsidised rates. FCI's responsibility will be limited to procurement of foodgrains for maintaining food security reserves and for such state govts., who will assign it the task on their behalf. However, given the poor financial condition of most states, it is difficult to imagine state Govts. adequately discharging this important responsibility. The Parliament's Standing Committee on food, civil supplies, and public distribution, in its report says that the states have neither infrastructure nor money for the job. The committee feels that there would be a greater likelihood of less procurement, even non- procurement, due to an inadequate infrastructure. As a result the farmers may end up as the real losers.

The Govt. is selling wheat to foreign nationals at a price which is half of FCI's economic cost (Rs. 8300 per tonne in 2000-2001). The issue price of wheat for supply to Indian nationals above poverty line has been Rs. 8300 per tonne in 2000-2001; whereas, it has been Rs. 4150 per tonne.

A large number of starvation deaths were occurring even though the Govt's godowns were overflowing with foodgrains. This was a violation of the 1962 famine code which provides that "in times of famine, every healthy person who presents himself for work as part of the 'food for work' scheme would be provided with work... all dependents, aged or unhealthy people, must be provided with gratuitous relief".

For proper monitoring of PDS, consumers involvement becomes essential. Because they are the ultimate beneficiaries. The consumer awareness on the essential commodities Act and Consumers protection Act will play a vital role in PDS monitoring. The consumers have to realise their rights and liabilities in utilising the PDS. The awareness on the consumer Protection Act will pave the way to the consumers to realise their right, thereby the malpractices in PDS, system should be curtailed.The committee suggested that the women and youth be given a proper representation in the Vigilance Committee. Proper monitoring agency should be evolved for ensuring adequate stock of essential commodities at fair price shops thro' the country.

We cannot expect the PDS to serve all the people in our country. It can serve and has to serve the vulnerable section of the society. It is the basic objective of it. Present coverage of PDS, is to be scaled down. Proper formula is to be evolved for PDS, targeting, so as to enable the Govt., to strengthen the PDS, network and enhance the supply of essential commodities.

While evolving National Policy for PDS, uniformity is to be maintained in the ration scale across the states. The food subsidy is to be distributed to the States on uniform basis. Further, subsidy for wheat supply must be at par with other foodgrains. In South rice is supplied at maximum. In North wheat is supplied at maximum in fair price shops. Though the item of supply is being changed, the subsidy must be uniform for rice and wheat. It is an important agenda to be considered by the expert panel while evolving national policy for PDS. Inter -state or inter-regional disparities should have no place in PDS

The demand and supply analysis may be done on commodity wise. For certain items, if the demand is lesser than the supply, such items could be stopped and highly demanded items may be provided in addition to the present supply. It helps to avoid unnecessary accumulation of unwanted commodities for longer time in the godown.

World Bank has suggested two strategies for maximum effectiveness in reducing poverty;

(1) Encouragement of broadly based economic growth that generates demand for labour and

(2) Requires the provision of services in the social sectors-primary education, health care, family planning and nutrition.

PDS does not come under the poverty reduction strategies of the

World Bank. So it is to be streamlined in phased manner in the near future. It is strongly stressed by the World Bank that the generation of employment and providing services in the social sectors will alone reduce poverty and not welfare programmes offering subsidy. In the Socialistic pattern of society like ours, to bridge the gap between haves and have- nots we should introduce welfare schemes (with subsidy element) to certain extent as a safety net to the have-nots.

International Food Policy Research Institute, Washington states that agricultural assistance to world's poorest countries from major Govts. and international institutions has declined drastically. During 1980-1990 US. Agriculture aid has decreased from 30 per cent to 15 per cent. ie., from 1.4 billion dollars to 388 million dollars during this period. World Bank is the largest single aid giver to agriculture. It's share is also getting down. Agriculture provided by the World Bank has decreased from $4491 billion in 1980 to $ 3012 billion in 1990. Borrowings from World Bank by South Asian countries for agriculture and rural developement is also reduced from $773 million in 1991 to $ 336.1 million in 1992. This scenario shows that we have to face food crisis in the years to come.

The projects on agriculture and irrigation are based on external aid in our country for agriculture development. The food crisis will affect the anti-poverty programmes of the Govt. Further, population is also on increasing trend in our country. So it is time to review and strengthen the PDS to support the anti- poverty programmes and to serve the deserving and needy people. In addition to the rapid economic policies anti- poverty policies are also needed to solve poverty and hungry.

"We are committed to effective public distribution system".

(Selected Thoughts of Indira Gandhi: 31st Jan. 1980.)

In short, the present PDS is beset with many serious problems. It needs reforms. But a subsidised PDS for the well- targeted groups still remains the best form of food security to the poor. Notwith-standing many economic, political and administrative factors which prevent the full realisation of its potential, the PDS is a highly relevant scheme which needs to be further strengthened. In order to effectively serve the purpose of providing food security to the poor, the price food-grains sold thro' the PDS should be kept at very low levels.

"Starvation is the characteristic of some people not 'having' enough food to eat. It is not the characteristic of there 'being' not enough food to eat."

(Amartya Sen: Poverty and Famines: An Essay on Entitlement and Deprivation (1981) Oxford, 1982).

16

Water Resource Management

"The earth is the essence of the elements, water is the essence of the earth, the herbs are the essence of the water, fruits are the essence of the flowers, and energy is the essence of man."

"Upanishads: 6:4:1."

For an agricultural community, water is life. That is probably what gave rivers their sanctity. Bathing is a ritual and also a purifying experience. Pandit Nehru paid homage to the following words: "The Ganga specially, is the river of India, beloved of her people, round which are interwined her racial memories and her hopes and fears, her sense of triumph and her victory and defeat. She has been a symbol of India's age-long culture and philosophy, every-changing, ever-flowing and yet ever the same Ganga."

Water is the finite source, and the tiny fraction suitable for drinking or irrigating is disbursed. Now the need for potable water is escalating because of rapid industrialization and increasing population, especially in the regions where the water is scarce.

Sustainable development refers to the process of development that meets the needs of present generation without compromising the ability of the future generations to meet their own needs. (The World Bank Commission on Environment and Development, 1987).

Hence, sustainable development strategies which protect the eco-system.

There are two main functions of water (1) Water is the unifying factor in most eco-systems and critical in maintaining the functioning of living organisms. Water plays a key role in the biological processes. It erodes, dissolves and transport substances, in this way making inter-connections among the components of an eco-system.

(2) The hydrological cycle is one of the main life supporting mechanisms of the earth system; as a consequence, in many cases, water is the key factor in environmental problems.

Water Resource Management refers to economies applied in the usage of water be it ground water or surface and ensures a judicious distribution of water to as many uses as possible. In Asia 86 per cent of fresh water use is for agriculture, 8 per cent for industry, and 6 per cent for domestic purposes.

According to a United Nations estimate, by the year 2025 two-thirds of humanity will face shortage of fresh water.

Some 200 million Indians do not have access to safe and clean water. An estimated 90 per cent of the country's water resources are polluted and untreated industrial and domestic waste, pesticides, and fertilizers (The Observer of Business and Politics, April 23, 2000).

Several experts in the National Commission for Integrated Water Resources Development Plan had urged that irrigation infrastructure status and conservation of water should be given top priority as India had already attained the status of water scarce country.

The situation is aggravated by the problem of water pollution or contamination. India is heading towards a fresh water crisis mainly due to improper management of water resources, and environmental degradation.

This fresh water crisis is evident in many parts of India, varying in scale and intensity depending mainly on the time of the year.

Ground water crisis is not the result of natural factors; it has been caused by human actions. During the past two decades, the water level in several parts of the country has been falling rapidly due to an increase in extraction.

One of the reports blamed the state governments for being a catalyst in accelerating the depletion of water resources by giving farmers cheap or free electricity who use it to pump water out of underground aquifers faster than rain that recharges them.

Rural habitations are classified into four categories:

1. 'Not-covered.'
2. 'No safe source.'
3. 'Partially covered,' and
4. 'Fully covered.'

Status	*No. of Habitations*
Not covered	nil.
No safe source	931
Partially covered	4085
Fully covered	61615
Total	66631

(*Source:* Periodical Survey: TWAD 2001).

The status of water supply is a dynamic concept rather than static one.

61,615 habitations as fully covered.

In reality, several of these habitations may get only partial supply due to the following factors:

(a) Increase in population; (b) Decrease in the performance of the local sources due to over extraction; (c) Quality degradation; (d) Deficient recharge of ground water due to monsoon failures; and (e) Failure of system units.

The constraints of the co-ordination model are formulated according to system identification:

1. Hydrological Constraints.
2. Agricultural Constraints.
3. Capacity Constraints.
4. Municipal Constraints.
5. Economic Constraints.
6. Environmental Constraints, etc.

Water resources development has received importance in India right from prehistoric down to the present. Historical records bear testimony to the existence of a number of old works in different parts of the country.

Water resources development received the highest importance after our independence. Many impressive storage works like dams, were constructed to augment irrigation facilities and hydro power generation.

Equally important is the ground water development especially thro' private tube wells. This has unfortunately been limited to the arid areas of north West India, and also in metropolitan cities.

India's substantial investment in rural development during the past five decades has not produced a matching transformation on the ground. The recent impetus to already-existing watershed development programmes is thus a policy response to reverse the prevailing malaise in integrated rural development programmes.

Watershed—is not about water and crops only. In theory, an effective watershed project must drought-proof the rural landscape from the human consumption and crop irrigation standpoint by capturing each falling raindrop.

The experiences with watershed projects are quite varied, ranging from about a dozen very successful projects to a large number of non-effective projects. As a result, there are situations where some of the successful watershed projects have not made even minimum provision for drinking water and fodder. Similarly, development of pasture land and diffusion of various soil-moisture conservation practices have often remained neglected in actual implementation.

In addition to the Central Government outlay for rehabilitation and development of micro watersheds, the World Bank, Danish Development International Agency (DANIDA), SIDA, SDC, Department, of International Development (DFID) and the Indo-German Watershed Development programme are supporting watershed development projects thro' direct funding support as well.

Since watershed development is associated more with technology, communities and local institutions have yet to come to terms with the philosophy of watershed development. With the technological approach having proved to be less than effective, the need for integration of local wisdom and traditional systems is becoming more important.

Despite a frequent review of the guidelines to incorporate compelling concerns, watershed projects fail to have the promised impact. Since the benefits of watershed projects do not get shared amongst a large number of households, their adoption by the community continues to remain a major concern. Technology fixes, on the other hand, distance the community even further.

In the requirement of water, the sectoral shares of domestic, irrigation, industry, energy, others have been 6.62 per cent, 85.83 per cent, 1.26 per cent, 0.31 per cent, 6.47 per cent respectively. The water requirement will be increased from 634 bcm in 2000 to 1092 bcm in 2025 and 1447 bcm in 2050.

Table Showing the Sectoral Water Requirement For India (In BCM).

Sectoral Water Requirement for India (In BCM)

Sector	*Year*		
	2000	*2025*	*2050*
Domestic	42	73	102
Irrigation	541	910	1072
Industry	8	22	63
Energy	2	15	130
Others	41	72	80
Total	634	1092	1447

Source: Central Statistical Organization: Compendium of Environment Statistics 1999, (CSO, 1999).

One of the major threats to water resources is water pollution. Water pollution arises from many sources.

The types and sources of water contamination include "Point" sources of pollution which refers to wastes being discharged from a pipe, and "non-point" sources, which means all other sources such as water run off, irrigation, leaks from storage tanks.

The effect of water pollution is indicated in the following Table:

Effects of Water Pollution on Human Health

Diseases	*Types of organism*	*Symptoms and Comments*
Cholera	Bacteria	Vomiting, diarrhoea/
Typhoid	Bacteria	Vomiting, diarrhoea, inflammed intestine, enlarged spleen
Bacterial Dysentery	Several species of bacteria	diarrhoea
Para-Typhoid fever	Several species of bacteria	Vomitting, diarrhoea
Infectious hepatits	Virus	Yellow jaundiced skin, enlarged liver, vomiting, liver damage
Ameobio dysentery	Protozoa	Prolonged diarrhoea

Source: RAMASAMYS: "Environmental Crisis: Causes, Consequences and Remedial Measures" Poster presented in the International Conference on Environment and Health, Bangalore, 1998.)

Large dams, heralded as the modern temples of development up to 1970, ended up as targets of a worldwide controversy over their development effectiveness.

Large dams have made substantial constribution to irrigation and agricultural development, power generation, industrial and domestic water supply and flood control.

As estimated 30 to 40 per cent of 268 m. hectares of irrigated lands globally rely on large dams and contribute to 12 to 16 per cent of food production. Hydropower accounts for about 19 per cent of the world's total electricity supply.

Hydropower is the major source of power in many countries and its share is more than 50 per cent in 63 countries.

Globally, 12 per cent of large dams are designed as water supply dams, whereas another 13 per cent of the dams have flood control function.

Table Showing Global Growth of Large Dams in the Twentieth Century

Global Growth the Large Dams in the Twentieth Century*

Decade	*Number*	*% to Total*	*Cumulative Number*	*%*
Before 1900	630	2.7	630	2.7
1990s	353	1.5	983	4.1
1910s	601	2.5	1584	6.7
1920s	809	3.4	2393	10.1
1930s	964	4.1	3357	14.2
1940s	913	3.9	4270	18.0
1950s	2735	11.5	7005	29.5
1960s	4788	20.2	11,793	49.7
1970s	5418	22.9	17,211	72.6
1980s	4431	18.7	21,642	91.3
After 1990	2069	8.7	23,711	100.0
Total	23,711	100	23,711	100.0

(***Sources:*** WCD, *Report of the World Commission on Dams,* Annexure V, p. 369, Earthscan, London, 2000.

*Excludes 90 per cent of large dams in China due to lack of decadal division of the data.)

The benefits of large dams have come with a large number of problems and at certain heavy costs to sections of population and environment.

The WCD Report discusses these problems as a part of the global review in the 2nd part of the report. The development effectiveness of large dams is questioned on grounds of technical, financial and economic performance as much as on social and environmental aspects.

Three-fourths of the sample dams show cost overruns. Cost overruns are higher in the case of multipurpose dams than single purpose dams. Cost overruns are much more in South Asia. 50 per cent of the sample dams show irrigation dams is below target.

The economic rates of return (ERR) are much lower at evaluation compared to appraisal.

In the case of power generation, performance is below target in more than 50 per cent of the projects. Two-thirds of water supply dams too show below target performance.

Out of the major issues that have sparked-off worldwide protest against large dams is the large-scale displacement of people, and livelihoods caused by these projects.

The WCD., differentiates the two dimensions of displacement, the physical displacement, and the livelihood displacement.

Often physical displacement is accompanied by livelihood displacement. The estimates of displacement of large dams globally vary widely. The WCD puts it between 40 to 80 million people, against Mc Cully's (1976) estimate of 60 million.

China and India, which built 57 per cent of World's large dams, also account for the largest displacement. The official figure of 10.2 million for China appears to be much of an underestimation. Yangtze basin alone is supposed to account for about 10 million displaced people. Unofficial estimates for China range between 40 to 60 million. Estimates of large dam displace people in India range from 16 to 38 million. The WCD., estimates of dam displaced people during 1950-1990 in India and China are placed between 26 to 58 million.

(WCD: World Commission of Dams).

The battle against large dams is fought on grounds of equity and sustainability. This challenging task of evolving a normative framework for equitable and sustainable development begins with the assumption that there is an emerging global vision of equitable and sustainable development that can be the basis for evolving a new framework for decision-making on large dams.

The WCD finds that there are internationally acceptable norms on human rights, as enunciated in the Universal Declaration of Human Rights (UDHR, 1947) right to development, as set out in the UN Delcaration on the Right to Development (UNDRS, 1986) and sustainability, as provided under the UN RIO Declaration on Environment and Development (UNDED, 1992).

The WCD effort is to fuse these three major landmarks as the premises for a rights-based development approach guiding decision-making on water and energy management.

The human being is to be the care of this approach, with no distinction between height and entitlement of all.

Towards the end of the report, the WCD sets out an ambitious "Agenda for Change" and the bits and pieces of legal and administrative initiatives may as well as be indications that with mass mobilization, a positive change is quite possible.

But such mobilization definitely has to be beyond the WCD framework, not only for the rights-based framework but against the unleashing of reforms that tend to annihilate the rights of the underprivileged.

Water resource development is to be planned in an integrated manner at the river basin level and effective basinwise programmes have to be evolved considering the inter-relationships of soil conservation, afforestation, land development, controlling grazing and so on and so forth.

The development of forests in upland of the water basin where the slopes are high will help in minimizing the landsides, leading to lesser sediment transport.

Environmental monitoring of the catchment area on continuous basis and soil conservation measures such as contouring, check dams, afforestation etc. to be practiced.

J.Cyril Kanmony (2001) has pointed out that the water demand for irrigation accounts for 94 per cent. Domestic demand constitute 5 per cent and industrial demand 1 per cent.

However, the demand for water for domestic purposes is expected to grow at a much higher rate than those of agricultural and industrial sector.

Again Kanmony quotes that the WHO has fixed the per capita requirement of water per day at 139 litres.

But in India, the minimum requirement fixed by the Government, is 70 lts in urban areas, and 40 lts. in rural areas.

But the actual supply on an average is only 66 lts. Further, in India there are cities with the supply of a maximum of 600 lts. and minimum of 7 lts. There are villages where the supply of water per day per person is only 3 lts.

There is much wastages in the distribution of water in agriculture, only 35 to 50 per cent of water reaches the crop.

The success of the watershed development programme depends on the large scale awareness among the various sectors.

Keeping in mind, the "Watershed Fortnight" in the month of June is celebrated on large scale since last four years in the State of Maharashtra. The special efforts are made to involve the local leaders, villagers, and development depts in this campaign.

The watershed is a comprehensive, integrated approach of land and water resources management. The main objectives of the watershed management involves; conserving soil and water, improving the ability of moisture holding capacity of soil, rain water harvesting at micro level, and natural and artificial recharge to approve the ground storage and growing greenery which involves aforestation, raising of crops and grasses. It should commence from upper reaches and progressively proceed towards levels.

The drinking water scenario in India is evolving into a major crisis and tough measures need to be taken to bring some respite for the people who face a crisis on the water front as a daily routine.

The synergistic effect of bad drinking water and diarrhoeal intestinal infections needs to be highlighted and hygienic water tapping and usage practices reinforced thro' appropriate and accessible multimedia channels, and campaigns.

(P. Durga Prasad, *op. cit*).

Last but not the least, political will of Government, to frame appropriate and sustainable water policy and equally vital indomitable conscience of water users to utilize water judiciously are imperative.

"We never know the worth of water till the well is dry."

(Thomas Fuller, Gnomologia, 5451).

17

The Impact of Globalisation

According to Manu Shroff, "Globalisation process is a process of moving away from the international economic order to what might be called a global economic (and political) order."

Global ageing as we all know, is a trend that is fundamental, irreversible and an established theme for the new millennium. Its imprint on international economics, politics, and diplomacy is transforming the world.

The crisis of global ageing is entirely new and unprecedented. There are no pointers from the past, no lessons from history, no premonitions from the collective memory of mankind. In the late 18th century, Economist Thomas Malthus had predicted that natural population growth would always outrun the carrying capacity of the earth, a dismal scenario in which human life could only be nasty, brutish, and short.

The term "Global Ageing" covers diverse trends, some that are good and beneficial as also others that are not. Increase in average human life spans that we are privileged to witness must count as one of the greatest boons of the 20th century. In India, apart from the fact that average life expectancy has gone up from 32 years in 1947 to 62 years today, the number of people aged 60 years or more has increased from 19 million in 1951 to 72 million today, and is estimated to rise further to 177 million by the year 2025. Yet the requirements of the elderly have never really been the focus on our public policy, the unstated assumption being that numbers would remain small and providing care and support for the elderly is the liability of their families, not of the State. The unfortunate fact is that paucity of resources and tremendous growth of population would not permit us to build a credible social security network.

We have to look beyond the physical destructions to assess the over all implications of the current global turmoil. It is a common knowledge and simple keynesian economics that with globalisation economics prosperity or ills of one nation has a propensity to spill over to other nations. Thus, the ongoing recession in the West, if deepened by the current crisis, will no doubt cast gloom on the world as a whole.

The process of globalisation that has been initiated at the behest of the World Bank and IMF, is aimed at integrating the Indian economy with the world's developed economies so that the capital flows of the latter may increase as they are seeking more profitable outlets. The capital flows that have increased have gone to the more developed states with better infrastructural facilities in high-tech industries with hardly any growth in employment. Agriculture is out of its orbit, and will have no effect on agricultural growth. On the other hand, it may harm the latter as liberalised imports of the highly subsidised agricultural commitments from the developed nations will have deleterious effect on Indian agriculture.

Everyday the population of the country is increasing by 55,000 persons and in the context of stagnant productivity in agriculture the most serious threat in the coming days will relate to food security.

Inevitably, across the political spectrum there has been the sense of "There is no alternative" (TINA) to globalisation and liberalisation. The Indian elite has seen globalisation as the opportunity to join the international elite and have pushed for it. They are freely able to consume the same goods that the international elite consumes and can freely move around in those circles; Indian businesses initially felt that they would be able to use liberalisation to generate larger profits. They have by-and-large been disabused of these misconceptions since they find they cannot compete against the Multinational Corporations (MNCs) due to their control over capital, and technology. Loss of control of Indian capital over its own markets is symbolised by the movements in the Indian stock market indices which are now being determined by the foreign investors and changes in NASDAQ.

Effectively, the advantage of liberalisation has accrued to foreign capital and the process of globalisation has been a one way traffic for the nation as a whole. It has affected economic, political and, social aspects of our nation. However, an illusion of prosperity has been created by the availability of goods and the spawning of casino mentality created by the capital gains in the world of finance. The new technologies being introduced in India under the process of globalisation are highly capital intensive. The WTO., has strengthened control over technologies by MNCs by creating property rights over them. The introduction of e-Commerce has the potential of eliminating a large number of jobs from the services sectors in both the developed and the developing worlds. Those propagating globalisation in India appear to have not considered the implications for not only the poor but also the middle classes. The nation needs a technology policy. .

Globalisation will naturally result in greater exploitation of our resources by foreigners. No doubt a minuscule minority at the top will benefit in this process with no benefit to the vast masses grinding under poverty and disease.

Eventually it is going to turn out to be a clash of civilisations. Where is the world heading ? Long-term turmoil or a quick turnaround ? Are the American way of life, their foreign and defence policies likely to undergo a change in the coming years ? The prospects for South Asia are grim given the uncertainty all around.

This will be aggravated by the growing economic crisis in India and the world.

Globalisation has greatly broadened the horizons of international co-operation in the economic sphere. However, has this benefitted every-one? Have famine and illiteracy been eradicated from the world ? Certainly not ! Rich states have really got richer by reaping the fruits of globalisation whereas poor states have found themselves even poorer.

If the current trend persists and wealth keeps building up on one pole only, the other one will see an inevitable rise of social tension and political extremism.

Even though globalisation has not resolved the problems of the people in the absence of alternatives, the TINA syndrome has prevailed and no effective challenge has as yet come up.

However, alternative models of development are feasible and Gandhi with emphasis on catering to the interest of the last man first showed the way towards building a just society. Fortunately, India as a large country is not in the same position as Mynamar or Albania and can do things differently. India with its long history has shown that it can at times also show the way to the rest of the world. For this is a vision and a political will needs to be developed.

Further, the only way to prevent is to enhance the social component of globalisation and put an end to discrimination in international economic relations. The new round of WTO., trade talks should work out more balanced rules of world trade. They are to reflect the legitimate interests of all countries, including those that are about to join the WTO., and provide an opportunity to ensure a more even development of their national economies.

Furthermore, it is of vital importance for relevant international agencies to develop mechanisms allowing to forecast and rapidly address international financial crisis. Cooperation should be expanded between the United Nations and the Bretton Woods institutions and other international financial and economic organisations.

We live in an age of sovereign equality and sovereign responsibility. If there is a genuine global equality, then there is also a duty for equals to work together towards removing the dangers which face all of us. Nuclear weapons are definitely a danger with anyone and hence for everyone. There cannot be a selective denuclearisation. We in India for long been lending our voice and weight for complete nuclear disarmament. Our engagement, from the beginning, in all the larger causes of the world affairs, has been to seek equitable order and for the removal of asymmetries between developed and developing nations.

However, globalisation is still far from an equitable process. We must dismantle the iniquitous order and have regimes which are universal and non-discriminatory. The existence of all weapons of mass-destruction is incompatible with civilised norms. We would rejoice when these scourges are eliminated, when the nuclear genie does not threaten the makind any longer.

Hence, we must seriously examine the prospects of de-nuclearisation in the 21st century.

What is to be done so as to fight the meance of globalisation with all its attendant evils ? In the Shakespearean parlance we can say: "To be or not to be is the Question" political parties in India appear to have surrendered to the dictates of globalisation and liberalisation. But there is always a silver-lining in a cloud of affliction. The grass-roots movements can take up the challenge.

The civil rights leader of the USA., the Late: Martin Luther King who lamented in course of his crusade against colour bar in the USA., said that he goes to other countries as a tourist but to. India he goes as a pilgrim. For him, as he said, India means Mahatma Gandhi and he learnt the techniques of "Satyagraha " from Gandhiji and put them into action in the USA, and succeeded in a large measure.

We were fortunate enough not to have succumbed to the pressure for expeditious full convertibility, otherwise during the South-East Asian currency crisis, we would have faced insurmountable difficulties.

"The rising tide of global economy will create many winners, but it will not lift all boats" (Global Trends 2015: Report, The US. Intelligence community).

The human beings, wherever they reside, are far being a burden on society. They are its core and fundamental strength. That is what the post-

Malthusian world must learn. The truth is that no worldly resource is as valuable and more creative than the liberated human mind.

In the so-called era of globalisation scenario the dispossessed of the world are actually its potential resource. We must always remember this and pledge to work together to protect justice and equity, security and dignity at all times.

French thinker Henri de Saint-Simon said:

"The golden age of the human species is not behind us, it lies ahead; it is in the perfection of the social order; our father did not see it; our children will one day achieve it and it is our duty to pave the way fors them".

18

Tackling of Non-Performing Assets in Commercial Banks (NPAs)

The essence of the economic reforms launched from July 1991 by the Government, of India has been towards creating a competitive environment as a means of improving the productivity and efficiency of the economic system. In the wake of implementation of these reforms, a high level Committee was appointed by the Govt., of India in Aug., 1991, under the Chairmanship of Shri. M. Narasimham to examine all aspects relating to the structure, organisation, functions and procedures, of the financial system. The Committee submitted its final report in Nov., 1991 which contained a number of recommendations for toning up the operational efficiency of the financial system.

Non-Performing Asset:

A non-performing asset in the banking sector is an asset not contributing to the income of the bank or one which has ceased to yield any income (interest). It is a zero-yield when applied on loans and advances.

Assets can be classified into:

1. Financial
2. Infrastructure and
3. Manpower.

A financial asset is said to be non-performing, where interest application has been stopped due to its identification or consideration as a sick account, under the guidelines of the Govt., Reserve Bank of India/ Term Lending institutions or the internal decision of the banks. These may include suspense accounts, clearing adjustment items, and investments which are not yielding incomes.

A study made by Reserve Bank of India in the industrial sector revealed the causes of industrial sickness in the Table-1.

Table 1

	Causes of Sickness	*Percentage of Units*
(a)	Mis-management, Diversion of funds and infighting among owners...	52
(b)	Inadequate marketing...	23
(c)	Improper initial planning and technical drawbacks...	14
(d)	Power failure and Non-availability of raw materials---	9
(e)	Labour problems...	2
		100

It may be observed from the above Table that 50 per cent of NPAs is due to mis-management, while 75 per cent is due to mis-management, and improper marketing facilities.

A major criticism of the recommendations of the Banking Sector Reforms Committee 1998 is that:

"In its overzealous attempt to cast the banking system in the image of American banking, the report of the Committee has lost sight of India-specific issues. A more meaningful perception of the ills of the public sector banks would have emerged if the Committee had applied its mind to these four issues: Political meddling; bureaucratic control; industrial relations; and governance in banks."

(N.A. Majumdar, 1998).

There are doubts about the manner in which the reduction has been brought about. The method that is largely adopted by most banks has been to negotiate compromise settlement, provide waivers and write off the balance.

However, the real issue is how to improve credit quality. And adequate recovery procedures are necessary for improving credit quality. Further, risk-management skills of the bank personnel need further strengthening.

By far, the most daunting challenge for banks will emanate from the need for advanced risk-management practice and their wider application. This is so esp., with regard to the high standards the IRB approach warrants from Banks. The standards are an amalgamation of international best practices which even very few international banks are likely to comply with.

As regards Indian banks, the task will be further uphill, esp., in view of relatively low level of technological absorption in their day-to-day operations on the technological front.

Risk exposures and measurement is yet to take deep roots in Indian context. Measuring and disclosing various risks calls for a sound MIS and comprehensive database.

The present trend of NPAs is given in the Table 2.

Table 2

Total Advances and NPAs Public Sector Banks

(in crores)

Year	*Total Advances Rs.*	*Gross NPAs Rs.*	*% of Gross NPAs of Total Advances*
1993	169181	39250	23.2
1996	259231	39583	17.3
1997	244214	43577	17.8
1998	284971	45658	16.0
1999	368264	58554	15.9

Source: RBI (1999) Report of Trend and Progress of Banking in India (1998-99) Mumbai.

Reasons for NPAs in Commercial Banks:

1. Lack of proper appraisal.
2. Wilful default.
3. Industrial sickness.
4. Natural calamities.
5. Diversion of funds.
6. Lack of follow-up.
7. Government policy.

Steps to be taken for tackling NPAs:

In fact, monitoring and follow-up is an integral part of the process of ensuring the quality of an advance. The problem of NPAs, can therefore be tackled thro' preventive measure such as credit investigation, appraisal and supervision. These steps would ensure a high quality asset management.

A number of measures if effectively taken can ensure effective monitoring and resultant recovery of the loans, and reduction in the volume of NPAs., The steps are: The volume of NPAs can be minimised to a large extent by a proper pre-sanction appraisals; following basic principles of lending; a constant strict vigil over large borrowal signals is necessary so that early signals of problem loans and other risks such as diversion of funds, deterioration of financial position, and dilution of security, are perceived early and investigated quickly for appropriate remedial action;

the Govt., should take necessary steps to recover the NPAs., of Indian banks thro' Revenue Recovery Act. This will create the fear of the borrower, and ensure larger repayment of their loans.

Presently, the banks follow equitable mortgage of the security for the advance granted. But now the banks think that they will go for English mortgages, which is going to give more tightened legal protection to the banker. If the banks are going to implement the English mortgage, the recovery will be more and keeping NPAs assets to the bearest minimum.

Write-off the loss asset is the last resort to the bank, getting the tax advantages of writing-off losses.

Banks have a host of decress. In many cases, the decress are not executed with cases, the result that the dues remain un-recovered. One of the reasons is the absence of any suitable machinery to probe the debtor's assets, get details, and file an execution petition. To overcome this, it is suggested that recognised auctioneers may be assigned the decrees at an agreed discount who would in turn execute them for their full worth.

The NPAs of the banking system are now in the region of Rs. 52,000 crore and it is clearly recognised that the drain on the system of such a large burden needs early resolution. It is expected that the one-time settlement for NPAs below Rs. 10 crore will be non-discretionary and uniform and a number of banks have focussed their energies on a one-point agenda of recovery of loans.

It is recognised that recovery of NPAs., is not an easy task and the sheer attention of time results in an accretion to NPAs as loans are down-graded on the asset classification ladder.

Legal infirmities are by far the most formidable impediments to a strengthened banking system. The Andhyarujina Committee has recommended the creation of a new law granting statutory power of possession and sale of securities directly to banks and FIs and creation of a new securitisation act which would confer legal sanctity to transfer of future receivable. Action on this front would be the most important measure in the second generation reforms.

A bank with low NPAs in its portfolio is considered as the best bank as per the CAMEL (C: Capital adequacy; A; for asset quality; M for Management efficiency; E: for Earnings; and L: for Liquidity. (Rating introduced by Reserve Bank of India for rating the banking system).

As can be seen a bank with low NPA will have all the above five attributes which will make it strong and vibrant in the country.

19

Scenario of Education Under Economic Reforms

Breaking out of the fetters of colonialism, India has chosen for herself the path of democracy to evolve peacefully towards economic development, equality and social justice. This path is that of national reconstruction thro' conscious and meaningful participation of people. Education has been considered as the most important instrument of social change, not merely a mechanism for generating manpower, but rather a process of conscientious responsible citizenry in our democratic society. Thus, when the Education Commission (1964-66) opined that the "Destiny of India is being shaped in her classrooms" it was not mouthing hollow-rhetoric, it was reflecting the aspiration of the young nation, though now it may seem to reflect wishful thinking. The national policy has been in favour of a major role for education in national development. This is amply reflected in the impressive quantitative expansion of education during these 56 years since our independence.

However, has this expansion been accompanied by greater equity in access, as well success ? Have the substantive aspects of education fared well in quality and relevance ? Has educational expansion resulted in manpower development in critical areas/sectors of development ? These are the questions we must address if we have to assess the strengthens and weaknesses of Indian education in the millennium era.

Education should create a new human being. It should enable us to relate to the world. It should radiate love and tolerance. It should give us strength to fight all sorts of darkness, violence and exploitation. It should create a humane egalitarian harmonic world. Perhaps the ideal meaning of education is inseparable from the experience of profound humanism.

The establishment of a caring society appears almost impossible. The modern educational system was an alien construct transplanted by colonial fiat, and the post-colonial experience has brought about no significant change in the value structure, whether in the world of the formerly colonised, or of the erstwhile colonisers. The seeds of destruction inherent in that educational system have taken root and, if not corrected, will spell impending doom in the near future for the whole of mankind, whether thro' nuclear explosion, internecine war or natural disaster.

Society does not generally follow the ideal we are talking about. Because what we call legitimate education is essentially a historical product; it cannot be separated from the philosophy of age. For example, when we look at the modern age we see how education-formal/institutionalised education seeks to serve the functions of modernity. What is important is how to reproduce modernity- its organisations and technologies.

With modernity society becomes increasingly complex and informal familial education, as it is argued, is no longer adequate. What is needed is formal/ institutionalised education. Because in the modern age nonkinship and universalistic considerations are of primary significance in the organisation of economic, political and other social relations. That is why, the assertion of formal education.

The fact in that is a modern complex society, as John Dewey wrote: "Much of adults do is so remote in space and in meaning that playful imitation is less and less adequate to reproduce its spirit. Ability to share effectively in adult activities thus depends upon a prior training given with this end in view. Intentional agencies schools- and-explicit material-studies are devised. The task of teaching certain things is delegated to a special group of persons."

The gathering storm in education across the world was perceptible to only the discerning handful, but a few years ago, when the youth was yet to assert a distinctive position in society, when university students were still numerically insignificant and largely preoccupied with prospective careers in lucrative jobs much more easily available than now-a-days. But the scene underwent a sea-change with the recent explosion in the educational institutions, as according to Eric Hobsbawn (The Age of Extremes-Vintage Books, 1996):

"It was obvious to planners and governments that the modern economy required far more administrators, teachers and technical experts than in the past, who had to be trained somewhere and universities or similar institutions of higher education had by ancient tradition, funtioned largely as training schools for public services and the specialised professions. And, of course, the newly independent ex-colonies which multiplied during the 1960s on their own institutions of higher education as a symbol of independence as they insisted on a flag, an airline or an army".

Universities and other institutions of higher education are facing a critical resource crunch. Thereby their continuity is at stake. Unless these institutions organise their funds, that is, strive towards financial and academic autonomy, they stand the risk of closure.

Swami Vivekananda had exhorted the privileged to ensure education for the poor, but to desist from indoctrinating them in any kind of programmed confrontationist ideology. He had anticipated that with proper exposure to the new information sweeping into India, the poor would eventually work out their schemes for salvation. They were to be given all material help, solicited wherever possible from the affluent, but no effort need to be made to control their mind. Their thoughts were to be unshackled from the cobwebbed part-enlightment would come naturally.

The major challenge before the teacher education system is to ensure its own regeneration and revitalisation. It has to ensure that it depends to culture specific, region specific, and change specific requirements and is futuristic in its content and transition. The programme should '*ipso facto*' enhance the efficacy of the system and convert the institutions into activity based partnership oriented, and enjoyable teaching learning situations. The social context and orientation towards individual needs must become prominent ingredients of such programmes.

There is need to develop sufficient research, database on which, the nature, structure, duration and content of teacher education programmes can be built. Same sould be applicable to the inservice education programmes which at this stage have become routinised and are conducted generally on models developed three or four decades ago. These are more oriented towards the resource persons or trainers and their preparedness than towards the needs of the serving teachers. The trend will have to be reversed and such a reversal is possible only thro' regular inbuilt surveys, assessments, and studies within the system itself.

There are three things that we can do.First, as educationalists we can broaden our horizons, and participate in many other struggles for liberation. Because the recovery of education is essentially the recovery of the larger society. Second, as teachers and students we can work within specific situations in which we find ourselves. We can bring some refreshing innovations in our educational practices. Third, we can remain perpetually self-critical. This restlessness leads to intervention. In otherwords, no situation is entirely dark; it is possible to intervene. Living meaning-fully is, after all, an attempt to broaden the scope of the possible.

While Sex education is regarded as a key element in stabilising growth in a number of developed countries like Australia, Denmark, France, Germany, the Netherlands, Norway, Sweden, Switzerland, and the USA., the recent researchers in the West though limited, suggest that access to information on the sex neither leads the children's moral degeneration, nor provokes them to indulge in immoral sexual activities.

Unfortunately, India in this regard continues to lag behind as here sex education has not been allowed in schools so far.

The main obstacles in the way of providing sex education in India are, not difficult to identify. In spite of the socio-economic development in the country, the prevelance of overwhelming illiteracy and a very high proportion of rural population have made the teaching of sex education in schools a complicated task.

The made the teaching of sex education in schools a complicated task.

However, in view of the grave population problem confronting the country, we can no longer afford to wait for the attainment of any particular level of social advancement, or economic development which automatically generates conditions conducive for imparting sex education to the children in schools.

In fact, in many developing countries like China, Thailand, Malaysia and Indonesia the planning for the small family is already in practice due to the people's awareness of the small family norm, and the birth control methods. Hence, it is high time that by deliberately including sex education in the school curriculum-the children are given an insight into the totality of issues connected with sexual behaviour and convinced that parenthood is the real parenthood. It is neither anti-child in approach, nor is it a matter of blind instinct. Instead, it is the source of mutual love, respect and harmony between husband and wife, and also between parents and children.

Although for controlling the country's future population growth the idea of poviding sex education in schools is highly appreciated, given the prevailing socio-cultural fabric of the country it is indeed a very radical step in the beginning-people are bound to be apprehensive of its implications. Hence, the Indian Govt., will have to take initiative in this regard by making necessary arrangements for its teaching in schools.

In a country like India where the whole social structure is based on institutionalised inequality, it is hard to teach human rights as a subject.

The worst human rights violation in India today is the illiteracy level which stands at more than 50 per cent and about which no concrete steps appear to have been taken by any organisations, either public or private. Thus any human rights education is introduced at best be addressing less than 50 per cent of the total school-going age population. If we take into account the inefficiencies of our school system, we can assume that not more than 15 per cent of the total children in this country will be actual, effective recipients of any new course. From such numbers, it is obvious that for the country as a whole education has very little to do with our attitudes in adult life. It has, in fact, contributed to a negative phenomenon, that of cynicism, and resentment against the education on system.

Why do we need to introduce human rights education ?

We may quote the following lines from a U.N. document on this subject:

"human rights education (is)...aimed at the building of a universal culture of human rights through the imparting of knowledge and skills and the moulding of attitudes which are directed towards the promotion for understanding, tolerance, gender equality and friendship among all nations, indigenous peoples and racial, national, ethnic, religious and linguistic groups."

From this objective, it is obvious that human rights cannot merely be a subject to be taught in the class-room. HR., must be taught in a manner that the recipient of this education is able to effectively disseminate it futher.

Notwithstanding the practical difficulties HR., education is a necessity. The focus of the NHRC Seminar was on HR., education down the line; this is likely to be of peripheral value only. Education is a way of disseminating knowledge and experience to improve the capacity to comprehend reality. The need of the day is HR., education as a part of a general, secular, moral education for people in positions of authority starting from individuals of the adult male population and going thro' minor and major officials of Govts., to leaders at the helm of every organisation.

In the grim scenario what is the role of education and the educationist? It is neither the mere learning of three "Rs"- or the attainment by a few the high mental ability to grasp philosophical concepts. Education has to deal with enabling every individual to lead a meaningful life, and engage in pursuit of happiness.

"Happiness depends on what you can give; Not on what you can get",-said his H.H. Swami Chinmayananda.

It is high time that educationists, both in the fields of formal and informal education, took up the task of bringing about social and economic changes by inculcating in young and old, a scientific temper so that we can fulfil the promise we made to ourselves half a century ago.

The evolution of the educational system in this country, as elsewhere, has been marked by elaboration, diversification and increasingly narrow specialisation of fields of thought. Many disciplines came into being and developed independently of one another; in some cases dividing into highly compartmentalised subject disciplines. However, the remarkable discoveries in science during the last few decades have broken down these frontiers. It has become imperative, in view of the complexity of areas of knowledge, to consider the essential unity of the various scientific fields and subjects. There is an emergence of new fields which do not fall within the traditional disciplines. Information theory which involves thermodynamics and fundamental biology as well as telecommunication is a good example of interdisciplinarity. We notice that the problems of the contemporary world such as famine and destitution of the entire population, threat of nuclear war, deterioration of the environment which need to be handled do not lie within one discipline and their solution requires inter-disciplinary approaches and collaboration between specialists and different disciplines.

—Advances in the human sciences have greatly contributed to the development of interdisciplinarity because they have to borrow theories or instruments from other disciplines. For example, the Games Theory, Factoral Analysis, the concept of Feedback and the complexity of their subject matter obliges them to have recourse to several disciplines simultaneously. Interdisciplinarity in teaching and research, therefore, is the foundation for sound education. This remains one of the weakest areas in Indian education.

Although a number of Committees and commissions have been set up, to look into the problems of education in the country, several of their redommendations either have not been implemented or have only been marginally implemented, and where implemented, effects have not been very impressive and lasting.

Education indeed is very slow to respond. Courses and curricula tend to duplicate what already exists, and there are very few innovations in this area.

It is a welcome feature that the NEP., 1986 has been enunciated which addresses itself to most of the problems relating to education. Unlike in the past, a programme of action has been brought out by the Government, Just after the release of the Policy which attempts to detail the recommendations indicating a reasonable time frame for effective implementation within the broader societal system. This document has emphasized the hitherto neglected element of "making the system work." It says, "Unless the system of education works properly at all stages of education, in all parts of the country the ambitious programme of education reform envisaged in the NEP, will come to a naught." Tremendous organisational efforts and resources are required. But "making the system to work" is the crux.

And, somewhere along the line, while thinking of development and nation building and viewing education as an instrument of social change we are sidetracking the main function of education, namely, learning.

"The direction in which education starts a man will determine his future life." PLATO: The Republic.

It is time to conceive of a paradigm that restores to learning its primacy and treats education as secondary of learning. In order to bridge the gap between our vision and reality, education should not be confused with learning, and whether we look at education as the end product, as content, or as a process, it should not be allowed to take central stage in any scheme of things.

In recent years, there has been a decline in gross enrolment ratios in primary and upper primary education Table: 1 The gross enrolment ratio in primary education was above 100 per cent in the beginning of the 1990s. It started declining since and reached the level of about 90 per cent. Marginal changes in gross enrolment ratio in primary education once it was 100 per cent, need not necessarily be a cause of concern. But the decline in enrolment ratio from 100 per cent to 90 per cent is a big decline. The number of out-of-schools still seems to be formidable.

More importantly, the decline in the gross enrolment ratio in upper primary education should be a matter of serious concern, as (1) it is nowhere near 100 per cent; (2) the decline is continuous and steady; and (3) the decline is steep. It is difficult to explain the continuous and steady decline. For example, the enrolment ratio in upper primary education in 1988-99 was 56.8 per cent, while it was 58.5 per cent in the previous year. It was above 60 per cent in the beginning of the last decade. This declining trend is somewhat universal all over India, (i.e.,) it could be noted in almost all states: educationally backward and advanced as well. Thus the exclusive focus on primary education has not resulted in increase in access to primary education, in terms of gross enrolment ratios; and it also led to ignoring upper primary education.

Table 1
Gross Enrolment Ratios in Primary and Upper Primary Education in India per cent

	Primary	*Upper Primary*
1990-91	100.1	62.1
1991-92	100.2	61.4
1996-97	90.6	62.4
1997-98	89.7	58.5
1998-99	92.1	56.8

When reform policies were introduced, it was hoped that the resultant benefit in terms of higher rates of economic growth, would allow higher allocation of resources to human development sectors like education, and health.

"There is no power in the world, only one wizard element that can reconcile and harmonise the natural conflicts of races and religions. And that is education". (Sarojini Naidu 1879-1949: Nationalist Leader and Poet: Selected Poetry and Prose: Harper Collins: 1993). But this does not seem to have happened.

20
Problem of Unemployment

One of the major indicators of India's failure in its initial development strategy was the widespread problem of unemployment.

The package of the new economic policies of liberalisation and globalisation has been adopted since July 1991 as a development strategy. This package has far reaching implication for labour employment in the country. The result of employment strategy of new economic policies is yet to come out in India, but this is borne out, by the evidences from the Latin American countries which have undergone structural adjustment programme-which is in progress in India that the growth of employment will be severely affected. Between 1980 and 1984 open unemployment in these countries has gone up from 7 to 11 per cent. In chile, columbia, Peru and Venezue, unemployment jumped 50 to 100 per cent and ranged between 14 and 20 per cent. In India, according to the projection made by Sudipto Mundle, the umemployment rate is likely to jump from 4 per cent in 1991-92 to 5 per cent in 1992-93, assuming a high growth scenario, and 5.9 per cent in 1992-1993 to 6.6 per cent in 1993-94 assuming low growth scenario. Hence, the additional unemployment due to stabilisation programme would be 4 million persons under high growth scenario and 10 million persons under low growth scenario (Veerasekharappa, 1993). The available trends of growth rate of 90s show the low growth scenario.

The attempt at macro-economic adjustment is one that work essentially through economic contraction as the recession already underway indicates. In such circumstances, economic activity and associated jobs does not increase but stagnates or declines. Govt activity esp., productive investment by the state, is in for a period of contraction and the impetus imparted by the State to the overall economy is therefore already on the decline. This means the slow down in organised sector employment is likely to be even sharper in the near future.

There is little to be happy about any sector growing in employment by 0.1 per cent when the labour force grows at least at 2.0 per cent.

The labour force participation rates, for the country as a whole, have fallen across the board for male/ female and rural/urban divisions. Further, unemployment rates based on all concepts have risen with few exceptions.

We may look at the scenario of workers who are there in labour force either with principal status or with subsidiary status. We may also look at people who are actually working and those who are not working but are available for work. We make a comparison between 1993-94, the year close to the beginning of the current economic reforms, and 1999-2000. Table: 1: presents a variety of participation and non-participation rates in labour/ work force. We may note that labour force consists of workforce employed and unemployed.

Table 1

Usual Activity Status of Persons for Major Categories

(per 1000 persons)

	Rural male		*Rural Female*		*Urban male*		*Urban Female*	
Year	*1993-94*	*1999-00*	*1993-94*	*1999-00*	*1993-94*	*1999-00*	*1993-94*	*1999-00*
LF-US	562	541	333	303	544	543	165	148
WF-US	553	531	328	299	520	518	154	139
UN-US	009	009	005	003	024	024	011	008
WF-SS	015	009	094	068	008	005	034	022
LF-PS	547	532	239	235	536	538	131	126
WF-PS	538	522	234	231	513	513	121	117
UN-PS	009	011	005	004	023	026	011	009
RUN-US	014	017	009	010	041	045	061	057
RUN-PS	016	021	015	013	054	048	067	061

Note: 1. LF=Labour Force; WF=Work Force; UN-Unemployment; RUN=Rate of Unemploymet; US-Usual Status; PS=Principal Status; SS=Subsidiary Status.

2. Last two rows represent unemployment rates in terms of 1000 persons in labour force.

The Economic Census of 1998 has provided information about employment. Comparing it with the data for 1990, it becomes evident that globalisation and liberalisation have resulted in job losses of the order of 7 million during 1990-98 about four million in the rural areas, and three million in the urban areas. (Table: 2)

Employment Situation in India (1990-1998) Table 2

	Sector	*Agriculture and Allied Activities**	*Non-Agricultural Activities*	*Total*
Rural				
	1980	2.45	22.02	22.47
	1990	4.32	29.06	33.29
	1998	4.88	24.42	29.30
Absolute	**1980-90**	**+ 1.78**	**+ 7.04**	**+8.82**
Change	**1990-98**	**+ 0.65**	**- 4.64**	**-3.99**
Urban				
	1980	0.40	28.80	29.20
	1990	0.53	38.25	38.78
	1998	0.68	35.06	35.74
Absolute	**1980-90**	**+ 0.13**	**+ 9.45**	**+ 9.58**
Change	**1990-98**	**+ 0.15**	**-3.19**	**-3.04**
Total	1980	2.85	50.832	53.67
	1990	4.76	67.31	72.07
	1998	5.56	59.48	65.04
Absolute	**1980-90**	**+ 1.91**	**+ 16.49**	**+18.40**
Change	**1990=98**	**+ 0.80**	**-7.83**	**-7.03**
Annual Average growth rate (%)				
Rural	1980-90	+5.62	+2.81	+3.13
	1990-98	+1.80	-2.15	-1.58
Urban	1980-90	+2.93	+2.88	+2.88
	1990-98	+3.15	-1.08	-1.01
Total	1980-90	+5.28	+2.85	+2.99
	1990-98	+1.96	-1.53	-1.27

Note: *Includes activities other than crop production and plantations.
Source: Compiled and computed from Government of India, *Economic Census 1990 and 1998.*

Moreover, "The World Investment Report", 1999 admits the lopsided character of the economic system. It says "because of their technology intensity and competitive behaviour they are likely to generate smaller number of jobs than other firms of equal output and size."

Very few workers in the World benefit unemployment protection. Workers in the rural areas and also in the urban informal sector have virtually no protection against unemployment. It is well understood today that globalisation has significant implication for social protection in the countries with open economy who are exposed to the cyclical movement of the global market. Also it is found that there are instances of reduction of social security expenditure in the countries where the share of trade in GDP., has increased.

After more than a decade in 1999, a study on the unorganised labour, migrant labour in Punjab, a Project sponsored by the ILO., had unfolded the grim reality. While describing the plight of a woman worker the report says:

"She was sitting in a dark damp room of 8x10 feet with her one week old baby and tying knots at the ends of a blanket. She earns Rs. 20 to Rs. 22 every day. The chawl she lives in has only three latrines and two hand-pumps for 150 persons. It is Hargovinda Colony of Ludhiana where drinking water is polluted with chemicals released from the factories around. Chest congestion is a common ailment affecting even the babies. She is the second generation migrant married to a seasonal worker from Bihar."

A decade of reform and development has not ended the agonising ordeal of the unorganised working class masses in the country. From Table: 3 we can see that during the decade of reforms on the basis of 1991 and 1999 figures, of a total net additional employment of 13.4 lakh, 3.2 lakh was by the public sector and 10.2 lakh by private sector. During these years, more than 10 crore might have entered the labour force. Can we really talk of downsizing ? We can note that part of the increase in employment in the private organised sector is just transfer of employment from the public sector in the wake of disinvestment.

Table 3
Employment in Organised (Public and Private) Sector

(In lakh)

Year	*Union*	*State*	*Quasi*	*Local*	*Public*	*Private*	*Organised*
1991	34.10	71.12	62.22	23.13	190.57	76.76	267.3
1992	34.28	71.90	63.93	21.98	192.10	78.46	270.6
1993	33.83	72.93	64.90	21.60	193.26	78.51	271.8
1994	33.92	73.37	65.14	22.02	194.45	79.30	273.8
1995	33.95	73.55	65.20	21.97	194.66	80.59	275.3
1996	33.66	74.14	64.58	21.92	194.29	85.12	279.4
1997	32.95	74.85	65.35	22.44	195.59	86.86	282.5
1998	32.53	74.58	64.61	22.46	194.18	87.48	281.7
1999	33.13	74.58	63.85	22.59	194.15	86.98	281.1

Full employment is the primary objective of our macro economic policy and all the Five Year Plan documents stressed the need for full employment.

But the strategies followed by various Indian governments appear to be counter productive. In areas like productivity, profitability, efficiency, the results of economic reforms are mixed but in the sphere of employment, it is really adverse. The productivity gains achieved 3.2 per cent had not passed on to the working class. The workers received only 1.2 per cent of the productivity gains.

The share of the organised sector in employment has plummeted from around 10 per cent in the late 1980s to 7 per cent in the late 1990s. We are talking of downsizing Govt., of voluntary retirement schemes, of rational lising labour laws so that they are serviceable to the private organised sector. Nobody would hold a view that we should have more people on a job than we require but very few people would agree that in the presence of so many hands we should go for such technology as would employ very few hands.

The sole point that Mahatma Gandhi made for opting for dear technology of "Khadi" in comparison to cheap technology of mills was that in the ultimate analysis, in a macro sense the former turns out to be cheaper.

We may add here Europe is now veering round to the view that growth and competitiveness by themselves have failed to open the development fully. Inspite of an impressive record in these two areas, unemployment in Europe has reached serious proportions. Solution to the unemployment problem has defied the standard remedies; higher investment, more mergers, expanded trade, and full throated deregulation. A 167-page White Paper (April, 1994) issued by the European Commission, titled: "Growth, Competitiveness, and Employment," calls for a new development model resting on a triangular relationship: growth, Competitiveness, employment, in which the employment policy is the centre-piece of the strategy.

The opening sentence of the White Paper says it all:

"Why this White Paper ? The one and only reason is unemployment."

"We are aware of the scale of unemployment and of its consequence, too, but the difficult thing, as experience has taught us, is to know how to tackle it. We know how to produce-but our manufacture often destroys jobs."

True, the dynamism the market can help boost growth, but experience has shown that:

"the market is not without its failings. It tends to underestimate what is at stake at the long term, the speed of the changes it creates affects the different social categories unequally, and it spontaneously promotes concentration, thereby creating inequality between the regions and the towns."

But the strategies followed by various Indian governments appear to be counter productive. In areas like productivity, efficiency, the results of economic reforms are mixed but in the sphere of employment, it is really adverse. The productivity gains achieved 3.2 per cent had not passed on ot the working class. The workers received only 1.2 per cent of the productivity gains.

Indeed in most European countries,

the proceeds of economic growth have mainly been absorbed by those who remained in employment, and have a large pool of unemployment who have been excluded.

The Paper acknowledges that though some progress has been made during the 1980s in reviewing the regulations that hinder job creation, and substantial wage moderation has lowered price of labour as a factor of production, the employment intensity of growth in the European Union has hardly changed.

It concludes, towards a new development model, both from the viewpoint of the effectiveness of the triangular relationship growth-competitiveness-employment the environment and the improvement in the quality of life.

It argues the community to create jobs—"to safeguard the future of our children, and social protection systems which are threatened by unemployment"

The challenge is of finding a new synthesis of the aims pursued by society and the requirements of the economy so as to lay the foundations for sustainable development of the European economies, thereby enabling them to withstand international competition "while creating the millions of jobs that are needed."

The paper also outlines some thoughts of a new development model relevant to Europe which includes such aspects as the need for structural links between environment and employment. It highlight the need for correction in the over-use of natural resources, and the under-use of labour resources.; the need for a strategic micro-economic policy, and instruments for sectoral level development including energy, transport, agriculture, and industry conforming to such a framework. Use of clean technology is a key aspect.

In India too, product growth is out-placing employment. The experience of the 1980s is that of a welcome sharp rise in the growth of the product (5.3 per cent from 3.5 per cent) but a sharper and disaster decline in the growth rate of employment (from 2.8 per cent to 1.5 per cent) This crisis of a glaring and growing mismatch between growth and employment generation facing the Indian economy, does noι figure in the analysis of our policy makers.

Hence, more serious thought is required as to how the employment objective can be made central to the pursuit of growth and competitiveness by the market and the state-in the wake of globalization of the economy. We too have to safeguard the future of our childrens.

"That is called national education which enables you to know your nation...If knowledge had been imparted to me in Marathi, I would have learned at 25 what I know at the age of 52".

(Bal Gangadhar Tilak, 1856-1920: Nationalist, educationist, editor)

21

Welfare Implications of Economic Reforms in India

The term welfare has been defined in a number of ways. The concepts 'welfare' 'economic welfare.' 'social welfare' are fairly elusive. Even a great economist like A.C. Pigou would not attempt to define welfare. He observe, 'welfare' however, is a thing of very wide range. There is no need here to enter upon a general discussion of its content. It will be sufficient to lay down more or less dramatically two propositions; firstly, that the element of welfare are states of consciousness and perhaps, their relations; secondly, that welfare can be brought under the category of greater or less.

The significances of the concept of Welfare Economics is spread to every nook and corner of the World by great Economists, Statesment, Social thinkers and philosophers. All the leaders do admit unanimously that establishment of Welfare Economics is the only way to drive-out 'poverty' from both developed and developing nations.

Many Economists and Social thinkers brought forth number of concepts to explain the theory of Welfare Economics. Among them the definition of Prof. Ernst Engle's suits to the present economy of our country. He defines Welfare Economics in a more apt way and states that "the socio-economic conditions of people could be identified on the basis of their total income, and the portion of their income spent on necessary articles such as food, clothing, shelter, medicine and education during a given period of time." This theory appeals much to developing countries like India, because of the fact that the majority of the population in these Economics live with very, very limited income with too much of necessary expenditures. Further, he adds that if too much of this limited income of a given group is spent on necessary items, esp., on food, these people naturally belong to the Low Income Group (LIG) of that particular economy.

William Beveridge, who is considered the Father of Social security has given another important concept to bring out the significances of Welfare Economics to the World. He defines it as" each Government or every employer should provide and ensure maximum social security to all the labouring classes. The Social security measures should be given from cradle to grave to each and every citizen of the economy."

When humanitarian considerations is coupled with economic principles, anybody can easily come out from the "vicious circle of poverty" and establish a better standard of living.

Under the impact of trenchant criticisms of Lionel Robbins, Hicks and others, the welfare economics lost its scientific purity. Its assumptions were challenged and so also its operational consequences as guide to welfare policy. But it still persists, esp., in the field of taxation, minimum wage policy, and social legislation. Like the "Fisher's Quantity Theory of Money," it is very defective, but we can hardly go without it.

Many nations experience economic growth and developments as time passes by. Lot of economic plans are evolved and implemented in these economies. But, the fruits of these development programmes do not easily reach the poor and needy people whose number is very large. The benefits of growth programmes of the Govt., do not tickle down, properly and reach the poor. Economic development with "Social Justice" has gone somewhere from the scene.

As we may recall during the last five decades of Centralised Planning, the Indian economy accorded a dominant role for state enterprises in many sectors, pursued path of industrialisation behind high protective barriers and suspicion of foreign investment, adopted the regime of multiple controls, restrictive regulations and various state interventions.

Major share of the country's resources were applied to finance public sector projects bringing low rate of return year-after-year. The Govt., expenditure in respect of subsidies, interest payments, defence services and populistic schemes registered a sharp increase resulting into deficit in the budget and increasing burden of borrowings. The fiscal syndrome of deficit financing leading to double digit inflation, mounting balance of trade and payments difficulties, erosion and dwindling of Foreign Exchange Reserves culminated into a vicious crisis which provided an opportunity to the Govt., to introduce a new model of development.

Inspired by the success stories of developing countries such as South Korea, Taiwan, and the erstwhile Communist countries like China, India too constructed an alternative new model of development on the postulates of Liberalisation and Globalisation.

The marginalism implied in marketism has been marginalised

everywhere as proved by the empirical evidences of Hall and Hich, Baurnol, Cyert and march and a host of others.

The argument that the market can deliver welfare services also does not hold water in the Indian conditions for the simple reason that nearly 40 to 50 per cent of Indians are "marketed out" due to lack of purchasing power to buy services as the market determined "mark up" prices. Perhaps, the market can provide a variety of consumer durables both Indian and foreign to the rich, "neo rich" and middle class people who can afford to enjoy the elite consumerism fostered by Economic Reforms.

The social responsibility which characterise the Western capitalists is conspicuous by its absence in the alter of Indian capitalism. It is true that they can organise production efficiently but not necessarily at a minimum cost, and distribute them at lower price.

Access to adequate food is an essential condition of welfare and hence deemed to be an universal human right and collective responsibility. The Universal Declaration on Human Rights (1948) recognised that "Everyone has a standard of living for the health and wellbeing of himself and his family, including food." The World Conference 1974 reaffirmed that "Every man, women and child has inalienable right to be free from hunger and malnutrition in order to develop fully and maintain the physical and mental faculties."

Unfortunately, In India, hunger and malnutrition due to inadequacy of food had become widespread and there are areas of the country were deaths by starvation occur every year. It is ironical in the tenth year of the operation of economic reforms, hunger deaths were reported. This underscores the failure of economic reforms to provide even the basic right of Indians and also underlines the need for ensuring food security to the people. In the Indian situation, expanding and strengthening the system of delivery of food in general, and subsidies to food in particular should be a matter of high priority for state Policy.

Processed foods are primarily derived from agricultural Commodities, which often incur multiple taxes at various stages such as Market fee, Mandi fee, Octroi, Entry tax, Cess, Sales tax, Turn over tax, Central Excise, etc., This multiple taxation has a cascading effect on prices.

In additon, there is a wide variation in the level of taxes across States from 4 per cent to 20 per cent. A simple solution would be to do away with such cascading taxes, and replace these, if need be, with a uniform additional excise duty to encourage free and easy movement of goods within the country, as has been done with tobacco and textiles.

Urgent and effective intervention is required to make this a reality. We as a country have responded to crises, thro' concerted action born out of national consensus. The success of the "Green Revolution" is indeed proof of this. Now, we need a "Food Revolution" to foster a virtuous cycle of regenerative, broad-based growth.

What kind of measures are needed to build up the rural economy at this critical juncture ?

The major measures needed are restructuring and re-tooling of the extension services. The existing extension staff need to be retrained in order to serve as Rural knowledge workers, who can take new technologies to all farm families, irrespective of the size of holdings or level of literacy.

Modern information and communication technology provides uncommon opportunities for developing a user-driven, and user-controlled extension system. The information provided should be demand-driven, and should be relevant to time, and specific farming systems.

Retaining and re-deployment and not retrenchment should be the pathway for developing an extension system which is capable of stimulating an evergreen revolution in our farms.

Restructuring the State Land Use Boards is another major task. If the extension service is to help small farmers adopt land and water use patterns linked to marketing opportunities, there will be need to restructure and strengthen the State Land Use Boards. If this is not done, our farmer's fate will increasingly become a gamble in the market. We have an excellent capacity in remote sensing, weather forecasting and information technology. Hence, there should be no difficulty in achieving a proper match between markets and land use. The State Land Use Board should be headed by leading professional.

Central and State Govts., should not expand of Tidal extension depts., if opportunities for remunerative self-employment are to become available to farm graduates. We need a new deal for the self-employed in terms of public policies which promote and not obstruct socially relevant enterprises. In their respective catchment areas, industry could provide a wide range of services, as is already being done by the tobacco, and sugarcane industries. For example, non-availability of good and disease-free seeds is still a major constraint.

The re-organised, extension system should help to make our agriculture environmentally sustainable and globally competitive. This will be possible only if it becomes a farmer- centred and controlled system.

The price level at which commodities, esp., essential commodities are available in the market is an important determinant of welfare of people. Price stability through control of inflation has been one of the avowed goals of New Policy. Curtailment of fiscal deficit, and monetary contraction aimed at this goal. But what happened was that inflation during the post reform period persisted and in fact accelerated. The annual price increase in the last ten years of reform has been of the order of 11 to 12 per cent.

In recent months, the price of rice and other essential commodities have been soaring, hitting the common man under his belt. The price increases have been widespread and substantial. This rising rigour of inflation has come as a fall out of the structural adjustment programme itself. The export promotion has pushed up the price of primary commodities in the domestic market. A reduction in subsidies of fertilizers, electricity and coal has contributed to a rise in cost and price. Decontrol of prices have also fuelled prices. The rise in procurement and support price is another major determinant of inflation. The experience suggests that inflations affects the poor adversely than any other categories and the welfare consequences of the poor are very severe.

A poor country like India can ill afford to the policy jolts and shifts. However, this is not the time to bemoan. A new system has to come to stay with us, and reversing it now may be costly but reforming the reforming may be a more productive and prudent step.

We need to bring strong correctiveness and mechanisms within the packages to effect a golden trade off between development and welfare. A strategy for economic growth that emphasize on people's development and their productive potential is the only way to open opportunities. New opportunities are needed to expand and improve employment opportunities so that people can participate in growth and benefit from it. A happy blend of both the public and private sector on pragmatic and not on dogmatic considerations should be worked out.

Decentralisation of powers at the village level, creating and enabling environment for the masses and explicit policy shift towards welfare promotion can contribute to the greatest happiness of the greater number.

"The king who is trained to be wise, disciplined and who is devoted to just government and to the welfare of all beings will enjoy the earth unopposed."

(Kautilya, 4th C.B.C., Classical master of Statecraft).

22
Foreign Direct Investment

During the early phase of the Planning era, the national policy towards foreign capital did recognise the need for foreign capital, but decided not to permit it a dominant position. Consequently, foreign collaborations had to keep their equity within the ceiling of 49 per cent and allow the Indian counterpart a majority stake. Moreover, foreign collaborations were to be permitted in priority areas, more esp., those in which we had not developed our capabilities. But in an overall sense, our policy towards foreign collaborations remained restrictive and selective. Consequently, during 1961-70, a total of 2475 foreign collaborations were approved, and the during the next decade 1971-80 an other 3041 collaborations were sanctioned.

It was only during the 80s that the Govt., relaxed its policy towards foreign collaborations. This was done specifically in respect of investors from Oil Exporting Developing Countries with a well-defined package of exemptions.

Countrywise analysis of foreign collaborations reveals that the USA was at the top, accounting for nearly Rs. 322.7 crores of investment. This was one-fourth of the total foreign collaboration approvals. This was followed by the Federal Republic of Germany 17.2 per cent, Japan, UK, Italy, France and Switzerland. Five countries, that is, the USA, West Germany, Japan, UK, and Italy accounted for nearly 63 per cent of total approved foreign investment. Even Non-Resident Indians (NRIs) contributed about Rs. 113 crores accounting for 8.9 per cent of total investment.

One of the major achievements of the new economic reforms was that they provided a big boost to the inflow of foreign investment.

The foreign investment flows for the period 1991-92 and 1995-96 Upto November, 1995 reveals that the total investment flows of the order of US. $ 11. 744 billion were made, out of which direct investment accounted for

US $ 3.694 billion. As against this, portfolio investment accounted for US $ 8.05 billion. What needs to be emphasized is the direct foreign investment is less than one-third of the total foreign investment and even out of it, 10.4 per cent is contributed by non-resident Indians.

Portfolio investment of the order of 8.05 billion appears to be speculative nature which can take to flight in a period of political and economic uncertainty. It may not be correct on the part of GOI., to permit portfolio investment because this has only strengthened the foreign business firms to contorl the share market. Such a course may not be beneficial to the country.

Unless the lag between actual inflow and approvals is reduced, the role of FDI., in giving a boost to our country remain a myth.

Whether under external pressure or not there is little doubt that India is following step-by-step, the direction of IMF-World Bank regarding stabilisation and structural adjustments. Our policy towards foreign investment has been changing over time from regime of controls and restrictions more recently to an opendoor policy of liberalization and globalisation.

Economic Reforms introduced thro' New Industrial Policy-1991, with a backdrop of severe foreign exchange shortage-about Rs. 2500 million worth foreign exchange reserves, is an attempt to do away with the rigours of industrial and trade regulations in a big way in order to make the economy more open and competitive, having well-recognised the urgency of inviting foreign investment, foreign technology and foreign ideas, hence our policy in a global way towards Global Reach.

India has everything that a country could possibly have. We have second largest reservoir of technical and cheap manpower, all kinds of raw materials, a huge market with an estimated population of 900 million and a rising consumer class offering ample market opportunities to foreign investors, the huge and diversified capital market, financial support and widespread banking and insurance networks as special inducement to FDI.

According to the Director of World Economic Forum: "India is the right place for long term investment."

The share of India in direct foreign investment when compared to China, Brazil and Mexico is very low. Secondly, transfer of technology can also be effected with more investment being made by the technologically advanced MNCs.

These gains are not disputed by the critics, but the fact of the matter is that there are aspects of FDI which seriously impinge on people's welfare and national sovereignty. It is these aspects which need serious consideration by our Govt.

First, 43 per cent of the foreign investment is in the nature of portfolio investment which only strengthens speculative trading in shares. This had led to an artificial boom in the share market and the BSE Sensitive Index touched a high mark on 4282 on June, 18, 1994.

Secondly, FDI is catering to the needs of the upper-middle and affluent classes, thus concentrating on the 180 million consumers in the Indian economy.

Thirdly, portfolio investment made in India is in the nature of hot money which may take to flight if the market signals indicate any adverse trends. Thus, it would be a mistake to treat portfolio investment as a stable factor in our economic growth.

Fourthly, a larger inflow of FDI, more so in the financial sector, will lead to the building of reserves which in turn will expand domestic money supply. Consequently, an inflationary trend in prices gets strengthened in the process.

The MNCs after their entry are rapidly increasing their share holding in Indian companies and are thus swallowing the Indian concerns.

All India Manufacturers Organisation (AIMO) have raised their voices-against the discriminatory policies of the Govt, to foreign capital at the cost of indigenous capital.

A Press release issued by the Ministry of Commerce claimed that the first two months of the year 2000 have seen FDI inflows amounting to $ 600 million, of which about $ 481 million have come in Feb, alone. This is against the average inflow of $ 230 million a month in the Past. Table: 1

Till recently, the industry Ministry did not include GDR inflows into FDI, calculation, but ever since the Finance Ministry freed GDR, clearances and left it to FIPB, to decide whether or not companies are violating the FDI cap, it has been included in the data. Mauritius continues to be the leading foreign investor in India.

Table 1
Foreign Investment Inflows

(US$ million)

Year	Direct Investment (A)	Portfolio Investment (B)	Total (A+B)
1990-91	97	6	103
1991-92	129	4	133
1992-93	315	244	559
1993-94	586	3567	4153
1994-95	1314	3824	5138
1995-96	2144	2748	4892
1996-97	2821	3312	6133
1997-98	3557	1828	5385
1998-99	2462	-61	2401
1990-00 (Apr-Jan)	1608	1840	3448

Source: Reserve Bank of India, Handbook of Statistics on Indian Economy, 1999. RBI Bulletin, April 2000 for the figures for 1999-00 (April-January).

In the world of growing interdependence of nations and diminishing importance of national frontiers, there is increasing mobility of capital internationally. Globally, private capital flows have replaced Official Development Assistance (ODA) as the dominant source of external capital for many countries. While official flows totalled $ 56 billion, compared to $ 44 billion private flows in 1990, by 1996, public flows declined to $ 41 billion and private flows grew to $ 244 billion.

Generally, private capital flows are mainly concentrated in a small, but increasing number of so-called "Emerging Markets." Overall about 81 per cent of FDI to developing countries goes to only-a dozen countries. India does not figure in this list.

While the various steps which the GOI, has taken in the context of FDI promotion in the country are welcome steps, the fact remains that India's share in the total FDI flowing to all the developing countries is relatively small. India's share stood at 0.5 per cent of the total FDI for all the developing countries in the year 1992. Even after an increase of FDI in India in the following years, the situation is not very satisfactory as India's share constituted one per cent of the total FDI for all the developing countries in the year 1994. The corresponding percentage increased to 1.9 in 1995 and is estimated at 2.2 per cent in 1997. It may be pointed out that China tops the list among all the developing countries of the world so far as FDI is concerned. Further countries like Brazil, Mexico, Argentia,

Indonesia, Chile, Venezuela and Malaysia attract higher investment than India.

There are certain aspects which need to be considered in the context of FDI, for developing countries like India. It is well known that developing countries like India are weak in economic terms. It may be opinted out that India's share in the International Trade is not even 1 per cent and that of imports is 0.7 per cent. Under such a situation, even to attract a small quantum of FDI, the country has to offer attractive terms. For instance, the investors in the power sector were offered 16 per cent post-tax rate of return in dollar terms.

While the FDI is desirable and useful in many ways for economies like India, it may, however, not come in areas in which it is most needed. The interest of the foreign investors and multinationals, by-and-large, will not coincide with that of the economy concerned because their objective is to maximise profit and they would thus like to invest in areas where the returns are the highest.

Rather than giving a blank cheque to the foreign investors, the GOI, should specify a time-frame for FDI, in the country.

Moreover, the GOI should not compromise the independence and autonomy of the country merely because of the fact that FDI, will flow in the country. If the flow of FDI, by the foreign investors is linked to any of the conditions that of the signing of the CTBT, the GOI, should not only make a flat refusal but condemn the same at appropriate forums.

Further, the GOI should also make provision for the safety cushions in case of deviation by the foreign investors from the agreed terms for FDIflows.

On the whole, while the overall liberalisation and globalisation policies encouraging FDIs have been widely acclaimed they have also come under criticism from other quarters, like opposition parties, labour unions etc, However, the fact is that a "New Era" has been ushered in the annals of Indian Economy. True, too much liberalisation and our approach to globalisation in an era of unbridled openness and competition, in an unequal and borderless world, MNCs need close monitoring and proper watch/vigil in order to keep the country away from their foul play.

While analysing FDI scenario in India, it is observed that there is a huge gap between approval of FDI and actual flow. There is delay for the inflow of approved FDI into India. GOI should take rapid steps for the inflow of approved FDI, instead of inviting fresh investment.

Total FDI approval in India during the period 1991-2000-Jan-to April is 2,16,171 crore, whereas the actual flow is Rs. 75, 852 crore only. The percentage of FDI inflow over approval is 35.09 per cent only. Our FDI policies must be transparent.

We should avoid delay in taking decisions regarding FDI, approval. There must be a healthy co-ordination among the concerned Ministries while giving approvals for FDI,

There is a gap between approval of FDI, and actual-flow of FDI, Table:2 shows FDI approved and actual inflow during the period 1991-2000.

Table 2

FDI in India-Approval and Actual Inflow

(Rs. in crore)

Sl. No.	*Year*	*FDI approved Rs.*	*FDI actual inflow Rs.*	*% of inflow over approval*
1.	1991	534	351	65.73
2.	1992	3888	675	17.36
3.	1993	8859	1787	20.17
4.	1994	14187	3289	23.18
5.	1995	32072	6820	21.26
6.	1996	36147	10389	28.74
7.	1997	54891	16425	29.92
8.	1998	30814	13340	43.29
9.	1999	28367	16868	59.46
10.	2000 (Jan-April)	6412	5908	92.14
	Total	216171	75852	401.25

Source: Economic Times, 16 July 2000.

The expansion of international production was facilitated by the on-going liberalisation of FDI, regimes. Over the period 1991-1996, about 95 per cent of a total of 599 changes in the regulatory FDI, regimes of countries were in the direction of liberalisation. They mostly involved in the opening of industries previously closed, to FDI, the streamling or abolition of approval procedures and the provision of incentives.

In the case of India, the numerous hurdles and irritants holding back actual fructification of FDI have to be removed. The Govt's proposed hand holding exercise has to be strictly implemented.

Moreover, FDI should be encouraged in new sectors like Real Estate, and Insurance. All this would encourage incremental investments.

The world is changing rapidly and it is clear that India has to face many challenges in the world affairs. In view of the New World Order it has become essential for India to reassess and reshape her foreign policy. We should remeber that foreign policies are not fixed for all times, rather they are dynamic in character and change according to the circumstances, hence, adjustment and variations are vital for them.

Today's world scenario has created great challenges for India which are severe, but their solutions are also available. The need is to detect them and include in the foreign policy of India.

Foreign policy must be based on an intimate knowledge of and feeling for current international developments.

Our foreign policy is based on the principles of non-alignment and peaceful co-existence. These principles are the best safeguard of the independence and integrity of developing nations. Our relations with the USSR, and other friendly countries have strengthened non-alignment. This policy is active.

The issue of financial liberalisation is now seen as much more complex than what was originally envisaged. Because the needs of the real economy can be met only through Liberalisation, the literature still holds as its ultimate goal the "Full Liberalisation" of the Indian Economy.

However, the speed and sequencing of liberalisation, the manner in which liberalisation should be integrated into macro-economic stabilisation and structural adjustment programmes, and the prerequisties for the eventual success of liberalisation are still matters of ongoing concern.

A well-planned stabilization and growth-oriented structural programme will provide a solid foundation for the continuing success of liberalisation policies.

"Accept your destiny and go ahead with your life. You are not destined to become, an Air Force Pilot. What you are destined to become is not revealed now but it is predetermined." Dr. A.P. Abdul Kalam.

Foreign Direct Investment

Table A

Overall balance of payments

($ million)	1998-99	1999-2000	2000-01	2001-02
A. Total Current A/c	-4038	-4698	-2579	1351
(a) Merchandise	13246	-17841	-14370	-12703
(b) Invisibles	9208	13143	11791	14054
B. Capital A/c	8435	10444	9022	9545
1. Foreign Investment	2312	5117	4588	5286
(a) In India	2412	5191	5102	5925
(i) Direct	2480	2167	2342	3905

(ii) Portfolio	-68	3024	2760	2020
(b) Abroad	-100	-74	-514	-639
2. Loans (External Assistance Commercial Borrowings, Short Term)	4418	1601	4531	-917
3. Banking Capital	698	2127	811	4607
(a) NRI Deposits	960	1540	2317	2754
Overall Balance (In. Capital and Current A/cs and Errors and Omissions	4222	6402	5855	11757

Source: Reserve Bank of India.

With regard to the current account, India has been experiencing a substantial deficit on trade account and positive inflows on account of invisibles, mainly represented by inflows in the form of services and transfers while investment income has been negative. After many years, India had a positive current account position during 2001-02.

FDI policies have to be in line with requirements of the domestic market. For example, if investments are required in are as such as estate and trading, then the policy should encourage investment in such areas. The applicable small sector reservations and limitations on investment in such units also remain a barrier to investment, including foreign investment.

In August, 2001, the Planning Commission constituted a Steering Committee on FDI, which had 12 members and was headed by N.K. Singh, Member, Planning Commission. Mr. N.K. Singh in its report recommended a ten point agenda covering on a whole host of issues relating to FDI, and the recommendations contained in the Report are given below:

(1) Consider the enactment of a Foreign Investment Promotion Law that incorporates and integrates aspects relevant to promotion of FDI, The Dept, of Industrial Policy and Promotion should administer this law as against the present administration of the Foreign Exchange Management Act (FEMA) by the Directorate of Enforecement. This will be in line with the approach that the activity of encouraging FDI should be a promotional one rather than a regulatory one.

(2) States should enact a special investment law relating to infrastructure to expedite all investments in infrastructure sectors. The purpose of this law should be to integrate, to the extent feasible, the various State laws, rules and regulations applicable to infrastructure sectors. Areas such as environmental clearances, industrial relations, and worker health could be covered under such an enactment. The

Committee has suggested that the A.P. Infrastructure Act could be used as a reference.

(3) Empower the Foreign Investment Promotion Board (FIPB) to give initial Central level registrations and approvals where possible, with a view to speeding up the process of project implementation.

(4) Change Government's Rules of Business to empower Foreign Investment Implementation Authority (FIIA) to expedite the processing of administrative and policy approvals.

(5) The aggregate FDI. target for the 10th Plan should be disaggregated in terms of sectors and relevant administrative ministries/depts, to increase accountability. The Committee feels that if an annual FDI., inflow target of $8 billion is to be achieved over the next five years, then such targets need to be set. The report also contains an indicative list of target amounts that could be set for various sectors. This, of course, assumes that a carrot and stick approach can be implemented.

(6) Sectoral FDI, caps should be reduced to a minimum and entry barriers eliminated.

(7) The Committee has also recommended that a number of exit barriers should be removed. This includes sale of shares by one foreigner to another foreigner, sale from non-resident to resident, the rule that premium on publicly listed share price cannot exceed 25 per cent and rules regarding minimum sale price in the case of unlisted companies.

(8) The existing stratgey for attracting FDI, should be overhauled. The emphasis should from a broad (scatter shot) approach to one of targeting specific sectors. The Foreign Investment Promotion Council (FIPC) should be reformed to implement this strategy. Modern marketing techniques need to be used to attract FDI,

(9) The special economic zones (SPZs) should be developed as the most competitive destination for export related FDI, in the world by simplifying applicable laws, rules and administrative procedures and reducing red tape to the levels found in China.

Domestic Policy reforms in the power, urban infrastructure and real estate sectors and decontrol/delicensing should be expedited to promote domestic and foreign investment.

(10) The Committee has suggested a number of Changes in present sectoral limits on FDI, The changes suggested in some of the important areas are provided in the Table: B

Table B
Proposed Changes in Sectoral Limits on FDI

Sector	*Equity*	*Limits*	*Entry*	*Route*
Manufacturing				
Petroleum Refining-PSEs	26%	100%	FIPB	Automatic
Oil Marketing	74%	100%	FIPB	Automatic
Mining & Quarrying				
Coal & Lignite	50%	100%	Automatic	Automatic
Infrastructure Services				
Civil Aviation	40%	49%	FIPB	Automatic
Basic & Mobile Telephone	49%	74%	FIPB	No Change
Pipeline: Oil & Gas	51%	100%	FIPB	Automatic
Financial Services				
Banking (Private)	49%	100%	Automatic	No change
Insurance	26%	49%	Automatic	No change
Investing Companies	49%	100%	FIPB	Automatic
Currently Banned Sectors				
Plantations	0%	49%		FIPB
Real Estate: Complexes	0%	100%		Automatic
Individual house/bldg/shed	0%	100%		FIPB

India's share in FDI inflows among developing countries has been varying between 1 per cent and 2 per cent. This is indeed paltry. During 2001-2002 FDI., inflows did show improvement as it grew by 65 per cent over the previous year. Even with this improvement, FDI contributes too little to capital formation in the country. FDI, as a percentage of total Gross Domestic Product (GDP) was only 0.9 per cent in the year 2001. Among leading developing countries, this is the lowest in the world.

We are aware that FDI inflows in India are low. The irony of the situation is that India has a liberal and transparent FDI regime. As pointed out in the report, the entry rules are well defined and equity limits on foreign investment in certain sectors are explicit.

India basically loses out at the altar of India's red tape and the hurdles of doing business in India. This is also responsible for the low levels of realisation of FDI., flows compared to the proposals cleared.

Delays also lead to time and cost overruns. Even though many foreign companies are attracted towards India, a large number of them reject India as a possible destination as the market for many products is not sufficiently large enough at present to merit the extra effort required to implement the project.

Overall, the report submitted by the Committee is an excellent one and suggests comprehensive reforms to continue the liberalisation process undertaken by different Govt, since 1991. In fact a few of the suggestions are quite radical.

In the final analysis, the efficacy of the report will be judged by the implementation of its recommendations.

The subject of FDI., continues to be in the news. Very recently the 10th Plan Document was formally adopted by the Planning Commission. As widely reported, the plan document lays emphasis on achieving an 8 per cent growth throughout the plan period 2002-07.

For that purpose, it visualises an investment of 28.4 per cent of the GDP... 26.8 per cent is expected to come from domestic savings but a crucial 1.6 per cent of the GDP is expected from external savings.

The larger FDI flows are attributable to certain capital market developments, that have not been entirely benign. The spurt in buybacks, creeping acquisition by MNCs operating in India has been the main reason. For 2001-02 there were 20 buybacks floated by the MNCs. Most of them have formidable names in the Indian stock markets.

Through buybacks, take-overs, creeping acquisitions and so on they were consolidating their shareholding pattern in India. The loser has been the Indian shareholder and the exchanges as most of the MNCs chose to delist from the domestic bourses. They might have their own reasons and current market regulations do not prohibit such activity. However, it is clear case of FDI figures being misconstrued; for greater benefit they ought to have gone towards creation of productive assets.

Additionally, in the instant case, it is obvious that further funds will not be brought in by the MNCs. So the rise in FDI flows might have been an one time boost.

The above reinforces a growing opinion that not all the FDI flows have the results expected of them; enhanced industrial competitiveness, technology transfer, access to capital and integration of domestic markets with global ones.

Empirical evidence suggests that those beneficial consequences do occur but only in specific contexts. What should equally matter in any evaluation of FDI flows into India is their quality and not just aggregates (Quantity).

23

Export-Import (Exim) Policy

The principal objectives of the Exim Policy 2002-2007 are as under:

(1) To facilitate sustained growth 1 per cent of global merchandise trade.

(2) To stimulate sustained economic growth by providing access to essential raw materials, intermediates, components, consumables and capital goods required for augumenting producing and providing services.

(3) To enchance the technological strength and efficiency of Indian agriculture, industry and services, thereby improving their competitive strength while generating new employment opportunities, and to encourage the attainment of internationally accepted standards of quality.

(4) To provided consumers with good quality goods and services at internationally competitive prices while at the same time creating a level playing field for the domestic producers.

The above objectives will be met thro' the coordinated efforts of the State Governments and all the departments of the Government of India in general and the Ministry of Commerce and Industry and the Directorate General of Foreign Trade and its network of Regional Offices in particular, with a shared vision and commitment and in the best spirit of facilitation, in the interest of promotion of trade in goods and services.

Exports and Imports shall be free, except in cases where they are regulated by the provisions of this policy or any other law for the time being in force. The itemwise export and import policy shall be, as specified in ITC (HS) published and notified by Director General of Foreign Trade as amended from time to time.

The Export-Import policy for 1997-2002 appears to be the first major policy announcement by the multiarty conglomerate presently ruling the country. Both in terms of its content as well as style of governance, this policy pronouncement gives some indications about the elements likely to define the approach, sympathies and commitments of the Govt,

One of the specific important features of the Exim policy of 2000-01 is the removal of Quantitative Restrictions (QRs). The withdrawal of QRs has to be carried out under the obligation of mutual agreement between the U.S., and India, within the provisions of WTO.,

Unlike most of the countries of the world, India's import has been subject to different types of QRs. These restrictions are in the form of non-automatic licences, import thro' canalised agencies, SIL, actual user criteria etc., These restrictions are imposed because India presumes that she has an unfavourable position of Balance of Payments (BOP). In early 1990s and even earlier years, India had a serious BOP., problem; however, this has declined significantly during recent years.

At present, India's current deficit is 1.7 per cent of the GDP and foreign exchange reserves cover more than nine months of imports.

In the General Agreement of Tariff and Trade (GATT), WORLD TRADE ORGANISATION (WTO) system, it was decided to remove all types of QRs, and India had also agreed to phase out its QRs on all commodities, except for around 600 commodity/ lines for reasons related to security etc., ie., under Article XX and XXI of GATT 1994. However, India maintained QRs on import of some more items, in its import policies of 1999-2000 and earlier years, under provisions of Article XVIII:B of the GATT/WTO system.

This article recognises that member countries whose economies can only support lower standard of living, and are in the earlier stage of development may "apply quantitative restrictions for balance of payments of position."

The article, relating to BOP mentions that a member country has to publicly announce the time schedule for elimination of QRs. India has presented a time schedule of nine years.Australia, Canada, Japan, the EU., New Zealand, Switzerland, and the US., had objections to this time schedule, and brought dispute settlement proceedings against India. India reached mutual agreement with all these countries, except the US., and also agreed to phase out her QRs over a time period of 6 years, ie., 1997-2003. But the US., filed a dispute against India.

India and the US signed a mutual agreement on Dec., 28, 1999 which has ended the dispute between the two countries on an earlier phase out of QRs. In this agreement, India has agreed to advance the date by two years to March, 31, 2001 on lifting the QRs for all the items.

The dispute settlement body of the WTO was set up in 1997, and India had unilaterally removed QRs on a large number of additional items under the import-export policies of recent years.

In the import policy of 1999-2000, 1,429 items were under the import policy of restricted items, canalised route or SIL as shown in (Table: 1:)

Table 1 Different Types of QRS for Indian Products, Maintained for BOP Reasons during 1999-2000[1]

Type of QRS	*No of Lines*[2]
Total	14293
Restricted	700[4]
Canalised	44
SIL	685

Notes:
1 As on December 28, 1999.
2 At 8-digit ITC-HS classification (i.e., Ex).
3 The corresponding number of lines at 8-digit or 10-digit level is, 589.
4 Includes one line at sub-group of 8-digit which is prohibited.

A large number of them (685) could be imported after acquiring the SIL, which can easily be obtained from the market. In 1999-2000, there were 700 items subject to the hard-core QR policy of restricted items. Effectively, these were the items that could have really effected India's import and hence balance of trade, or BOP positions.

In the meeting of WTO at Seattle-there was almost a consensus on "Market access negotiations on non-agriculture products." The draft declaration took up a number of issues like peak tariffs, tariff escalation, tariff bindings, elimination of non-tariff barriers and reduction/elimination of tariff. As a part of modalities, it was also decided "...the bound rates, and where there are no bound rates, base rates to be agreed shall be used as the basis of negotiations." Hence, if the Seattle draft on "Market Access on Non-agriculture Sector" had been adopted, it would have become very difficult for India to raise the present level of tariff for any commodity of industrial sector, including those for which QRs will be removed.

A basic consideration which could enable us to uncover spaces enlarging our options can be obtained by analysing the linkages of the trade policy with other policies and sectors. The trade Policy's links with savings, investment, exchange rate, domestic price, inter-sectoral linkages, esp., those connected with industry, agriculture, infrastructure and areas, methods and costs of seeking competitiveness in the global arena need to be examined and coordinated prior to rushing in for an Exim policy.

Some aspects of this policy show a glaring absence of coordination with other related policies. Without an external economic intelligence network, the proposed anti-dumping agency may as well get dumped as inconsequential. No commodity can be viably exportable unless there is a reasonable and fairly stable home market, because the former is clearly far more uncertain and beyond our control and thus necessitates the latter as the cushion. Without reliable and appropriate prices, incomes and wages forecasts and or control mechanisms, our presence in the external markets would remain volatile.

With growing import-intensity, may be more pronounced for the non-traditonal items of export than for the traditional ones, esp., in the midst of huge and chronic trade deficit, the choice of thrust areas of exports has to be very carefully calibrated.

OGL consumer goods imports are a sure device for globalising our domestic prices, that is, bridging the gulf dividing world market prices from our prices. With growing nominal income groups between the rich and the poor nations, that is, the failure of domestic incomes to move to levels closer to the global levels brings about a situation of globalised prices in the framework of non-globalised sticky Indian income levels.

We may recall how the USA during the 1970s used to mobilise her economists to undertake and popularise pseudo-theories maintaining that impacts amount to "Market Distruption," that is, finishing off the home market for the domestic industry's ineluctable adverse effects on domestic labour. This was their response to recession and the consequential need to adopt super-protection policies. But today when countries struggling to provide some space to their poor adopt even mildly similar policy stances they invoke super-301 type measures challenging the sovereignty of others.

This Exim Policy (1997-2002) has been hailed by advocates of free trade as being "Politically Savvy" as it "walked a fine line between opening up the domestic market and reassuring domestic producers."

(Financial Express: April 1 and 2, 2001.)

Moreover, provision of "adquate safeguards " through such institutional mechanisms as adjustment of tariffs and imposition of anti-dumping duties, reportedly, has not only pleased the major "chambers" of industry but also has "deflected political criticism" for the moment.

(Economic Times, April, 2, 2001:

(Business Standard, April, 2, 2001).

Economics will have a chance to establish itself at academic level as well as policy areas both in the government and corporate, provided there is a new awakening on social realities and the amends we need to make in the broad content of Economics.

If we analyse capitalist economics today, the power technology and newer markets created by elements of Western modernism and gainful exploitation of the scenario by multinational organisations, they are placed on a pedestral of economic prospects.

We are not saying that the world of Globalisation is going to be in that pattern. We are just trying to focus how theoretical estimates warrant a careful and meticulous re-examination because of the changes in a broader social scenario.

In this context, what is really important is to identify the concepts that will be relevant to our country inter-alia work out the costmetics for the new innovative economic reforms and of course, with the determination to translate visions into reality, the convert the dreams about the furture into facts of the present.

24

Economic Stabilisation and Growth

The Structural Adjustment Programme (SAP) has been imposed with the underlying logic that the process of globalisation and liberalisation would free the production from exogenous constraints and endogenous inertia. Initially as the controls are removed the prices shoot up, but as the economy adjusts to the globalised liberalised state, the claim is that the output will gear up to the requirements and the prices will be automatically controlled.

The experience of the Latin American economies tell us a different story. Not only has the per capita income declined, the people in these countries have had to live with an annual inflation rate of 10-10,000 per cent for more than a decade.

Table 1

Inflation in Latin American Economies After SAP

(Percentage change in wholesale prices)

Year	*Argentina*	*Bolivia*	*Brazil*	*Mexico*
1980	75.4	49.3	106.4	24.4
1981	109.6	35.2	103.2	24.5
1982	256.2	227.9	93.2	56.1
1983	360.8	416.0	167.4	107.4
1984	575.1	1695.4	236.3	70.3
1985	662.9	10,446.9	229.0	53.6
1986	63.9	172.8	140.2	88.4
1987	122.9	10.5	207.1	135.6
1988	412.6	19.0	697.2	107.8
1989	3432.8	19.2	1268.4	16.1
1990	1606.9	20.0	2703.8	23.3
1991	110.5	19.2	401.4	20.5
1992	6.0	—	987.8	13.4

Source: International Financial Statistics, IMF.

The prices in Indian economy have not gone berserk like those in Latin America. In fact, the inflation rate in India had entered double digits (10.5 per cent in Nov., 1990) even before the structural adjustment was imposed. It reached a peak of 16.3 per cent in sept., 1991)-just as the reforms started-declined to a single digit soon enough (9.4 per cent in Aug., 1992) and came down to 6.9 per cent in April, 1993. Since June, 1993 it started rising again and was 8.2 per cent in Jan., 1994.

The Govt., claims that controlling inflation is a major achievement of its stabilisation policy-that is, curtailment of fiscal deficit. The Indian economy can now look forward to increased output and prosperity. The critics, however, point out that the single digit inflation is an outcome of good monsoons, and not of good fiscal management.

What is good for the gander is hardly ever good for the goose. What is relevant for a developed economy is, therefore, rarely recommended for a developing country. We may consider the following statement from the London Economist of July 11, 1992 in regard to the US commercial bank lending: "By the end of May (1992) commercial and industrial loans had fallen by $ 42 billion from their peak, in November 1989, of $ 644 billion. Bank holding of Govt., securities had increased by half, to about $ 599 billion. Figures realeased at the end of July will probably show that the two crossed over in June."

The economic literature on development over the past 56 years was dominated by four major leading thoughts: (1) The linear stages of growth models: (2) Theories and patterns of structural changes; (3) The international dependence revolution and (4) The Neo-Classical free-market counter revolution.

The 1980s saw the Neo-Classical counter revolution which emphasized the beneficial role of free markets and the heavy economic costs of Govt., intervention in promoting development. It is the last line of thinking that is behind the IMF and the World Bank suggested medicines for the ills of the needy and sick developing countries of the world under the guise of structural adjustment. These structural changes in the economy as a consequence of development is common to all the four lines of thinking.

According to W.A. Lewis, underdeveloped economies consist of two sectors: (1) A traditional, overpopulated rural subsistence sector characterized by zero marginal labour productivity, meaning that there is surplus labour; (2) A high productivity modern urban industrial sector into which labour from subsistence sector is gradually transferred. Both the labour transfer and modern sector employment growth are brought about by output expansion in the latter. The speed with which this expansion occurs is determined by the rate of industrial investment and capital accumulation in the modern sector. Such investment is made possible by the excess of modern sector profits over wages, the assumptions being that the capitalists reinvested all their profits. And the level of wages in urban industrial sector was assumed constant, and with constant urban wages, the supply curve of rural labour to the modern sector would be perfectly elastic.

The Western countries through the Fund-Bank combine, have been harping on these reforms and many countries including India have succumbed to the pressures and have undertaken these reforms. To what effect were these undertaken ? Countries quoted as examples of success, Malaysia, S. Korea, Taiwan, Thailand and to some extent Indonesia had governments which ruled the people by the Iron Law; and further these countries were small. The successes reported are just a few, but the failures are many in Asia, South America, and Africa.

Moreover, the world of yester years were a bipolar and its dictates were very different; the objectives then were development and providing assistance. The present world is emerging as a G-7 hegemony, which is looking for markets; and the developing world is expected to serve the interests of the developed world. And so, in India the hopes for transformations are not taking place. It is alleged that the West through these international organisations, is using the conditionalities for its open entry into the populous and demand hungry Third World, and find a market for their recession affected products. But the developing countries, this would only help destabilize these economies, and get them be continuously dependent on the West. Hence many developing World politicians and economists accuse the West of open practice of Neo-Colonialism, with hardly any interest in the economic development of the Third World countries.

Examining the theoretical basis of the Fund-Bank combine, it is obvious that the basis is the Ricardian and Heckscherohlin theory of competitiveness. This competitiveness is primarily in cost-efficiency, and its determinants are found in the structure endowments. In these traditional models, competitiveness is rooted in a set of initial conditions, that is, the state of technology or factor composition which are the conditions a country starts with. Normally globalisation would allow specialisation according to competitiveness and alter the division of labour, but within the same initial conditions. But in an underdeveloped economy, the initial conditions are underdeveloped milieu, and competitiveness gets grounded in under-development itself. Since development is meant to undermine systematically these conditions and create a new set of conditions leading to self-sustained growth, in an underdeveloped country this does not take place, and competitiveness gets eroded as the economy develops.

A review of Indian economic policy would indicate that, controls and Govt., intervention were not the only faults that derailed the economy of the country. It was more the approach to planning that was faulty. We planned for an ambitious programme of industrialisation, neglecting agriculture and not caring to provide the basic needs of the vast majority of the people.

Secondly, our planning models, licensing and control systems wer such that demonstration effect had the field day, which helped inculcate in the people, an unnatural appetite for and appreciation of Western thought, western education, western technology, that "Indianness" was despised and devalued; anything foreign was taken to be the ideal to be reached; consequently self-esteem of self-worth were completely set aside or ignored altogether among all sections of the people.

Mahatma Gandhi wrote way back in Aug., 1947, "I will give you talisman. Whenever you are in doubt or when the self becomes too much with you, apply the following test. Recall the face of the poorest and the weakest man whom you have seen, and ask your self if the step you contemplate is going to be of any use to him;will he gain anything by it ? Will it restore him to control over his own life, and destiny ? In other words, will it lead to Swaraj for the hungry and spirituality to starving millions?"

The irony with these stalilisation programmes is that since they were essentially based on restraining aggregate demand which had a depressing effect on the real output of economies. Various studies have built up models of economic growth and stabilisation programmes which show that the rates of growth of output initially decelerate if not actually fall, then after a few years would pick up and accelerate faster than the rate of GDP. The eventual acceleration of the growth of output primarily results from the structural policies when they complement the usual demand restraining stabilisation policies.

However, the initial phase of deceleration of output is a result of certain inherent problems of adjustment under an overall restraint on demand. Even if the initial conditions were marked by excess demand or expenditures exceeding output, the reduction in expenditure would not just reduce prices or the rate of inflation but also real output or atleast the rate of growth of real output. The effect is more explicitly brought if we consider changes in relative prices because the stabilisation policies are complemented with other policies such as devaluation and deregulation of prices, which change the relative prices between different sectors. A devalution which changes the relative price between tradeable and non-tradeables. In the long run resources will move from non-tradeable to tradeable sectors improving national income.

The current economic reform programme being carried out by GOI., has been described as basically a shift from central planning to a market driven economy. It does involve a move away from the centralised allocation of resources in some key factors by the Govt., to allocation by the market forces. In fact, a basic feature of the economic reform programme is the open recognition that many constraints and controls were not working and that others were distorting allocation rather than improving the performance of a free market. Markets not only cannot easily be suppressed out , and they cannot be always avoided. The policy framework for future must give more attention to the better and proper use of human resources technology and self propelling self reliant strategy.

There is a need of firm commitment for rural development on the part of the Govt., and on the bottom top approach. In the efforts of poverty eradication stress should be laid on proper implementation, administration, funding and evaluation. Thus, Govt, should make efforts, to raise the rate of investment for a quick expansion in the output of wage-goods sustantially above the rate of growth of population and for achievement for Triple full employment at full efficiency, minimal wage on full year basis.

The State has to play its role alertly and effectively to achieve these targets even in this era of Liberalisation. it would not be proper to throw the baby of wage-goods in the bath-tub of Liberalisation and market mechanism, without constant monitoring and proper policy formulation and implementation.

The monetary policy has to be evolved to meet the credit needs of the growing economy in order to keep in check inflationary forces. Moreover, while making any change in the structure of interest rates, public debt policy considerations will have to be kept in view while it is true that most of the economic progress we see around us would hardly been possible without the productive use credit made possible thro' the lending of investible funds by the banks and other financial intermediaries. It is no less true that credit has been mainly responsible for economic debacles in the past. Thus, the need for exercising proper control over the supply of money is evident in the interest of maintaining economic stability in the system.

We should now bend our energies to make India prosperous and economically vibrant country with its vast resources and huge market.

25

Emerging Contours of Health Sector Reforms

It is becoming clearer day-by-day that the health status of the population is one of the most important factors in the process of economic development. There are two reasons for it: First, health as and indicator of economic development, shows the success or failure of a country in providing the most basic needs of the people like food, shelter, sanitary conditions and so on.

Secondly, health is a form of human capital and helps as a factor in further development of the country. According to Strauss, Delalikar and Behrman, health influences the supply and productivity of adults in the labour force, and the enrolment performance of children in schools. And Kruegar, Wheler, Hicks and Balassa view that high infant and child mortality rates greatly influence fertility rates, which in turn play a crucial role in development.

One of the best established epidemiological findings is that the prevalence and distribution of diseases is strongly influenced by economic factors. A crosstabulation of incidence of diseases by economic class in a population group would show that most infectious diseases common in developing countries can really be considered as "Diseases of Poverty." As living conditions improve they tended to disappear spontaneously.

As economic conditions improved, people are able to take better care of their health problems. Morbidity gets reduced, because they can provide better nutrition, enjoy greater resistance to infection, and infectious diseases, as housing conditions, sanitation and water supply get improved; and when sickness overtakes them, they are able to provide better medical care. At the same time, economic improvement might lead to sheer consumerism and conspicuous consumption styles which become health hazards. Such a situation can co-exist with "diseases of Poverty" and found in most devloped countries.

In this context, it is good to recollect the well-established finding regarding relationships between health status and economic development. First, it is not automatic that improvement in education and health will trickle down to the poor people in due course as the economy develops. For the upper and middle classes do often prevent such filtration to maintain their position and continue to exploit the poor

Secondly, the synergism between poverty, malnutrition, and increased morbidity and mortality is well established. Hence, to improve health, it must be attacked directly and integratedly to improve the health of the people.

Thirdly, given the social and political factors, even a comparatively limited economic growth can lead to outstanding improvement in health status, as it happened in Cuba, and China and also in Kerala, while the affluent Punjab and Rajasthan were not blessed with good health status. This shows that integrated programmes of economic and social and political development would make health services far more effective even at lower levels of economic growth.

Conversely, improvement in health statuts does lead to economic development. For instance, when the endemically Malaria infected Terai region was eradicated of it, there was rapid economic development in that region. Further, general health improvement increased worker's productivity and thus contributed to economic growth.

Whatever be the nature of the economic revolution that has been taking place in India during the last 56 years, unfortunately, the structure and pattern of health care delivery has been a "continuum " from the colonial period. After our Independence, no attempt was made to radically restructure health care services. Though India has a significantly large public health sector, private sector has grown enormously, since 1970.

Hospitals were 3862 in 1971, which rose to 11,174 in 1991; Beds available in 1971 were 3, 48, 655; and they rose to 6, 64, 135; dispensaries were 12, 180 in 1971, and 27, 431 in 1991. Since the 7th plan, a boost was given to setting up Primary Health Centres (,PHCs) so that there would be one PHC for every 30,000 population. This number shot up to 22, 243 in 1991 from 5131 in 1971. The number of allopathy doctors available in 1971 was 1,51, 129 and this number rose to 3,98, 238 in 1991. out of these, 42.6 per cent of hospitals were in the public sector, while private sector hospitals were 57.4 per cent. 40.4 per cent of dispensaries were in the public sector, while private sector owned 59.6 per cent. The trend was reversed with regard to the number of hospital beds. Private sector claimed only 32.2 per cent of these beds, while the public sector owned 67.8 per cent of the hospitals beds.

As per data supplied by Human Development Report 1996, in India annual expenditure on health services is 1.3 per cent of GDP which means that per capita public expenditure on health is very low in comparison to developed and most of the developing countries. On comparing the trends in the total financial allocations to health sector by Govt., we find by-and-large, financial decisions are broadly consistent with policy strategies. However, the financial availability for the health sector cannot be considered to be adequate enough to translate the goals of "Health for all" into actual practice.

Table
Public Sector Plan Outlay on Health, FWP, Safe Water Supply and Sanitation

(Rs. Crore)

Plan		*Health*	*FWP*	*Safe Water Supply and Sanitation*	*Grand Total*
I	Plan	65.2	0.1	11.0	76.2
		(3.3)		(0.6)	(3.4)
II	Plan	14.8	2.2	74.0	217.0
		(3.0)	(0.1)	(1.58)	(4.7)
III	Plan	225.9	24.9	105.7	356.5
		(2.6)	(0.3)	(1.2)	(4.1)
Annual Plans		140.2	70.4	102.7	313.3
(1966-69		(2.1)	(1.1)	(1.6)	(4.8)
IV	Plan	335.5	278.0	458.9	1072.4
		(2.1)	(1.8)	(2.9)	(6.8)
V	Plan	760.8	491.8	1091.6	2344.2
		(1.9)	(1.3)	(2.8)	(6.0)
VI	Plan	1821.1	1010.0	3922.0	6753.1
		(1.9)	(1.0)	(4.0)	(6.9)
VII	PLan	3392.9	3256.3	6522.5	13171.7
		(1.9)	(1.8)	(3.6)	(7.3)
VIII	Plan	7575.9	6500.0	16711.0	30786.9
		(1.7)	(1.5)	(3.8)	(7.0)

Source: Draft VIIIth Plan (1992-97).

Note: Figures in brackets indicate percentage to total plan outlay.

From the above Table: it is evident that financial allocation to health is gradually decreasing, whereas it was 3.3 per cent of total plan outlay in I Plan; it is 1.7 per cent in VIII plan. However, the share of plan outlay on safe water and sanitation has increased from 0.6 per cent during I plan to 3.8 per cent in VIII plan. It implies that govt., has stressed on preventive aspect of health care facilities.

The overall performance of India's HRD through health and nutrition has been far from satisfactory, and it may have implications for the income earning prospects of so developed human resources. It is, therefore, necessary to focus attention on utilisation of thus developed human resources in terms of employment and unemployment levels in the Indian economy.

The problem of utilisation of developed human resources is more formidable than faced in development of human resources itself. It is disappointing that Govt., has not fully utilised this slender stock of scientific and technical manpower and this is evident from large scale emigration of the scientific and technical manpower from India to developed countries. There is an imperative need for adopting an appropriate strategy to tackle the problems of unemployment, underemployment, and misemployment of highly skilled persons. For this, a comprehensive human resource development policy, which encompasses all programmes or activities, directly or indirectly related to the development, maintenance and utilisation of human resource is needed.

The 9th FYP, of its kind not to make any financial commitments for health for the full plan period. Those who studied the plan had to depend upon the annual budget allocations that kept getting reduced with every revision. (Table:1).

Table 1

Central Plan Outlay for Health and Family Welfare

(Rs. in crores)

	1997-98		1998-99		1999-2000		2000-2001
	(BE)	(RE)	(BE)	(RE)	(BE)	(RE)	(BE)
Health (including ISM & H).	955	918	1195	981	1195	1062	1378
Family Welfare	1829	1829	2489	2253	2920	3120	3520

BE=Budget Estimate; RE=Revised Estimate; ISM&H=Indian System Medicine & Health.

Source: Economic Survey 2000-2001.

In the planning process health care is being considered less and less important is evident in the 9th Plan objectives. where only a passing reference has been made to "Providing...primary health care facilities." Similarly, while the total outlay on Health and Family Welfare has remained aroudn 2.8 per cent to 3.3 per cent of the total plan expenditure from the Ist Plan onwards, the percentage outlay on Health has decreased from 3.33 per cent in the Ist Plan to 1.75 per cent in the 8th Plan, while that of Family welfare increased from a mere 0.10 per cent to 1.50 per cent.

The Economc Survey 1999-2000 talks of zero incidence of polio by the end of 2000. through oral immunisation. This is remarkable since it is well known that oral vaccines can also cause polio, and that polio is transmitted by contaminated water. In this context, we may to point out that despite the success of the pulse polio campaign, there has been a recent spate of polio cases in Delhi (TOI., 28th March, 2000).

Policies followed under SAP., cause a skewed pattern of investment in communicable and non-communicable diseases. In addition, increasing emphasis on privatisation is also affecting health services.

The 9th FYP., as well as the National Population Policy (NPP) 2000 both emphasise the importance of improving interventive services, equipment, technologies, and emergency care to decrease maternal mortality and morbidity and to improve child survival, but they do not even mention the fact that poverty, malnutrition and potable water as well as sanitation play an equally important part in health status. This increasingly medicalised view of health does not bode well for the goal of "Health For All."

Significantly, while the 9th Plan talks of improving primary health care services, increasing health personnel, and providing improved urban health services, the funds for infrastructure have stayed about 8.5 per cent of the budget of the Dept, of Health (Expenditure Budget 1998-1999 to 2000-2001). In fact, in the 90s, there has been only marginal expansion in the health infrastructure as is revealed in the "Economic survey" 1998-1999.

The population-Control centered technocentric health sector planning is a part of the reforms that are creating increasing unemployment, a decrease in people's real wages, increasing incidence of poverty, and setbacks to the food security of the poor and vulnerable people (A.E.S, 1991-1998).

In the absence of any genuine attempt to tackle these problems, people's health will become worse. The lack of social security nets, increasing dis-investment in public services, and health services that seem to focus on needs of donors rather than on epidemiologically assessed needs of the population, will be reflected in a reversal of the health indicators of the people.

In fact, the Infant Mortality Rate (IMR) that is said to be the most sensitive indicator of a population's health is already sounding an alert. Not only did the fall in IMR slow down in the 90s (Table: 2), in comparison to the previous decades, the latest SRS reveals that IMR is on the rise. (Table 2 and 3).

Table 2

Trends in Infant Mortality Rate in India 1951 to 1998

	1951	*1961*	*1971*	*1981*	*1991*	*1994*	*1996*	*1998*
IMR/1000	146	146	129	110	80	74	71	72
Fall in IMR	-	0	17	19	30	6	3	-1

Source: SRS India cited in Economic Survey 1998-1999 and 1991-2000.

Table 3

Trends in Infant Mortality Rate in Different States in India Over Three Years

State/UT	*1996*	*1997*	*1998*
Andhra Pradesh	65	63	66
Assam	74	76	78
Bihar	71	71	67
Gujarat	61	62	64
Haryana	68	68	69
Karnataka	53	53	58
Kerala	14	12	16
Madhya Pradesh	94	94	97
Maharashtra	48	47	49
Orissa	96	96	98
Punjab	51	51	54
Rajasthan	85	85	83
Tamil Nadu	53	53	53
Uttar Pradesh	85	85	85
West Bengal	55	55	53
All India	72	71	72

Source: SRS India.

Unless public Health planning follows epidemiological evidence it will ultimately fail in its objective. If the health sector does not improve its approach and carry out health reforms based not on instructions from the IMF/WORLD BANK, but on the needs of the people, for many Indians it will be too late.

Hence, there is a need to develop an alternative system of health care. In this system, a community based health care system would be evolved with one community health centre for every one lac people, and a sub-centre for every 500 population. The health problems of each community would be solved by that community, with the people of the community meeting half the expenses, and the other half coming from the State. Such a system can succeed under Panchayat Raj system of local Govt,

The community Health Care Centre would be managed by qualified people drawn by the community. Qualification should not be just the modern system of medicines but an integrated system which would include cheap medicines. Studies show that the utilisation of homeopathy and Ayurvedic medicines have been increasing steadily in India.

And there is no room for complacency. We cannot afford to rest on our oars. The demographic and health picture of the country still constitutes a cause for serious and urgent concern. The high rate of population growth continues to tell on the health of our people and the quality of their lives.

To put an end to the existing situation, it has been found necessary to restructure the health services, to provide, within a phased time-bound programme, a well-dispersed network of comprehensive primary health care services that work with voluntary organisations all over the country.

We have, therefore, to work to a definite time-frame for effecting a quantum-jump in terms of providing easy and inexpensive access to medical and family welfare facilities in rural and urban areas alike.

We need many more doctors living and working in our villages and the purposive involvement of the entire medical community in the family welfare and allied programmes in order to move nearer to realising Bapu's vision of a progressive and prosperous India, free of want, deprivation, and disease.

"Health is the starting point of all welfare. The health of the nation depends on the health of the individuals. Without it we can have no progress in any direction that would be enduring or meaningfcel, So the provision of adequate health services is one of the first responsibilities of any Government."

(Smt. Indira Gandhi: 15 June, 1981).

26

Risk Management in Banks

The financial sector reforms has brought in a number of far-reaching changes in the operational arena of banking., both in respect of approach and procedure. On such important dimension is Risk Management be it deposit mobilisation or extending credit or investment or Forex business entail a future orientation.

Peter Drucker in one of his articles on future says:

"We have only two things about the future it cannot be known; it will be different from what exists now and from what we now expect...The best we can hope to do is to anticipate future effects of events which have already irrevocably happend."

Walter Wriston, Chairman and Chief Executive of citicorp (1970-84) remarks:

"The fact is that Bankers are in the business of managing risk, pure and simple that is the business of banking."

There might not be two opinions about this remark on the significance of risk management in banking. For, the assumption and management of risk is the very essence of the banking business. For example, at board and executive management levels there is the ultimate responsibility of ensuring protection and reasonable yield on capital base. This could be discharged by managing/minimising risk of loss. A failure in this regard would result in reduction of bank business and a fall in the value of the institution. This has an adverse impact on the image of the bank. Within the treasury area there are various kinds of risks such liquidity risk arising from mismatch between inflow and outflow of liquid funds (cash) market risk, credit risk etc., Besides fiduciary risk, physical security risk, risk arising from lack of integrity in computer data, and information system, so on and so forth, would also cause substantial risk of loss to the banks.

With globalisation and happenings like BCCI Barings and Daiwa, consciousness about the 'risk' factor is gaining prime importance.

Adherence to capital adequacy standards, accepted under bastle committee worldwide has given further fillip to the concept of 'Risk.' In the context of Indian Banks, asset classification norms pronounced by Narasimham Committee have brought the risk factor into sharper focus.

Concept of Risk

In their process of financial intermediation, banks use the financial, physical, organisational, human and technological resources to deliver banking products, ie., financial and non-financial services. Both the input acquisition and output generation are conditioned by environment the surroundings-within which the banks operate. Like opportunities from outside the organisation, the environment and strength within the organisation, the environment is also endowed with external threats and internal weaknesses. These facets get reflected as risks while undertaking business. The chance of what is visualised or what ought to happen, does not happen, or does happen, but not in a required measure, gives rise to an element of uncertainty, i.e., 'Risk.' With the globalisation of financial sector operations, the contours of risk have also broadened multifold. When the thrust of operations is on profit, i.e., reward, emphasis on risk is bound to go up. The uncertainty of future, impact of past, and instability of present, all give rise to risk.

Bank-Risk Classification

(1) Liquidity and Funding Risk

Being unable to meet the repayment demand of depositors is a contingency that bankers seek to avoid at all costs. On the other hand, storing liquidity is not a solution to the problem either, since it involves loss of profitability. To achieve a proper balance, liquidity needs must be planned taking into account likely gross cash inflows and outflows on a daily basis. In addition to such daily management, an overall liquidity balance should be secured as well as by tailoring the bank's lending and investment portfolios to thetype and basis of finding that it commands. Our reference to the asset portfolios in this context also covers off-balance sheet items in the nature of direct credit substitutes which could impact on the banks's liquidity.

(2) Interest Rate Risk

Indian commercial banks are moving, albeit, in a phased manner since May, 1989, to an era of "Total Deregulation" in regard to interest rates. Now, all the money market instruments such as Call money, Term money, Rediscount money, Certificate of Deposits, Commercial paper etc., are freed from the regulations relating to interest rates and the rates are now freely determined by the market forces. Similarly, the RBI has also allowed freedom to banks to determine the interest rates on domestic term deposits for over two years and also on advances with a credit-limit of Rs. two lac. Consequently, risk associated with the deregulation has also increased manifold.

A glimpse of the interest rate risk associated with the deregulation was faced by most of the banks during Sept., 1995, when the call money rates zoomed to around 60 per cent ot 70 per cent on an average and to even more than 100 per cent occasionally. The impact of volatility in call money rates also spread to the exchange market wherein the forward rate for Dollar rose phenomenally.

With a view to reduce the cost of forward cover on Dollar and also to bail out borrowing banks from the consequences of very high call money rates, the RBI, initiated several measures such as reduction of CRR by half a percent point, pumping money thro' securities Trading Corporation of India, removal of CRR on increase in NRE, FCNR (B) and NRNR, deposits over a base date, etc., with the competition getting more intense, the interest spread between the deposits and advances is also likely to come under heavy strains in the ensuing years. Hence, the survival of banks will hinge upon-effective management on the interest rate risk.

(3) Currency and Foreign Exchanges Risk

Any numeraire mismatch between liabilities and assets gives rise to currency risk. Even in the same currency book, mismatches among different maturities could arise in the course of business that will mean a foreign exchange risk. Bank managements need to satisfy themselves on an ongoing basis that the open positions that so arise are within the limits earlier set from a prudential standpoint.

In the light of the above circumstances, bank management would need to monitor:

(1) (a) Cash in/Cash out for managing liquidity and reserve position; (b) liability and assets composition to monitor the overall liquidity position.

(2) Classification of assets and liabilities according to their repricing basis, to ensure that an approximate balance is achieved.

(3) Status and behaviour of the loan portfolio for determining the general health, with special attention to large loan accounts; timely completion of the limit review for all loan accounts; Portfolio composition, made of group, industry exposures etc., to prevent undue risk

concentrations; efforts for dealing with non-performing assets; current market value of investments, and their maturities.

(4) Equilibrium between assets and liabilities in different currencies in the aggregate; equilibrium between assets and liabilities in different currencies of specific maturities.

(4) Market Risk

Market risk is the risk to bank's financial condition that could result from adverse movements in market prices. There are many types of market risks, that impact the portfolio value primarily, these risks involve forward risk, and for those involving options, changing interest and currency rates give rise to forward risks. These changes occur for specific commodities or financial instruments, and due to local and world economic or political events. Options risk emerges due to the same factors as also evolving perceptions of the volatility of price changes, the passage of time and the interactive effects of other market risks.

Market risk exists on the system either deliberately or accidentally. Active trading in currency, equity or investment markets, mismatches in maturity patterns of overseas subsidiary, lending to a particular industry, etc., are the potential areas for market risks. Generally, the inadvertently taken market-risks bring the financial institutions in trouble.

(5) Capital Risk

Due to the very nature of activities undertaken by banks, they need more capital, from economic rather than from regulators' perspective. Greater risks associated with: Credit, liquidity, interest rates, and market necessitate the adequacy of capital. Each bank has to assess how much capital it needs, economically, as also to persuade the outside world that its calculations of the needed capital are valid. What happens when the capital is low, is concerned rating agencies, reluctant counterparties, and in a deregulated environment, tentative depositors who impose a high cost of funds.

It is imperative for every bank to understand importance of having sufficient capital, as also the quantum of economically related capital. A bank further needs to have a management and measurement system for ensuring holding of appropriate level of capital.

(6) Technology Risk

The entry of new private sector banks and foreign banks has set the process of upgrading the technology in use in Indian commercial banks. Being new entities, these banks are able to start their operations based on the latest technology and, hence, in a postion to offer variety of products using these upgraded technologies. As the technology, esp., in the fields of computerisation and communications, are fast changing banks will be running a high technology risk in terms of frauds the obsolescence. Prior to 1990s, banks in India were using (with the exception of foreign banks and a few private sector banks) very little computers in managing their day-to-day operations. But in the coming years banks may have to introduce technology so as to effectively manage (manage major chunk of business) thro' such technologically upgraded means. This would call for proper assessment of technology risk, and adoption of suitable strategies and measures to overcome the impact of all these risks.

Risk Management System:

Like any other system, the success of Risk Management largely depends on the fulfilment of certain prerequisites. Addressing the issues described here under may reduce the risk of the system becoming dysfunctional:

(1) The imperative need is to understand the inherent characteristics of Risk, its definition and quantification.

(2) Awareness about the Risk encompassing all its manifestations at different levels of management hierarchies.

(3) Since Risk is essentially a group characteristic creating the necessary MIS, at different levels to enable the management and line people to anticipate first and advise effective measures to reduce the same.

(4) Exchange of Risk Information at different levels.

(5) Since Risk is essentially a matter of profitability, the theories of stochastic process should be extensively used by designing effective models for risk management and control.

(6) It should be necessary to draw lessons from the experience of other countries, industries, institutions etc., thro' the research based on secondary information or to conduct research studies based on primary sources of data which would be more country-specific-industry-specific-institutions-specific. Research support is a Must.

Presently, the Indian banking sector is passing thro' a testing, challenging, and exciting period. We could call the change paradigm shift in Indian banking.

In June, 1999 the Basel Committee on Banking supervision issued a new consultative paper on New Capital Adequacy Framework, and a second revision in Jan, 2000. The paper is open for discussion and comment till March, 2002, and the final Accord will come into effect by 2005. The new proposals once finalised will replace the 1988 capital adequacy framework.

By far, the most daunting challenge for banks will emanate from the need for advanced risk management practice and their wider application. This is so esp., with regard to the high standards the IRB approach warrants from banks. The standards are an amalgation of international best practices which even very few banks are likely to comply with.

As regards Indian banks, the task will be further uphill, esp., in view of relatively low level of technological absorption in their day-to-day operations on the technological front.

Risk exposures and measurement is yet to take deep roots in Indian context. Measuring and disclosing various risks calls for a sound MIS, and comprehensive database.

The biggest change is proposed in the system of risk weighting so that the rate of interest that a borrower is charged must reflect the riskness of the underlying asset. Hence, instead of a one-size-fits-all approach (100%) the committee has proposed reduction in risk weight for certain quality assets (20%, 50%) and increase in risk weight for lower quality assets (eg.,) venture capital and private placements (100 per cent, 150 per cent).

Weights have also been proposed for Asset Securitisation (ie)., companies rated AAA or AA-would be risk weighted at 20 per cent. A + to A - would be risk weighted to 50 per cent, BBB + to BBB - would be risk weighted at 100 per cent, BB + to BB - would be risk weighted at 150 per cent and those rated B + or below or unrated would be deducted from capital.

Regarding the treatment of operational risk, the details are still being worked out. But it is doubtful if a meaningful quantification of operational risk is possible. In any case, the 20 per cent capital charge suggested by the committee appears to be high and could be reduced. Also, are the various risks additive or independent.

It is difficult to separately quantify precisely the importance of each and every risk mitigation effort and allocate capital.

Despite adverse and unacceptable developments in certain segments of the financial sector, by-and-large, our financial system as a whole has shown considerable resilience in facing the new challenges. There has been some progress in reducing NPAs, in accelerating the recovery process, in setting new standards of asset-liability management, and in meeting capital requirements.

However, we still have a fair amount of ground to cover.

There are three mutually reinforcing pillars which are currently being considered as part of the new Bastle Accord on capital adequacy viz.

(1) Minimum Capital Requirements.
(2) Progress of Supervisory Review.
(3) Market Discipline.

India has been working closely with other major countries on the Bastle Committee as well as the Financial stability Forum in order to ensure that the new Bastle Accord and capital adequacy norms are practical for emerging countries also.

In addition to increasing their capital base, once the Accord comes into forcebanks would also need to develop internal systems for management of risk, and for adhering to adequate internal exposure limits to particular sectors and groups of inter-connected borrowing entities. Capital allocation will also have to be more risk sensitive.

For the future of the Indian banking in a deregulated environment, there is no alternative to technology upgradation coupled with the implementation of efficient risk management, and security procedures.

Further, OBSA., contribute substantially by way of fee, based income in the banks P & L, but owing to their complex nature they present a high level of risk, which, if not properly monitored, could be catastrophic for the bank. Hence, the implementation of Central Risk control Systems and alerts cannot be dispensed with.

And, the risks are different and the adequacy of capital should be to the extent of business done. Indian Balance sheet is as risk prone and vulnerable as any other in the world.

What we need is, steps to be taken to manage large volumes of non-performing assets in the Indian financial system. What we need is a large surgical incision and transfer some of their assets to Asset Reconstruction company, and recapitalise the banks. For that, a lot of vital tough decisions have to be taken-as our Balance sheets are vulnerable more to the legacy of the past, and it requires a surgical legacy.

In addition to risk management and capital adequacy norms, a lot of progress needs to be made in improving the quality of banking services and internal processes.

Time required for cheque clearances, information on customer accounts, tracking of credit risks or major borrowers, systems integration are some of the areas Indian banks could benefit from benchmarking against global practices.

Improving risk management systems in banks along with better regulation and supervision is crucial for the safety and soundness of the financial system. However, we need to press forward with overall economic reforms, otherwise problems in the real sector, for example, sick, industries, will spill into the banking system.

The thrust should be along parameters which anybody can judge us by Efficiency-that is return on capital, satisfaction of employees, long term growth, and strategy. For all these, there are international benchmarking available.

Today, we may not measure up to international standards, but we must be clear as to what will be the strategy for meeting them within a time-frame. If we are going to use technology as a driver for better services and costs, then what should be the kind of technology, how do we get the technology, and then focus on the marketing, so that we get the right kind of marketing with the right risks; we should know what kind of employees we need, and how to keep them satisfied.

So the thrust will depend on the end result the bank is looking for, where it is today and how to measure up to where it wants to go. Macro environment has to be provided to the bank to help them execute what is needed for benchmarking and reaching that level. This has to be done by the Regulators and the Govt., machinery.

Indian financial management is quite comfortable with enough resources and competent people. What is needed right now is, implementation and accountability. We already see some financial organisations which are becoming shining examples to bring about global standards in achieving benchmark in the financial sector. This is only going to improve with time.

The globalisation and the consequent technology-leap clearly spells out the message for every organisation; benchmark and progress or remain static and perish. Benchmarking is not a drive for just excellence in business results in the short run, but it includes a social responsibility of ensuring functional stability of corporations by strictly adhering to the fundamentals.

We must keep in view all the aspects emphasized above to ensure sdurability of the banking reforms.

In 'sum', sensitivity analyses would serve the purpose admirably.

27

Economic Liberalisation and Globalisation

In recent years India's widespread ranging microeconomic liberalisations in foreign and domestic trade has resulted in increased flows of foreign investment hitherto experienced in post-Independence India.

Since the assumption of office by Shri Rao-Singh Govt., in July 1991, there has been a number of far-reaching economic reforms. The Govt., surprised every one by throwing its support behind a set of dramatic economic reforms that were totally odds with India's socialist "Licence Raj." The new policy was based on broad economic parameters of liberalisation, privatisation, globalisation, relaxations, and integration of Indian economy with the rest of the World. The way in which the economic miracle started ten years ago is an old story.

The Western models of development, competitiveness is rooted in a set of intial conditions that is, the state of technology or factor composition which are conditions which a country starts with. Normally globalisation would allow specialisation according to competitiveness and alter the division of labour but with in the same initial conditions.

In an underdeveloped milieu, the competitiveness get grounded in underdevelopment itself. Since development is meant to undermine systematically these conditions and create a new set of conditions leading to self-sustained growth, in an underdeveloped country this does not take place, and competitiveness get eroded as the country develops.

If therefore and underdeveloped economy globalises on the basis of competitiveness, then the change in the division of labour that it entails has the tendency to be antithetical to development process by reinforcing initial conditions. It may in effect reinforce underdevelopment itself.

"Michael Porter" of Harward Business School cautions against the use of wrong kind of globalisation in less developed countries. According to him, whenever genuine competitiveness has been achieved it is by overcoming the initial conditions in which the country found itself in the beginning. Sustainable advantage demands that its sources be upgraded and expanded by moving up to the hierarchy of stages, that is, moving from less to more sustainable types of sources. Important factors which contribute towards this movement are investment in infrastructure and education, domestic rivalry, a large home market, and a natural commitment to success.

Globalisation of the basis of existing structures of competitiveness must be endorsed by the market and should be accompained by an on-going process of investment driven restructuring of the economy; otherwise, it will have a strong tendency to perpetuate a structure of fragile, fleeting competitiveness. Globalisation and consequent international division of labour might thwart any dynamic process leading the economy to the next stage, for globalisation might favour those industries which are essentially more dynamic to the background because they may be at this point unable to stand the test of the market.

Hence, liberalisation, globalisation and opening up the economy would definitely lead to some kind of structural adjustment, which might turn out to be maladjustment leading to aggravation of the initial conditions of underdevelopment. And so what is required is that prior to globalisation or along with that process, the offending intial conditions need to be removed or rectified. Otherwise, development efforts would fail. And, the existing underdevloped conditions are such that the Govt., planning and directing activities are necessary. It is not right to leave the economy to fend for itself basing on the doctrine of "less government, the better."

We know from the experience of many countries in South America and Africa that the globalisation and liberalisation experiment failed or did not bear much fruit. The Indian experiment for the past ten years or more also is not very much encouraging either. Hence, we should investigate the reasons for these failures.

In recent years, many third world economists have come out with the real reasons for such failures. They seem to find fault with the basic approach to development. According to them, so far the development approach has been in terms of planned alteration of the structure of production and employment, so that the services industries increased. These have usually focussed on rapid industrialisation, often at the expense of agriculture, and rural development. Only casual references were made to non-economic social indicators such as gains in literacy, schooling, health conditions and services, and provisions of dwelling houses-the stock of human resource.

These economists, therefore, have in recent years redefined Economic Development in terms of reduction of elimination of poverty, inequality, and unemployment within the context of a growing economy. Underdevelopment would in this context mean widespread poverty, existence of large scale unemployment, and inequality. Over three billion people of the world are estimated to fall in this category. Such conditions of underdevelopment in its totality is a consciously experienced state of deprivation rendered esp., intolerable as more and more people acquire information about the development of other societies, and realize that technical and institutional means of abolishing poverty, misery, and disease do indeed exist.

The correct way of looking at development is that it is a multi-dimensional process involving major changes in social structures, popular attitudes, and national institutions, as well as accelerating economic growth, the reduction in inequality, and eradication of poverty. In essence, development would involve a whole gamut of changes in the social groups within that system and moving of individuals and social groups within that system towards better conditions of life both materially and spiritually.

What is this transformation of social system leading to better or more humane life ? There are three basic components of "Cor Values " which constitute the above transformed social system. They are:

(1) Life sustenance.
(2) Self-esteem.
(3) Freedom.

These are the basic needs sought after by individuals and society.

The first component is "Life Sustenance," which is the ability to provide basic needs. These are basic because without them life would be impossible. They include food, shelter, health and protection. When and where these are absent or in short supply, then and there the conditions of absolute underdevelopment exists. Hence, a basic function of all economic activity is to provide as many people with the means of overcoming the helplessness and misery arising from lack of food, shelter, health and protection. This is a necessary condition for improvement in the quality of life which is development, but not a sufficient condition.

The second is "Self-Esteem." It is the sense of Worth and Self-Respect and on not being used as tool by others for their own ends. All societies and peoples seek some form of self-esteem, which may be called 'Recognition' or 'Identity' or 'Honour.' The nature and form of this self-esteem may vary from society to society and from culture to culture.

Today many Third World countries suffer from this malady when they come into contact with economically and technologically advanced societies-for nations prosperity has become more or less synonymous with or the measure of a country's worth. And so, countries which had previously a profound sense of this worth have come to suffer grievously in the context of persistent poverty, and economic dependence experienced by them.

Material values and well-being in the developed countries and the consequent political power they wield seems to have completely turned "topsy-turvey" or upside down the hierarchy of values and worth and have conferred worthiness and esteem increasingly on those countries possessing economic wealth, and technological power. So countries today seek development in order to gain esteem and economic development is legitimized as goal because it is an important, or even an indispensable way of gaining esteem. Hence the Second "Cor Value" is to reinstate and recapture the original "Self-Esteem," and "Self-Worth." Once this is established, the process of economic growth would gather momentum.

The third "Cor Value" is Freedom from servitude or the ability to choose. Freedom here does not refer to political or ideological meanings. It refers to a more fundamental sense of emancipation from eliminating material conditions of life and also from social servitude to nature, ignorance, other people, institutions, and belief. This freedom involves the expanded range of choices for the societies and their members.

In Arthur Lewis words, "the advantage of economic growth is not that wealth increases happiness, but that it increases the range of human choice."Wealth enables a person to have control over nature and physical environment, but what is important is that it gives freedom to choose greater leisure, to acquire more goods and services, and to deny all these material comforts and choose a life of contemplation. Thus fundamentally, it is necessary for the third world people to be free from servitude and to have real freedom of choice for any development effort to bear fruit. Development, therefore, is both a physical reality, and a state of mind in which the society has, though some combination of social, economic and institutional processes, secured the means for obtaining a better life.

In the above approach to development, the focus shifts from things to people. The basic raw material are the people who should have their basic needs met and should be confident or conscious of their worth or self-esteem, and are really free to make their choices.

Looking at the Indian economy, our approach was faulty-heavy industrialisation, controls and licensing unlimited, which helped the demonstration effect and conspicuous consumption to have a free field day, which further helped inculcate in the people unnatural appetite and appreciation for Western thought, Western Education, Western Technology, and Western Values so that "Indianness" was despised and devalued.

The consequence was that self-esteem or self worth was completely set aside or ignored altogether among all sections of the people.

The issue of financial liberalisation is now seen as much more complex than what was originally envisaged. Because the needs of the real economy can be met only thro' liberalisation, the literature still holds as its ultimate goal the full liberalisation of the economy.

However, the speed and sequencing of liberalisation should be integrated into macroeconomic stablisation and structural adjustment programmes, and the pre-requisites for the eventual success of liberalisation are still matters of ongoing concern. Much of the work on these transitional problems has arisen from the experience of liberalisation in a number of developing countries and it is on such experiences that we must draw upon if we are to determine whether or not there might be actually be limits to the liberalisation process.

We may add here that a well-planned stabilisation and growth-oriented structural adjustment programme will provide a solid foundation for the continuing success of liberalisation policies.

However, the recent Southeast Asian evidence suggests that regardless of the soundness of such a framework, if complementary policies are poor, if financial intermediaries are poorly regulated, a country can still experience a serious currency crisis resulting in an economic meltdown.

And when something goes wrong on the external front, as it clearly did for India in the early 1990s, concern with macro-economic policy dominates everything else. History may never repeat itself and the Southeast Asian currency contagion may never affect India, but the lessons learnt should help us to be prepared for any eventuality. For when formal models by themselves fail to provide guidelines for the conduct and implementation of liberalisation policies, it is such lessons alone that will help make the final diagnosis.

28

Population Explosion

Harvard Professor Edward Wilson, writing in the New York Times, quoted as under; "Population growth? God for the economy—so let it run. Land shortages? Try fusion energy to power the desalting of sea water, then reclaim the world's deserts...by towing icebergs to coastal pipelines...Species going extinct? Not to worry," the skeptics say. "That is the nature's way. Think of humankind as only the latest in a long line of exterminating agents in geological time. Resources? The planet has more than enough resources to last indefinitely."

We are confronted with a baffling and big question mark on the threshold of the 21st century. The question mark is quite obvious for each one of us which concern the world of human beings and their environment.

But not many really express serious concern or make dedicated effort to find a suitable answer to it. This is nothing but the problem of rapid population growth taking place around us. The people really are not concerned about the prognosis of their future as either bleak or rosy.

Ehrlich in his book, "The Population Bomb," sees the global crisis in the following terms:

"The human population is not only too large, it is growing at a mind-boggling rate about 2 per cent a year. At this rate, the population doubles every 35-40 yrs. Every year seventy million people are—currently being added to this planet—every three years and equivalent of the US. As a result roughly 15 per cent of the people in the world live in affluence and that about 60 per cent in utter misery and rest on the border line."

World today support about 6 billion people. The 1991 Indian census recorded a population of 844.3 million people at an annual growth rate of 2.1 per cent. Today we see not only unprecedented population growth but unprecedented consumption of resources, an unprecedented number of people living in poverty; and an environment water, air, and the land itself threatened by human action.

Population growth	*From*	*To*	*Period taken*
Ist billion-1-2 billion	1830	1930	1 century
2nd billion-2-3 billion	1930	1960	30 yrs
3nd billion-3-4 billion	1960	1975	15 yrs
4th billion-4-5 billion	1975	1987	12 yrs
5th billion-5-6 billion	1987	1997	10 yrs

Source: Population Headline, ESCAP, July 1992.

The World Bank, in a study on the population growth of India, has said that "if the country succeeds in universalising the two-chldren family norm within 2000 AD., the growth in population of the country would stop at 150 crore. In case this is delayed by another 10 years, the growth of population would stabilize only at an astronomical level of 300 crore." This may inevitably lead to mass starvation. The country needed 185 million tonnes of foodgrains by the end of 8th plan and around 220-230 million tonnes by 2000 A.D. These projections have been made on the assumption that by the turn of the century, the country will have a population of one billion.

It must also be recognised that poverty is the fundamental cause which make people over-exploit the natural resources of the country.—for meeting the basis needs. Besides, increase in population brings in its wake all the problems of pollution with which humans beings have to suffer in their survival.

All efforts which helped bring people above the poverty line also put greater pressure on the natural resources of the country. Irrigation facilities also produced salinity in the land. Industrial development creates products but also pollutes water and air. Medical facilities improve the health of the people, but also increase the population, thereby creating more demand for the production of nature, which is why our national income has been growing at a meagre rate since independence while the per capita income has been going up hardly by 1.5 per cent per annum on an average.

All development results are being neutralised by the growing population. Health facilities which are supposed to be important for effective family planning have become inadequate and poor. In fact, all social services have become quite meagre in supply in comparison with their demand. And now the XI Plan may also not give any major thrust to the problem of population control.

It is high time to ponder, to act swiftly in the form of a movement for population control as otherwise all our economic strategies are going to be of no avail.

Why the industrial powers, the so-called countries of the world, are so conspicuous about population growth in the poor, developing countries? Why do these countries continue to blame the population growth in the developing countries as the cause of all ills in the world? Why do these countries so overwhelmingly advocate reduction in the developing countries. The answer lies in the protection of the world economic order that these countries have nurtured for their own advantages and benefits. It may be pointed out that all the negative aspects of political growth as ascribed in the capitalistic economy can be avoided by a proper reorganisation of the economic order.

Karl Marx was the first person to evolve an economic order that was based on the productive utilisation of labour-the population and it prompted him to persent an alternative economic order in which population played a positive role. But this alternative economic order jeopardised the vested interests of the industrial powers and was opposed blatantly.

World Bank and IMF imposed conditionalities associated with Structural Adjustment made the situation worse with respect to population control. During the past ten years many changes have been made in the programme and policy which spell doom for the health, and welfare of women and children of India.

Budgetary cuts imposed elsewhere did not apply to population control for which allocations have been increasing. Although Family Welfare is supposed to include immunisation and MCH programmes, significantly, these two areas have faced cuts. The World Bank has extended credit to these aspects of Family Welfare, suggesting that the GOI., is unable to keep up expenditure under these heads due to budgetary restraint.

Population control policies are promoted in the name of emancipating women and protecting their reproductive rights and freedom. Contraception is supposed to save women from mental mortality and help them have healthier children, as assumption belied by the experience of all-countries which have had SAP, imposed on them. Today, population control has been accepted as an end itself.

The year 1994-95 witnessed two global conferences—the International Conference on Population and Development and the Social Development Summit. India is a signtory to the statements at both conferences, which give primacy to the market. Population growth has been projected as a major threat to the post Cold War world calling for severe measures to take care of this problem.

The inability of the International community to decide on the desirable numbers of human beings which can safely inhabit this planet, did not stop the Earth Summit from proposing a doubling expenditure for population control of which only 25 per cent is incurred by the North while the figure of external assistance to India is even lower. At the ICPD., the threat of population explosion was reemphasised and the financial institutions proposed to write off loans in lieu of meeting demographic targets. The conference aimed at enhancing the flow of funds for population control.

Obviously, clear demographic goals need to be defined. To each of them, as well as to integrate family planning with the overall strategy of socio-economic development, a number of programmes need to be initiated as part of the policy. There has been an inadequate recognition of interaction taking place between population and development in programmes to limiting the rate of population growth.

However, experience with growing numbers has exploded the fallacy that development is the best contraceptive and that it will take care of the growing numbers. Socio-economic progress may contribute to adoption of small family norms by couples. But if there is a strong in-built between fertility control measures and economic development processes, the battle against the growing numbers will be won than expected.

Population is India's number 'One' problem. We relied completely on voluntary family planning measures but our expectations have been belied. Hence, we have to make some bold attempts if we are serious in uplifting the economic and social conditions of the people. We have to stabilise the population immediately.

Population reports for the pre-modern era are both fragmentary and incomplete., Most demographers agree that total world population did not pass the 500 million mark until sometime after 1500 AD (Carr-Saunder, 1936). The population problem during this early period was characterised by high birth rates, high mortality rates and a relatively short average span of life.

With the beginning of agricultural revolution, the some what static population situation that had prevailed began to change. The increase in food production paved the way for an upward trend in population. This trend was accelerated by the industrial and sanitary medical revolutions of the next two centuries. Increasing trade and commerce the settlement of new areas, the trend towards the industrialisation and higher productivity per man, and the success with which modern medical science tackled the problem of high mortality rates—all added up to new incentives for population increase.

The Table: 1 shows the population growth of some major populous countries from 1950-1990 and projections to 2030. China, which already has one of the lowest population rates in the developing world, is projected to add 400 million people over the next four decades.

India will add 590 million people by 2030, even more than China, as its population increases to 1.44 billion.

Table 1

Population Growth in Some Selected Countries 1950-2030

(in millions)

Country	*Population* 1950	1990	2030	*Increase* 1950-90	1990-2030
Slowly Growing Countries					
1. United States	152	250	345	98	95
2. Russia	114	158	161	34	13
3. Jappan	84	124	123	40	-1
4. United Kingdom	50	58	60	8	2
5. Germany	68	80	81	12	1
Rapidly Growing Countries					
6. Nigeria	32	87	278	55	191
7. Pakistan	40	118	260	78	142
8. India	369	853	1443	484	590
9. Brazil	53	153	252	100	99
10. China	563	1134	1624	571	490

Source: USDA, World Population by Country and Region, 1950-90 and Projection to 2030 Economic Research Service, Washington, 1993.

The real "dichotomy" focussed by mankind today is the ever-increasing degradation of the natural environment as a result of development, which however must be also recognised as a major instrument of progress and an intrinsic element of our civilisation.

About 60 per cent of the world's people who live in high-growth-potential areas, the prospects of the future are not so bright. Their numers are steadily increasing. And thus far they have hardly begun to experience the shift from high mortality and fertility rates, that will be necessary if they are to use their present resource base in raising their average levels of living.

Population is pressing against supply in these areas, and although great potentialities exist for increasing food production, it is neither logical nor practical to assume that the world can go on indefinitely providing adequate substance for an ever increasing population.

The entire issue of population and environment should be viewed in the context of political dominance at the international level. Per capita use of resource and the size of the population are the only two proximate determinants of the enviromental problems.

Since the world today is dominated by a consumption oriented economic order, propagated by the so-called market economies of the world, it is the population size which become the major issue in the Western ideology in dealing with the environmental problems. This line of thinking gives an additional teeth to Western Powers in blaming developing countries for all ills of the world.

But there is little hope of a better world if current ideology of material advancement and unlimited increase in consumption continues to prevail. It must be recognised by all that the role of resource use is even more important than that of population in the deterioration of the environment. The politics of blaming population growth for saving the case of unlimited consumption may not lead to the sustainability of the environment. If it is to be made habitable for future generations, the world should—identify the issues in proper perspective.

"The quality of life cannot improve in India as long as the population keeps on increasing at the present alarming rate. In the time I shall take to deliver this lecture, the population will have increased by 2000."

"Nani Palkhivala, b. 1920. Constitutional Lawyer: ib-p.7"

"Population, when unchecked, increases in a gemotrical ratio."

(Thomas Robert Malthus: 1766-1834: English Minister, Economist: Essay on the Principle of Population: 1798.)

29

Areas of Retardation in the Economic Reforms

Since Independence, India has become a long way towards building a self-reliant modern economy to make its political freedom secure and meaningful to the vast humanity that inhabits this ancient land. Looking back at the situation on the eve of Independence, nobody will disagree that the economy has undergone a radical transformation and come a long way.

However, what we witness today is a hegemonic Globalisation. Besides this economic reversal, Globalisation has created new and serious challenges for the democratic decision-making power into the hand of transnational institutions like the WTO, the IMF., and WB., has severely reduced the sovereignty of the national Governments.

Franck Amalrick says in his study:

"Influencing national institutions and policies becomes openly one objective of development cooperation policies....The WB and the IMF intervene at the national level under the banners of "sound macro economic policies" and "good government" "technical banners that fit well the technical nature of these organisations while bilateral donors intervene under the banners of "democracy" and "partnership."

The ongoing Globalisation is based on the Washington Consensus. John Williamson coined this term in 1990 to express the common approach of the US Treasury Dept., the IMF., the World Bank and the Inter-American Development Bank.

Later GATT., and its successor, the WTO., came to join hands. In the words of Joseph stilglitz: It was a consensus formulated between the 15th and 19th street in Washington." The countries that were to implement the Washington Consensus had no say in its formulation.

Liberalisation of interest rates, trade, and inflows of FDI, privatisation, the reduction in the role of state in economic affairs, de-regulation, and secure property rights are some of the key elements of the Washington consensus. In the emerging scenario of Globalisation, the less developed states are unable to benefit much from the processes and policies associated with Globalisation because of their poor economic status. Indebtedness has increased to a point where debt servicing is not without its costs for the health and basic needs of the people.

The total debt of the developing countries amounts to nearly $ 2.5 trillion. Even the World Bank admits that 88 countries are faced with the problem of unsustainable debts and need help in the matter. Yet, not much relief has actually been provided in this direction. Only 14 countries have been considered from some relief under the HIPC, and this too comes only with tough conditionalites, which may not really help the State of the poor.

Davi Held observes ".... in this hyperglobanist account the rise of global economy the emergence of institutions of global governance and the global diffusion and hybridisation of cultures are interpreted as evidence of radically new world order or order with prefigures the demise of the nations-state".

(1) Fiscal Deficit

The Centre was able to keep its fiscal deficit under control at Rs. 83, 394 crores during the first eight months of this fiscal, which was 61.5 per cent of the budget estimate fo Rs. 135, 524 crores for the entire fiscal.

The deficit till Nov., 2002, which works out to 3.26 per cent of GDP., was relatively lower on account of better revenue mop up even at the centres spending was comparatively higher.

During April-Nov., 2002, the centre raised Rs. 123, 629 crores in revenue while total expenditure was Rs. 224, 579 crores leaving a fiscal gap of Rs. 83, 394 crores, according to figures released by the Controller General of Accounts.

The Govt., collected Rs. 80346 crores in taxes during the first eight months which amounted to 46.5 per cent of the budgeted Rs. 172, 965 crores. Non-tax revenue amounted to Rs. 43283 crores, which was only 60 per cent of the estimated Rs. 72140 crores for 2002-03.

Total receipt was Rs. 141, 185 crores, which was somewhat dampened by the relatively lower non-tax receipts and accounted for 51.4 per cent of the budget target of Rs. 274, 785 crores.

On the expenditure front, the centre's spending was relatively higher so far this fiscal and amounted to 54.7 per cent of the Rs. 410, 309 crores budgeted for 2002-03.

Plan expenditure was squeezed to Rs. 57, 710 crores, accounting for

50.8 per cent of the budgeted Rs. 113, 500 crores. Non-plan expenditure was Rs. 166, 869 till Nov., 2002 which was 56.2 per cent of the estimated Rs. 296, 809 crores.

The Centre's Non-plan spending surged mainly on account of higher interest payments, which was Rs. 67, 184 crores till Nov., amounting to 57.2 per cent of the budget target of Rs. 117, 390 crores.

The revenue deficit of the centre stood at Rs. 67888 crores, which is 71.2 per cent of the budget estimates. The primary deficit was Rs. 16210 crores accounting for 89.4 per cent of the budget target.

Most of the deficit was financed through market borrowing, which was Rs. 79548 till Nov., The centre completed 83 per cent of the borrowing till Nov. 2002 against the target of Rs. 95859 crores for the entire fiscal.

(2) Quest for Leadership

"Nicholas Kalder" of the Cambridge University emphasized that the effectiveness of any economic and social system is determined fundamentally by the character, motivation, ethical standards and the midset of all those who make the crucial decisions of the nations' social and economic life.

The quality of a polity depends on its leadership. As pointed out by the International Commission on Global Governance in their report", the world today requires enlightened responses to the many challenges it faces and to that end it needs credible and sustained leadership, a leadership that is proactive and not simply reactive, that is inspired, not simply functional, that looks to the longer-term and future generations for whom the present is held in trust; leaders made strong by vision, sustained by ethics, and revealed by political courage that looks beyond the next election."

"Men make history and not the other way round. In periods where there is no leadership, society stands still. Progress occurs when courageous, skilful leaders seize the opportunity to change things for the better."

(Harry S. Truman: This Week: Feb., 22, 1959.)

The nation requires a firm sense of direction and a leadership which is committed to making the future happen. The course of the trading regime in future will be characterised by the WTO., in all its operational aspects.

HRD., Technology, IR., and customer service and the four pillars of the banking system of the future. Each of these issues deserves a full fledged and exclusive revaluation and any meaningful assessment of the financial sector without taking cognizance of these vital matters would be incomplete.

The fear, of course, must be that a series of missteps by the large economies will precipitate a full-blown and protracted global recession. This is the time for the Indian Financial Institutions to sit together with the international financial institutions and develop a global stability plan.

The implementation of the policy decisions in India have to be taken beyond the overwhelming concentration and liberalisation. The focus on Govt., policy seems to be exclusively concerned with the need to remove counter productive regulations. Hence, the policy decision needs radical change for which dynamic leadership calibre is a "must" in the wake of the globalisation of the economy.

India's vast human and material resources if properly mobilized, ought to make India the most successful story of the First Half of the 21st century. Here then is a challenge for all of us; to nurse and encourage the right type of leadership so vital for the well being of the country.

The new urgency is how to prepare the nation to meet the future. The nation requires a firm sense of direction, and a leadership which is Committed to making the future happen.

In fact successful nations are those where the people do not have to be "led" but lead themselves.

In exceptional times leadership has a special place but we must learn to emphasize collective achievement, collective heroism, and the collective will to work. One of the functions of education is to produce this kind of mature will adjusted and responsible citizen who thinks not of this opportunities, but of his obligations.

"We are good as well as bad. But, by-and-large, if the leaders act right, people will get the proper lead. Practice is always more-ımportant than precept."

(Lal Bahadur Shastri: 1904-66. Prime Minister after Nehru.)

(3) Women in India

When the Indian govt., began to tread the path of Liberalisation in 1991, and started opening the economy and initiating economic reforms on the labour market, the proponents of reforms reflected on the consequences of these processes of labour including those sections of the work force, such as women.

A profile of women in the work-force bring out the gender differential significantly. This is evident from the fact that a major share of work force belongs to male category of population. Women lag significantly behind males in terms of work participation, employment etc.,

The majority of the working women participation in the labour market means working in the informal economy with no social or economic security or protection and in the least regulated of work places.

The work of women in the informal economy is often viewed as marginal, peripheral, temporary and supplemental. However, more and more micro studies are pointing out to the fact that women's work is a source of security for households.

Millions of women in India are working in that part of the economy where the distinction between paid and unpaid labour in the home is blurred; their contribution is hidden in toto from economic policy. Here, ideological bias and cultural sexism both are at work.

India's integration into the WTO., will hasten the negative development. The Singapore meeting of the WTO., advocated rules for capital flows and investment and national treatment for MNCs. Trade related social clauses are likely to follow.

These policies will further marginalise women, push them into informal sector, and stress related jobs.

While office related jobs have grown because of the kind of liberalisation, the overall work situation for women has seen no significant improvement.

The Economic Survey 1999-2000 underlines the need for women's empowerment. But the State's commitment to women empowerment can be gauged from the place accorded to it.

The section "Development of women and Children" appears at the fag end of the Last chapter of the Economic Survey. The State's commitment to women's empowerment is underlined thro' assertion and listing, largely, programmes for mother and child welfare. Scholars inspired by women's movement, have been vociferously arguing that there is more to women's contribution to the economy, society and the process of nation making than producing babies and there is more to women's contribution that their maternal capacities as the centre places of their service to the nation. It is disappointing to see the agenda of gender empowerment reduced to and clubbed with sections with special needs thus denying the structural dimensions of gender inequality.

Globalisation is accompanied by ideological transformations. In-India, this involves a sustained attack on the values linked with socialism and egalitarian ideologies. The collective memories of the ideals of the national movement, and other progressive movements are sought to be weakened.

Analysis of the working class women the world over show how the sexuality of women is commodified and controlled in ways which furthers the economic strategies of individual men and capital as a whole in the era of Globalisation.

In the context of economic liberalisation and globalisation, the quality of women's employment will depend upon umpteen factors. First, access to education and skill development training. In both these areas women continue to lag behind.

The solution lies in creating conditions and opportunities which are conducive for women to work in increasingly productive and remunerative sectors of the economy with freedom. These issues require high priority attention in the years ahead of us so that the negative effects of globalisation could be reduced and benefits of it could be optimised and realised. Social and political gains by women as a consequence of the women's movement need to be guarded and enhanced in the light of structural adjustment polices.

Women have won some victories as a consequence of the democratic movements. But again, large sections of women have not been the beneficiaries of these gains. Much of the gains remain restricted to the urban elite, middle class, and some others.

Women among the landless poor continued to be weighed down by social pressures. While studies show now these women...negotiate their daily lives to make partial gains for themselves, the fact remains that social measures need to be stepped up.

Further, effective growth strategy rests on patterning national revenues, and expenditures to contribute to equity. In terms of micro-economic policicies and state finance, several pressures are shaping the responses to change within the country.

No authentic feminism is possible unless the dominant perception of "meaningful work" is challenged. What ought to be seen is that behind this notion of-"meaningful work" lies almost an unbridgeable separation of culture from nature. This requires an anthropological imagination.

In India, a majority of women workers are concentrated in the unorganised sectors and low income groups. Despite such informal nature-we could discern some order. Any rapid changes in the present regulatory mechanism, it is feared, many indeed heighten the vulnerability of women primarily due to increasing unemployment and (or) exploitation. Here, exploitation may be understood as equal wages for equal work among males and females, overt or covert barriers to entry (or) to upward mobility of female labour, unequal access of females to factors of production, to technology, to information and to social and family resources.

Legal rights to property is yet another area gaining repeated articulation in the recent past.

Despite the constitutional goal of socialism, Indian society denied of its population an effective say in the decision-making mechanism of the country thus leaving the social structure as inegalitarian as we inherited it in the year 1947.We hope that this single gesture by our political class would prove quite revolutionising for the Indian society and would have a catalysing effect for the Indian body politic, and body social. The WRB., is supposed to have several positive spin-off effects in various spheres. With women sharing the high-pedestal in the decision-making system, many urgent social issues like population, gender disparity, and literacy are likely to receive enhanced attention than they have so far.

Women's empowerment should not be narrow and onesided limited only to the political participation.

It must expand its base in terms of knowledge, education skills besides social, economic, and political empowerment.

*Our Former President: Shri K.R. Narayanan was right when he said: "women have waited for centuries without striving hard to acquire their rightful position and status. They should strive seriously to unshackle themselves from the chains".

(*India Today: July, 1998).

The pre-reform and post-reform era and the whole set of arguments cannot be flawed just because a short time recession has emerged on the economic scene.

Short-term measures pertaining to revival of demand may have to be exercised but still the way out of the predicament lies in making a frontal attack on the basic maladies the economy is afflicted with.

Economic policy is not likely to change much. However, we must necessarily do something about the country's horrendous economic problems, so that citizens do not have to wait for another fifty years to get what is their due:an improvement in the standard of living of the average Indian and freedom from poverty, and economic deprivation.

We have been exploring various possibilities within whatever time that was available to us. We explored then and we are still exploring. We did not come across anything which is substantially better than what has been done.

We are still saying that although we consider this policy absolutely right and we feel its irreversibility would be useful for the country, as we go along, we can always, make small corrections, mid-course corrections. That is always possible.

But the point is, the direction has to be the same, the objective has to be clear. As India faces the new century, the Indian economy stands at cross roads. Either it can take the "Business as Usual" road which means continued poverty and low growth trap (or) take the high road to achieve prosperity, global prominence, and more egalitarian society through accelerated reforms, and by energizing the national innovation system.

"Women are supposed to be specially perspective, able to see nuances in a changing situation and this is the quality that is most needed in life today."

(Smt. Indira Gandhi: 7 March, 1973.)

30

Privatisation

'Privatisation' is not the word found in any well known dictionaries of the English Language. It is a process which reduces the involvement of the State or the Public sector in the economic activities of the nation. Actually, there is no unanimity about its definition. Some prfer the narrow definition and equate it with Divestiture or Denationalisation. It imples divestiture, which means sale by the state of the whole or part of its holding of the equity shares of a Govt., owned enterprise to private share holders and denationalisation which broadly means a change of ownership from the state to the private sector.

In the broad sense, privatisation would imply much more than divestiture and denationalisation. According to Dr. R. Pandse, privatisation has a very broad scope for developing countries like India. It would involve: (1) Divestiture; (2) Denationalisation; (3) Under Indian Industrial Policy Revolution certain industries are exclusively reserved for development in the state sector. Any relaxation in respect of such an exclusive reservation would be a part of privatisation process; (4) Closure of liquidation of any state owned enterprises (SOEs) (5) Leasing of SOEs to private party; (6) Transfer of management and control of SOEs to Private Sector individual or agency, more so if it includes share of profit; (7) Abandoning or postponing proposals (a) to start new SOEs or (b) to expand or diversify activities of any existing SOEs and (8) Farming out to private contractor or agencies needed by SOEs instead of these being provided or produced departmentally by the SOE., itself.

Privatisation refers to a class of institutional reforms, liberalisation refers to change in the relative prices operating in the economy. The effects of privatisation both on economic efficiency and Govt., expenditures are likely to be modest. Privatisation psychological impact is more important as a way of preparing the way for more fundamental liberalisation measures.

As of today, the distinction between the two is much confused, and it is difficult to reach definite conclusions regarding relative impacts of privatisation and liberalisation since the two reforms have been promoted together in practice. It could be suggested that in at least some cases, liberalisation or regulatory reform is better able than privatisation to bring about gains in economic efficiency.

In other cases, such reforms must accompany privatisation, if it is to have any impact. But it cannot be taken for granted that privatisation is a sine qua non for successful liberalisation, or vice versa. In certain circumstances, privatisation may turn out to be the pre-requisite for other reforms; in others, liberalisation alone will make subsequent privatisation redundant. There are also other cases in which privatisation will not be effective until after liberalisation measures have been implemented. In the absence of other policy reforms which increase competition, (liberalisation), in the economy, the impact of liberalisation on economic efficiency is likely to be modest.

Privatisation is to a developing economy, what a specific medicine is to an individual ? There are basic needs like air, water, food, clothing and shelter absolutely necessary to individuals. But individuals suffer from ailments or suffer injuries. For all these specific medicines are required. Depending on the seriousness of ailments, medicines may be more important than basic needs. For developing economies basic objectives of economic policy may be removal of poverty, or unemployment, provide basic needs etc., in pursuing these objectives, the economies might encounter ills and distortions and unless these are removed, objectives might not be achieved. Privatisation is this medicine meant to cure such ills.

But unfortunately, many have not diagnosed their ills, others refuse to admit the presence of ailments, still others are ignorant of the medicines available, moreover, not all medicines are useful and curative, there may be adverse repercussions and allergies also might erupt. And so we might say, that though privatisation is not a panacea of economic ills, many patients in the developing world suffer from maladies which require privatisation medicine.

One of the major ills are the ever increasing deficit budgets and inflation, which hit the common man very hard. Another ill is the ever increasing and irreversible non-development expenditure and non-plan govt., expenditures which result in significant cuts in the FYP., targets. The govt., consumption expenditure has been growing enormously, this is aggravated by poor returns from SOEs.

These ills exist and they are becoming significant and more and more serious. But at the same time, it should be emphasized that privatisation is not to be linked with poor performance of SOEs. This is meant to be only a remedy and expected to have both the enterprises and the Govt., in better hands. Besides, it is not against the PSU., because privatisation is supposed to release funds for the Govt., treasury and help undertake more and better public sector investment.

The global survey of privatisation shows a broad spectrum of countries experimenting along these lines; Great Britain, Italy, Sweden and Japan in advanced countries, and in the developing world, Bangladesh, Pakistan, Thailand, Malaysia, Taiwan and South Korea have experimented with privatisation with some success.

Many of the crucial decisions which shape our economy are taken in the private sector. If these decisions go awry, it is the economy which has to bear the consequences.

It is no good privatising and just allowing things to emerge. We have to have a conscious programme so that we may get the right price.

Secondly, the structure of what the industry will look like after privatisation needs to be thought about well in advance. It is no good privatising an industry and leaving it in monopolistic hands. What we should do is to create a regulatory and legislative framework, which eventually creates competition in areas of private monopoly.

In the case of water, the British Govt., went to great lengths to privatise water using concept known as "Yardstick Competition" where the regulator would have information about all the water companies. This helped the regulator draw up league tables to show which company is more efficient or more productive. Since no company wanted to be at the bottom of the league table, companies competed with one another to be higher up the league table.

However, the Govt., has gone down the franchise route like in the case of British Rail. Grounds of justification for privatisation are: (1) It will activate wider share of ownership (2) It will introduce an element of competition in specific industries; (3) It will change the relative importance of the private and public sectors; (4) it will improve further the performance of erstwhile SOEs; (5) It will release the Govt's administrative and policy making talent for the job of running the Govt; and (6) It will reduce the far-too-common political meddling in the affairs of SOEs.

India was an inward looking economy so far, creation of infrastructure etc., of course, these things have helped, but today for us, we need to be part of the Global Economy and that is the idea behind privatisation and liberalisation.

Privatisation needs to go hand-in-hand with globalisation is to bring the two things: IT., and mind set change-we need to create a competitive environment. In any area where there is competition, the consumer is the beneficiary. Customer actually sees value and privatisation alone will make us competitive and keep the consumer as focus. Hence as globalisation is happening if privatisation does not happen, then we will not be able to compete.

By becoming global, does it mean we lose focus of social obligations? We don't think these two are mutually exclusive. We think, automatically, social obligation will no longer means subsidies and handouts. It means giving all people an equal opportunity to be able to participate in any wealth creating opportunity.

Further, by globalising we have the opportunity. We need to be India centric in our resources and global in our market. We have talents and abilities here, so we use India centric resources to compete globally. Automatically, wealth will be created here which will ease the pressure on the Govt., to give handouts.

What is happening today is, when we talk of IT., we are talking of convergence of the computer today with the Information. Hence, it becomes a powerful tool. The reason for a software development to take off is because there is a common link between our market place, and development centre. So when we talk of IT enablement, we talk of an integrated enablement of the PC., and the telecom.

So far, there has been agricultural revolution, industrial revolution, now it is knowledge or information revolution. If we don't use IT., today, then we will lose out in this revolution because the knowledge revolution is being catalysed or powered by IT., These are some of the ways. India being computer literate or the ability to be computer literate, if we can focus on empowering our people on IT skills or IT infrastructure, we think sitting here in India we can offer many value added services, IT, enabled services throughout the world. It's an unique opportunity for the next ten years. We should not ignore it.

We think there is no problem with Indian business. Where we do have a problem is that as we go out of the major cities, the infrastructure, IT related ones like telecom, PC penetration is still very low. If we take retailers, distributors etc., a pre IT enablement and IT infrastructure is not there. Telecom is not there, costs are too high, PC penetration is very low. So in the main cities, we are reasonably ready, but when we go out of these cities, we are not yet ready.

IT's services today, as per NASSCOM's forecast is expected to give some $87 bn, in the next five years. That we think it is significant opportunity, but we think it is only a small portion of the opportunity. If we look at IT enabled services for example, doctors sitting here being able to use IT to give consultancy or advice across the globe; So too with engineering services insurance etc., IT enabled services can definitely create significant wealth for India.

We need Govt., to be a facilitator. When the Govt is opening out a sector, they need to first let us know what the rules are and then standby. Price of telecom and computers need to come down. Privatization in infrastructure and telecom needs to happen and this has to be encouraged. Only then will they be cost-effective tools for us to compete. We need to have cyber laws to create a favourable environment.

What was good under certain conditions is not always good for all time. Thanks to the planned economy sedulously fostered during the last many years. Indian economy has come out of the clutches of shortage. In the vastness and variety of our production, we have achieved remarkable progress. Our public and private sector industries have made phenomenal growth/progress during the last several years. We now rank within the first fifteen industralized countries of the world. The system of controls and regulations has become superfluous and even hurdles to the momentum of growth that has been generated in the economy.

There appears to be no need for any regulation of any industry which does not require foreign exchange either for machinery and equipment or for raw materials. In such cases competition will become a self regulatory mechanism. The GOI, has been steadily removing restrictions and liberalising the industrial policy. It is now for the industry to take advantage of these measures and go forward with dynamism. In fact, the ball is now in their court.

The private sector has shown remarkable strength and ability to handle multicrore sophisticated projects which were beyond them a few decades ago. It is for them to take advantage of the buoyant capital market and play an effective role in their own and national advantage.

In this context, it will help accelerated industrial growth if the Govt., can formulate a set of parameters regarding foreign participation, royalty, and other payments for technology transfers etc., so that a lot of delay and uncertainty—caused in fixing these issues in each may be avoided. Dramatic changes are overtaking the global economy. Countries that had adopted controlled system of production and distribution are changing over to market economy and renouncing the shackles. They have realized that both internal and external competition is necessary to improve efficiency and reduce cost. Industries in India who have enjoyed a sheltered, Sellers' market will have to gear themselves up to face the change in national and international trade.

Our share in the international trade is negligible and hence every effort should be made to increase it if we have to survive as an industrial country. While our exports are expanding our Imports Bill is much larger and trade gap is widening. A solemn responsibility, therefore, rests on the mercantile community of India to pay special attention to this national problem. sound industrial relations are a pre-requisite for higher production and productivity. We have enacted a plethora of laws to safeguard the rights of labour. But they are not by themselves a panacea for all our problems. Laws cannot bring about harmony and understanding between the two vital sectors of production. Development of human relations on the basis of mutual respect and accommodation are absolutely essential for peace in industry.

A nation which is preparing itself for a quantum leap into the 21st century can ill afford to neglect the health and well-being of its industrial relations system, for, in the ultimate analysis, it is the men and women at work that produce the wealth, with science and technology functioning as supports to this effort.

It has only been latterly recognised that development does not consist merely of an increase in the GNP or per capita income. The currently accepted concept of development rejects the purely statistical view earlier held and recognises the importance in the development process of strategies and programmes of employment promotion, reduction, of disparities in income, satisfaction of minimum needs sand improvement of the quality of life. Planners in developing countries recognise that social objectives have an important place in overall development.

Further, the need is to strengthen the public domain and place governance there in.

In fact, the performance of any organisation does not depend on 'who owns it' ? but 'how it is managed' ?

However, the privatisation experimentation would not be free from all problems of implementation. There would be innumerable problems. Problems should not deter us from undertaking an experiment which has succeeded in many places. None of the problems could be termed beyond our capacity and ingenuity to resolve. Other countries have crossed the bridges as they came, and we too can surely cross them equally well. official circles now acknowledge that there has been a significant shift in India's strategy for Privatisation. It is good to remind ourselves of some of the policy guidelines in this matter:

First of all, in India, what we need is not so much Privatisation but "Publicisation." For many of us SOEs., and their operations are shrouded in mystery and secrecy. The Balance sheets of may of them never see the light of the day. When these are published, and the general public has opportunity to know, and then there is every chance of better performance and this is the first Privatisation Process which we should set in motion.

Secondly, successful privatisation calls for a broad based programme rather than a preoccupation with getting the best price for individual companies. It is only when the returns to not just the Govt., but also consumers and ordinary shareholders are taken into account that privatisation becomes a programme with both economic and political benefit.

Finally, we should be confident that Privatisation is not a loss of face to any avowed past ideologies. It is neither "a panacea nor a tonic; it is a simple and practical measure, a specific medicine, which will go a long way in curing the ills and accelerating economic growth."

First of all in India, what we need is not so much privatisation but "Publicisation". For many of us SOEs., and their operations are shrouded in mystery and secrecy. The Balance sheets of many of them never see the light of the day. When these are published, and the general public has opportunity to know and then there is every chance of better performance and this is the first Privitasiation Process which we should set in motion.

31
Energy Crisis

India is not blessed with plentiful supplies of indigenous energy resource. But the progress and economy of our country in the major fields of industry and other spheres to a large extent have to be dependent on the energy resources.

Today electricity is a common resource like water, air and coal and other fuels. It is critical to industry, agriculture, health, education and almost all other sectors. The framers of the Indian constitution recognising this placed electricity in the concurrent list. All other infrastructure such as railways, Airlines, Aerodromes, port, and Telecommunications were made the exclusive responsibility of the Central Govt.,

"Electricity" is one of the most important facets of a multidimensional energy problem in the economies of the Central and State Governments, of India. According to the British Electricity Authority, "A nation's economic power can indeed be measured by the expansion of electricity supply."

Electricity is the most preferred form of energy and the demand for it has been increasing at rates much faster than other forms of energy. The steep rise in the per capita consumption of electricity is due to a number of factories in operation. The growth and pattern of power based industries like basic metals and chemicals constitute the larger consumers accounting for a share of about 62 per cent of electricity consumption.

Again, agricultural development, rural electrification and the rapid pace of urbanisation have enhanced the use of electricity in this country.

The Power Ministry has announced major concessions in 1994 for inviting foreign investments in the power sector. It is contended that foreign investment in absolutely necessary in order to increase power capacity, and that in the absence of such investment the country will be facing serious shortages.

In fact, the concessions given to the foreign investors are of such nature that they will defeat the very purpose for which they are sought; outflows from the economy will be far in excess of the increases in the output that these investments in new power capacity can promote; and the guaranteed price are going to be such as to cripple the State Electricity Boards and the rest of the Electricity Supply Industry in the country.

Several problems in this context need to be highlighted; First, the Govt., of India's investment for the VIII Plan is well below what was initially envisaged. Secondly, private sector investments projected to fill in the gap have not materialised beyond marginal amounts; Thirdly, the advance action required for the IX Plan is not being taken by the Govt., and there seems to be a belief that the requisite investments for the IX Plan power needs will be forthcoming thro' foreign investments; Fourthly, the terms on which approvals have been given to a few foreign investors are such as to drain the already depleted resources of the Indian ESI., Fifthly, since the required foreign investment flows to meet the power needs of the country are not likely to materialise, there will be an inevitable constraint on growth.

The high cost of power resulting from the induction of only one foreign investor, ENRON, for the Dabhol Power Project in Maharashtra are ruinous for the Indian economy, and that unless there is a determined effort to reverse the current trend and allocate state resources for the power sector, at a much lower cost than involved in the "Fast Track Foreign Investor Promoted Power Projects" (FIPPs), the future of India would not be bright. The VIII Plan target in power generation was to add 30, 358 M.W. As against this, the likely addition is likely to be less than 20,000 MW., Even this target will be difficult to achieve.

The SEBs are currently deeply in red, with their annual losses running at around Rs. 8000 crores. With this huge current account deficit, the SEBs are in no position to even maintain their units properly, let alone new investments.

The Table: 1 gives the targets approved by the National Development Council, in each of the years of actual additions to power capaicty during the recent, past and coming years.

Table 1
Power Capacity

	1992-93	*93-94*	*94-95*	*95-96*	*96-97*
Targets	4458	5651	5143	4749	10537
Achievements	3537	3500	4000*	4500*	4500*

Source: National Working Group on Power. *estimated

The Electricite de France in a round table with the World bank on "Power Supply in Developing countries: will reforms work ?" stated;

"Modern economic theory tells us that competition is more difficult to introduce in network infrastructure than in other industries, and more difficult in electricity that in other networks. it is odd that the World Bank derives no consequence from this, and treats electricity as any other commodity...We also know that competition does-not streamline regulation but makes it on the contrary more complex and burdensome. Introducing competition creates "half-free, half slave" sector...Marginally, the idea beyond our discussion about privatisation and competition may be to open the power sector of developing countries to foreign operators, expertise and capital..."

There are significant diversities and imbalances in the extent of power development among states. Even with a conscious planned effort the ratio of power available to the people in the most developed state of India is five times the ratio of the least developed states. If market forces should determine investments, this gap would certainly widen.

At the level of consumers there are income differentials between various classes of consumers—agriculture, industry, domestic and within each class of consumers.

The principle of cross subsidy was a vital instrument to ensure a modicum of development with equity. Since the World Bank led reforms are against cross subsidy and de-merit subsidies, the possibility of fruits of reforms reaching the weaker sections of society esp., farmer is increasingly becoming difficult. It is inconceivable that given such diversities a single common legislation, based on the World Bank dogma- would be able to meet all societal requirements as well as retain the federal character of the Indian Constitution.

Since the imposition of the World Bank's structural adjustment loan conditionalities and the consequent 1991 Power Policy, the GOI., announced a wide range of policy measures that liberalised the power sector in order to facilitate private foreign investment. To permit power generation by private sector companies registered in India, the Indian Electricity Act 1910 and the Electricity Supply Act, 1948 were amended.

The power sector has somc important characteristics that make it distinct for other sectors. Power cannot be stored. Generation has always to equal demand. The stability of the power system depends on imposing a cooperative functioning between generation, transmission and distribution agencies.

In order to maintain a grid discipline, the natural pattern in the power sector is not competition but cooperation. The major improvement in efficiency of the ESI (Electric Supply Industry) in developed countries came out of the integration of their power systems, and evolving a disciplined functioning within the system.

There have been criticisms of the high costs of foreign investor owned projects. Almost all the projects cleared for foreign investments have equipment manufacturers as part of consortia-setting up the plants. it is not surprising therefore, that the capital costs are so high—Rs. 4.5 to 6 crores per MW.

Both BHEL and the Industry Ministry have contended that BHEL can set up these plants at a cost of 3.0 to 3.5 crore per MW. The cost of projects can be brought down even further thro' standardisation and economic designs. However, given the nature of the concessionary package offered by the Power Ministry, it is advantageous for the investors to inflate capital costs.

Prof. Kirit Parikh, Director of the Indira Gandhi Institute for Development Research, has dubbed these power projects as (GOLD PLATED INVESTMENTS)

The Central Electricity Authority which is a unique organisation, built up over years, comprehensively involved in; planning for power development, design and technology development, techno-economic appraisal of projects, construction and plan progress monitoring of operations of power plants, technical consultancy, monitoring the performance of State Electricity Boards, power policy formulation, and grid management. Some of its functions are regulatory, some advisory, some innovative, and some are consultative.

The CEA., is organised in such a manner that there is complementarity between its responsibilities and functions. It has been working with the entire industry in a participatory mode-which is best suited to the concurrent subject. The concept behind this instrument was that in a developing country like India, expertise would be scarce and should be shared with the entire industry in areas of project formulation, project operation, and advising on techno-economic aspects.

Continued involvement with engineering, design and the latest Technology enables it to independently plan and appraise projects without depending on any other agency. It must be appreciated that electrical power has no finished goods inventory and is entirely on line. Hence, in a capital scarce developing nation a situation of acute power shortages can be minimised or eliminated only through meticulous planning and advance planning.

The above aspects need to be carefully examined when proposing a stand-alone regulator. A non-partisan evaluation of CEA would suggest that CEA's contribution to technology development and self-reliance has been phenomenal not only to supply industry but also the equipment manufacturing industry. Even the world Bank has acknowledged it. In fact far from emasculating it, there is ample scope for strengthening CEA., esp., in the matter of tariff, which at present is largely limited to nuclear power and central sector power.

We may quote here the submission of the Institution of Electrical Engineers 30th Oct., 1996 made, in the context of the reforms in the British Power Sector, to the Committee of the House of Commons:

The precept in law that "a man is deemed to be innocent until proved guilty" has an analogy in most technological developments, namely, project is deemed not to work, until tests demonstrate that it does. In other words, trials are essential part of project development, and necessary in order to elucidate unforeseen problems. The committee could explore the possibility of integrated preliminary trials with a phased induction to the market. Trials would constitute the first phase, with ideally, an interval before subsequent phases, to take account of lessons learned."

The Govt., has to make a bold bid to overcome the adverse effects in power planning in the ensuing years. For this purpose, following suggestions are put forward:

(a) The Govt., must undertake a crash programme which must be time-bound to meet the actute power shortage in the State.
(b) Steps must be taken by the SEB to identify the problems and constraints in technical and non-technical areas of activities of power management.
(c) The SEB should also undertake an effective distribution of power of various categories to consumers so that no power wastage or unproductive use will be encouraged in the State.
(d) Both the Central and State Governments, must formulate programmes to harness new sources of power, and the best way in which largescale increase in electricity generation can take place is by harnessing Nuclear Energy for the purpose.
(e) The roadmap of the reforms in the electricity sector is less clear today that what it looked like till the midninetees. Unless the issues related to the high commercial T & D losses, cross subsidies, metering and direct subsidisation of agricultural consumption and tariff reforms-Cost reflective tariffs are sorted out, no credible competition or privatisation can be thought of.

Since this requires active State Govt., support and co-ordination across the States, only the Union Govt., can pressure them to move in this direction. Some of the steps taken by the MOP., such as the draft Electricity Act, APDRP and MOUs., are rightly predicted on this belief. These steps need to go further to be more effective.

The threat of withholding power from the gird is an incredible one and should be replaced by measures, which affect the State control on the sector directly. Even there, caution needs to be applied. Eventually, the reforms in the sector should ensure that the sector moves out from the control of the State and is vested with the regulators based on sound-techno-commercial principles and under the gaze of public eye.

(f) Astounding arithmetic on demand and supply has been a pronounced characteristic of the power sector for the past so many decades, marked by an unquenchable thrist for funds and physical performance falling far below the promises. The power sector is not without its achievements but target setting and investment need projection while physical performance needs to be improved enormously.

(g) The challenge for the sector is as much of bringing pragmatism to capacity planning as of implementation of generation projects, not to mention the problems faced by schemes for improvement in transmission and distribution, which calls for a high degree co-ordination between planning and political systems.

(h) The capacity additions in the Indian power sector are not expected to meet the targets envisaged by the Govt., in the 10th FYP., 2002-2007.

The current restructuring measures envisage only "competition for the market," thro' competitive bidding, and not "competition in the market" for the supply of electricity. This would be in effect just replace the existing vertical monopolies comprising integrated generation, transmission and distribution functions, with horizontal monopolies (separate generation, transmission, and distribution companies with geographical monopoly) CRIS INFAC believes that the introduction of competition, at least at the bulk supply level (generators to distribution companies, without intermediation by the transmission company) is necessary for boosting efficiency and partially offsetting the impact of tariff increases on consumers.

(i) The hope that private investments would flow into power generation, popular during the past decade, was result of a simplistic understanding of the problems of the power sector. Some of the American power companies looked at India because the monopoly electric utilities of the U.S., were forced out of their traditional business due to de-regulation of the industry in the U.S. Conditions in India were not exactly welcoming to these investors.

We must therefore create conditions for the public sector, Central and State, to consolidate their presence in power generation. The fundamental condition is the rationalisation of tariffs and fixation of tariffs on the basis of commercial and technical considerations. Power tariffs should cover the cost of production at a reasonable level of efficiency and there must be scope for earning surpluses thro' improved performance, for investment in expansion.

(j) There must be a paring down of subsidies in a short time and cross subsidisation done away. The view that some subsidies may be inevitable becuase of socio-economic equity and should be a charge on the State budget is appealing but few of the States may have the financial resources to bear the burden.

(k) Reforming the SEBs into bankable, commercially and professionally run corporate enterprises, is a far simper proposition than to create conditions conducive for the private sector to take on the task of further expansion of capacity. These entities can then access funds both from India and outside, in the form of equity and debt. This transformation is essential to add 40,000 MW in the 10th Plan, and the more challenging 60,000 MW in the Eleventh Plan. Only then is there a hope of our progressing towards the objective of "POWER FOR ALL !"

32
The New Economic Policy and Corporate Governance

The mantra of Corporate Governance became a gosha in Japan, the US., and England, where, under the inspiration of the London Stock Exchange, Lord Cadbury outlined the basic contours of a good company from the point of view of the stock exchange. It is in this background that the Indian approach to corporate governance should be understood.

It is ironic that at a time when corporate governance has become a buzzword globally, some of the so-called citadels of corporate governance are falling apart. And the fall from the corporate grace is not an emerging market issue any longer.

Rightly, the role and importance of Corporate Governance are being re-emphasized even as the actual systems and practices of corporate governance are crumbling in places where that was least expected. It is only logical for stake holders to call for a replacement of general perceptions of corporate governance with independent analytical evaluation.

The core principle of Corporate Governance as laid down by the Organisation for Economic Cooperation and Development (OECD) Advisory Group are the four pillars on which the edifice of Corporate Governance in built.

These are: fairness; transparency; accountability; and responsibility. Without any iota of doubt, these are essentially qualitative and subjective issues, and hence, may not be easily amenable to clear-cut objective analysis.

There are certain specific statutory and regulatory requirements governing the economic management of corporate entities, which also define the codes and standards with particular orientation towards protecting the interests of diverse stake holders.

The Cadbury Committes' recommendations, the OECD principles, the confederation of Indian Industry, (CII) Code, the Securities and Exchange

Board of India directive through Clause 49 of the Listing Agreement, and the recent changes in the Companies Act provide the guiding principles of Corporate Governance. These could be excellent starting points within which a corporate entity's quality of Corporate Governance may be assessed.

In the 20th Century, corporate law makers were guided by the principle that the essence of Corporate governance is the disclosure of information to the sharholders. The more voluminous is the level of corporate governance.

Obviously "Padding Up" the balance sheet which is otherwise a disappointing story, with an overload of non-material information is certainly not a vindication of the honesty and competence of the directors.

The economic impact of the recent corporate scandals was worse than 9/11 was the commonly shared view at the India Economic Summit's session devoted to "Learning from crisis: Business ethics for a new era" (New Delhi, Nov. 25, 2002)

Addressing the session, Azim Premji, Chariman Wipro, revealed some interesting statistics on the impact of the recent scandals that rocked the U.S. business when he pointed out that the US. GDP., had reduced to 0.36 per cent and $8 trillion of wealth has been lost with long term implications for US., and other economies.

He said strong corporate governance was indispensable to resilient and vibrant capital markets and was an important instrument for investor protection.

While comparing the scenarios in India and the U.S., Rahul Bajaj, Chairman and Managing Director, Bajaj Auto, said the salaries of CEOs had not become an issue in India because management and ownership were closely linked and laws requiring disclosure of CEOs salaries has been in place for long.

However, he suggested transparency and full disclosure were not just ethnical issues but essential requirements for the survival of large corporates.

On good corporate governance, he said though guidelines were necessary but there was no substitute for good character.

George Ugeux, Group Executive Vice President, N.Y., Stock Exchange, said even as there was a general agreement on the need to have ethnical standards in business, a consensus on specific standards was difficult to achieve.

Though it was possible to set up rules to override and check personal interests, it was impossible to legislate against human greed, he added.

ICRA's corporate governance rating, for instance, limits its scope primarily to the interests of financial shareholders. The basic parameters are built around the shareholding structure, governance structure and management processes, including board-level issues, inter-relationship of shareholders, and quality of financial discipline, reporting, transparency and disclosures. Also, issues related to creation and distribution of corporate wealth are captured in the process, albeit indirectly.

ICRA's focus is predominently on substance over form. It is more the spirit than the letter of the relevant rules, procedures and codes that is important.

The sets of valuables that have been identified are drawn from different guidelines, codes of governance and committee recommendations on the subject. These variable reflect the distribution of rights and responsibilities among the constituents of the corporate management including the shareholders, the board of directors, the executive management and of course, the committees constituted for specific purposes.

There is a possibility that the corporate governance rating and the conventional credit rating for the same corporate entity would not converge. But they may not necessarily do so in all cases. The parameters, methodologies, target audiences and objectives of the two rating exercises are not identical although they share certain common features.

It is possible that a corporate entity following excellent corporate governance practices is unable to generate the kind of cash flows that would merit a high level of credit rating. Thus, credit rating and corporate governance rating are not necessarily co-directional.

Having said that, we must still argue that in the medium to long term, the two ratings should converge. A corporate entity does not carry on its business perpetually to demonstrate excellence in corporate governance. Good corporate governance is the means and not an end by itself.

ICRA's corporate governance rating exercise does not take a rigid view of the various evaluation parameters. A certain amount of flexibility is maintained, given the nature of some of the issues involved.

Corporate governance is still a new concept worldwide, and the process is evolving. In the Indian market, a beginning has just been made with the recent announcement of the country's first corporate governance rating.

It is felt the time is ripe for most countries, including India to have a re-look at the whole system of corporate governance and audit needs according to Kashi Memani, Chairman and Managing Director of Ms. Ernest and Young India.

He said every country was looking for better role models for corporate governance, and establishing better audit committees.

In India also he felt there was need to strengthen the Companies Act as in his opinion it did not have enough provisions to initiate desired levels of action against erring management. The whole system of corporate governance and audit needs to be strengthened, he reiterated once again in relation to India.

When the New Economic Policy of deregulation and liberalisation began in 1991, the general expectation was that many obsolete laws enacted during the British period would be repealed.

If stimulating corporate investment is the national goal, what we need is a set of prudent macroeconomic policies of governance which inspires confidence among investors in India and the overseas markets including NRIs.

33

Impact of WTO on Indian Small Scale Industries

The SSI sector occupies an important position in the industrial economy of the country because of its advantages of low investment, high potential for employment generation, and wider dispersal of industries in rural and semi-urban areas.

Thirtyone lacs SSI units spread over the country contribute 36 per cent of GDP. The Value of production by SSI sector has increased from Rs. 178699 crores in 1990-91 to Rs. 538537 crores in 1991-92 to 574488 crores in 1998-99. Employment has also increased from 130 lacs person in 1991-92 to 172 lacs persons in 1998-99.

In terms of capital outlay, the sectors has been using local raw materials and local manpower to produce goods and services, which are demanded locally as well as nationally and sometimes internationally.

The contribution of SSI to national economy has been well recognised by the various industrial policies of the country from time to time. The recent new policy initiative for the SSI sectors announced by the Govt., of India in 1999-2000 which emphasis to coordinate the latest development with regard to the WTO., a cell has been set up in the office of DC (SSI) to disseminate information to SSI Association and SME., units, regarding recent developments, prepare policies for SSIs in tune with the WTO agreement.

Today, there is a global recognition for the small and medium enterprises (SMEs) as they have an important role to play in the greater resource use efficiency, capacity for employment generation, technological innovation, promoting inter-sectional linkages, raising exports and developing entrepreneurial skills. Their locational flexibility is an important advantage in reducing regional imbalances. The future of SMEs is of major policy concern in the case of India, as it has the longest histories of govt., support to the small-scale industrial sector since Independence compared to most developing countries.

One of the objectives of WTO., is to reject all forms of protectionism, elimination of discriminatory. Hence, it would be very challenging for the SSI to survive and adapt to the future provisions of trade. What needs to be done? Given the contribution in terms of output, employment and growth, more than one-third of exports, and overall growth rate of SSI sector of 7.4 per cent as against 4 per cent growth rate of industrial sector, it is necessary that this sector must be prepared to face the challenges comfortably. The fact is that this sector is not being aware of the provisions and conditionalities of WTO. Majority of the Units are single man show, not found in clusters losing the benefits of economies of scale and common on facilities.

It is pertinent to mention some of the problems facing the SSI sector. These could be summarized as lack of coordination between SFCs and banks, which has resulted in the lack of flow of working capital to the SSIs leading to industrial sickness, and lack of finance for marketing.

Forescasting a substantial growth in the output of the SSI sector during the Ninth Five Year Plan, one more aspect of the operations of SSI units needs specific mention, viz., marketing support. The SSI units would be required to considerably enhance their marketing efforts if their increased production and products are to be sold profitably.

At the domestic front, the SSIs which are competent to export the product to global standards may be encouraged to do by the Govt., As an effort to generate more employment, efforts to develop sub-contracting based, establish linkage between large and small units of both domestic and global industries may be the need of the hour. Modernisation, diversification, technological upgradation, enhancing competitive ability, facing the challenge of protection to free trade etc., are the areas of concern. But it is to be mentioned again that the reality is hardly a 5 per cent of the SSIs may be prepared to face and the 95 per cent would be struggling to face the challenges of WTO., as they are far below the standards of SME. sector in developed countries.

The implication of the WTO regime on global economic environment could be felt in the form of near dismantling of tariff barriers, rapid expansion of free trade, replacement of national competition policies by a global competition policy, harmonisation of trade policies and procedures, free movement of factors of production and new business risks and new challenges of management in a highly reworked global economy.

The large number of one lac SSI units is not prepared for the sudden exposure to competition and liberalisation. This means that the competition both in the domestic and international market is going to hot up. The basic weakness of SSI lies in very small size by global standards, vulnerability due to lack of financial strength, highly diversified products increased competition from imports, export difficulties, problem of Technical know-how etc., eroding competitiveness and less complementary the large organised sector. Hence, there is a need to anaylse the Impact of SSI in India.

In the Ninth Plan document: Planning Commission, Ninth FYP., 1997-2000. Vol. II: Thematic Issues and Sectoral Programmes, Govt., of India, New Delhi, 1997-the SSI sector, producing about 8000 items, has matured and is in a position to face the competition from large industry, including multi-national companies. In the post-reform period, this sector has grown at a rate more often above those of both the overall manufacturing sector as also large-scale industries. Even then since the mid-1990s, growth of the manufacturing sector has been particularly slow, small enterprises, it is generally held have kept up the dynamism.

The malaise of the SSI sector, is reflected in the persistent high incidence of industrial sickness, a fact the Economic Survey 2000-01 also has emphasized.

From the Table: I it is clear that 99 per cent of total sick units are small enterprises and the absolute number has grown between 1995 and 1999; there were as many as 3.06 lacs such firms in 1999. These small firms account for close to a quarter of the total amount outstanding with the banks. Despite schemes to revive the potentially viable units, the problem of morbidity and mortality of large number of small units is a disturbing fact, so far as their role in generating employment and producing relatively less expensive goods for the masses are concerned.

TABLE I
Industrial Sickness in SSIs, 1995-99

(Rs. billion)

	No. of Sick/ Week Units			*Outstanding Amount*		
Year	Both SSI & Non SSI	SSI	%	Both SSI & Non SSI	SSI	%
1995	271206	268815	99.12	137.89	35.47	25.82
1996	264750	262376	99.10	137.48	37.22	27.07
1997	237400	235032	99.00	137.87	36.09	26.18
1998	224012	221536	98.99	256.82	38.57	24.60
1999	309013	306221	99.10	194.64	43.13	22.16

Source: *SIDBI Report 2000,* p. 128; and *RBI Report on Trend and Progress of Banking in India,* relevant volumes.

As the new economic policy approaches the 13th year, industrial sickness continues to grow at an alarming pace. More and more industrial units are became forced towards sickness as the opeations of the financial sector became more stratified. A large section of small and medium industry is being pushed out of the money market. Despite this, the Govt., is determined to implement the recommendations of the Committee on Industrial Sickness and Corporate Restructuring (CISCR).

In 1994 alone the Board for Industrial and Financial Reconstruction (BIFR) registered 193 companies as sick, which is a 27 per cent increase from the previous year. At the end of eight years of the functioning the BIFR, 1639 industrial companies were registered as sick with the BIFR. The accumulated losses of 1294 of the 1639 companies i.e., excluding 345 non-maintainable cases adds up to Rs. 29945 crores. The total number of workers in the 1294 companies is 989208. The industry wise distribution is given in the Table: II.

TABLE II

Industry-wise Cases Registered with BIFR

(As on December 31, 1994)

Industry	*No. of Cases registered*	*Dismissed as non-maintainable*	*Scheme sanctioned*	*Winding up recommended*	*Others*	*Balance*
Metallurgical	280	51	78	78	5	68
Textile	278	52	85	62	2	77
Paper and Pulp	130	25	38	36	0	31
Chemical	106	28	30	26	1	21
Electrical Equipment	69	12	23	11	0	23
Cement	60	7	18	6	2	27

(*Source:* BIFR).

While going slow on any substantive amendment to SICA, the Govt., has been making the necessary administrative changes recommended by the CISCR. Despite the CISCR's pious assertion of creating the environment for industrial growth and protecting labour, it sought to open a new route rather than the Industrial Disputes Act, the amendment which has been unfeasible for Govt., Rather than creating the CISCR's "FAST TRACK FACILITATOR", what is required is a body that is empowered to ensure the managements and Banks/FIs execute their responsibility in reviving sick industry.

What is required is not a piecemeal approach by a Govt., but a creative programme that takes into account the interests and concerns of all sections of society.

The volatility of exports with reference to fluctuating exchange rates is a critical phenomenon that significantly influences the SSI sector. An analysis of the trend in export earnings from the small firm sector during the 1980s points to only negligibly significant growth.

"From the point of view of export potential, what is actually needed is to enhance the relative export capability of the SSI sector. This is because, in a context to enhanced competition, the small scale sector is likely to be greater victim of competitive forces both within the international and internal markets" (P.M.Mathew: Towards a vibrant small Enterprise Economy in India, Institute of Small Enterprises and Development, Cochin, 2000).

How effectively have we dealt with the very many handicaps of the SSI and tiny sector?

We have failed to generate a reliable database of unorganised manufacturing sector, which would not only reflect the dynamics of informal production but also its actual contribution to the economy (K.Das).

What implications will the new regulations for the Indian small enterprises, given the nature of their preparedness. We shall have a glance at a few vital industries which are faced with the challenges of the WTO., regime.

(1) Pharmaceutical Industry

WTO., regime is a reality and with only two more years left for 2005 which marks the end of the transitional period meant for initiating reforms. Indian Pharmaceutical industry might be affected by new patent laws, as part of Trade Related Intellectual Property Rights System TRIPS agreement, negotiated under the WTO regime.

This agreement increases the area of coverage under the patent system such as drugs, agricultural, plants and animals etc., This agreement also increase the patent right to twenty years. It also provides for the grant of exclusive marketing rights in another country. All these provisions may affect the growth and stability of Indian companies.

Globalisation of the markets will lead to dumping of the products in different countries. Exclusive marketing Rights will pave the way for exploitation thro' advanced countries.

(2) Textile Industry

Indian textile industry's presence in the international trade is already very low and is prominantly cotton based, while world over, the trend is shifting towards synthetics, wollen and blends. Besides, the unit price realisations of Indian exports is one of the lowest. It is well known that a majority of the Indian textile machinery across spinning, weaving and processing is obsolete.

To compete effectively in the world maket, our country has to take stern action to develop infrastructure facilities, permit duty free imports of inputs etc.

(3) Garment Sector

The garment sector, predominantly small firm based and an important foreign exchange earner, will be adversely affected, as of the 714 items on which QRs., have been removed in the Exim Policy, as many as 322 relate to textiles. Already reeling under the pressure of competition from China, which plans to raise its share in Global trade to almost 50 per cent by 2005-06, a "non-competitive duty structure and no value addition duty are slowing the pace of growth of the industry in India." (Financial Express, April 11, 2001).

The rejection of inflammable skirts from India by the US., in a bitter example. The proposed abolition of the Multi-Fibre Agreement in 2004 will also severly dampen India's share of garments in World exports.

Out of Rs. 5, 82, 732 Crores worth of production in the SSI sector, goods worth Rs. 525916 crores were sold in the domestic market and the balance Rs. 56, 816 crores was sold in the international market. The SSI sector today is facing the major problem of competition in marketing their products.

Many of the SSIs may close down because of competition due to easy imports in the present era of globalisation which may add to NPAs.,

Hence, innovative schemes/ programmes need to be evolved so that the SSIs are not only promoted but they can thrive on their own. There is an urgent need to revamp the existing institutional framework supporting the SSIs to bring them in line with the need and requirements of this sector in the changed scenario. And, much more needs to be done in the policies and programmes of the Govts., so that the institutions become vehicles for ushering in an era of growth of SSIs.

The SSI sector deserves liberal institutional credit to its unique contribution in terms of creation of employment, foreign exchange earnings, reduction in regional disparities etc., But in reality, such supply of institutional credit is too meagre and often delayed.

There are many factors, both internal and external, responsible for the same. External factors may include a mild dose of industrial recession in the corporate sector, liberal import policy, increasing Govt., duties and other levies, weak infrastructural support and unhealthy competition, Similarly, organisational aspects of lending function with spl. reference to Banks, development of entrepreneurs, integrity of owners etc., may be considered as internal factors.

While external factors will continue to dominate for quite sometime internal factors need to be attended to on a war footing to revive the low credit off-take situation. In this regard, much is required to be done by banks during the second phase of reforms.

It is high time that the Govt., should address the generalised problems facing the industry as a whole: finance, technology and marketing. Marketing strategies which include pricing, branding, and the maintenance of international quality standards for products will be crucial in the new economic environment.

Joseph A.Schumpeter, had insisted for three important attributes required for an entrepreneur which are:

(1) Innovation; (2) Risk-Taking Ability, and (3) Leadership Qualities.

This is quite applicable in our today's economic scenario.

As against the present, a comprehensive plan with focussing on business dynamics is required. Business birth rate and death rate are equally important aspects for the planners viewed from this angle, more transparency and accountability are the immediate imperatives to salvage this crucial subsector of the economy from the onslaught of WTO/ Globalisation.

In short, to be a global player, the country needs to change many of its concepts, attitudes and priorities. These changes have to take place in the industry in the Govt.,-both Central and State, and in the administration.

It is a slow and difficult process, and will call for sustained efforts to guide, educate and lead the different segments. India has a potential but what it needs is consistency, objectivity and purposefulness.

"India will transform into a developed nation before the year 2020. A billion people are our resources for this national transformation."

Dr. APJ. Abdul Kalam.

34
Disinvestment

"Disinvestment should not be viewed purely from the revenue perspective. It must aim to unlock the productive potential of PSEs. Besides, disinvestments should galvanise these enterprises to promoting high quality employment as well as competition in the market place": Mid-term Economic Review. (2002).

Disinvestment has been delinked and is working in isolation. The sole purpose being touted as the philosophy of disinvestment is that "a greater focus has been placed on shifting assets out of Govt., hands than on seeing on whose hands they would fall." Frank Vogel of the Transparency International had warned against this in 1996.

Disinvestment policy and its implementation during the 90s shows how in its quintessential form it is arguably the most telling example of market fundamentalism. 'Disinvestment' say the Disinvestment Commission of the GOI., has been viewed as a tool for bringing down the budgetary deficits of the Government" (Disinvestment strategy and Issue, Dec., 1996).

During the period 1992-97, equity of PSEs., was disinvested in proportion ranging from 0.27 per cent to 48.94 per cent (with average of 22.20 per cent of the shares disinvested, and in the case of 20 PSEs off-loaded shareholding was below 10 per cent of the total). An overwhelming portion of these 39 PSEs are profit making ones. According to the Working Group on Disinvestment Issues the interest saved as a result of transfer of disinvestment proceeds as capital receipts to the GOI., from 1992-97 would be Rs. 94643 crores as against the return foregone (computed on the net profit after tax as given in the GOI's Public Enterprises Survey, 1996-97) is Rs. 178391 crores because of the sale of equity on the market (Mainstream, May 20, 2000).

Actually with our thin and narrow capital markets only in the case of four highly profitable PSEs, the disinvestment amounted to 40 to 49 per cent of their equity. The position of the PSEs in terms of share of equity disinvested is: 3 PSEs between 5 to 10 per cent, 6 PSEs between 10 to 1º per cent and 10 PSEs between 14 to 20 per cent upto 1997.

Disinvestment of PSUs

TABLE

PSUs in which disinvestment decision has been taken and disinvestment is in progress (Profit/loss for the year 2000-01)

(*Amount in Rs Crore:*)

Hindustan Organic Chemicals Ltd	(-) 39.06 :
National Fertilizer Ltd	(+) 27.31 :
Balmer Lawrie & Co Ltd	
	(+) 6.01 :
Braithwaite & Co	(+) 1.74 :
Burn Standard & Co	(-) 45.22 :
Bharat Heavy Plates & Vessels Ltd	(+) 0.94 :
Engineering Projects India Ltd	(+) 17.76 :
Fertilizer and Chemicals Travancore Ltd	(-) 1956.58 :
Hindustan Salts Ltd	(-) 2.19 :
Hindustan Cables Ltd	(-) 71.41 :
Hindustan Copper Ltd	(-) 105.80 :
Instrumentation Control Valve Ltd Palakkad	(+) 0.16 :
Madras Fertilizers Ltd	(-) 29.76 :
MECON Ltd	(-) 51.36 :
Minerals and Metal Trading Corpn	(+) 12.39 :
National Aluminium Co Ltd	(+) 655.83 :
National Instruments Ltd	(+) 0.09 :
NEPA Ltd	(+) 4.86 :
State Trading Corpn of India Ltd	(+) 26.65 :
Shipping Corporation of India	(+) 382.56 :
Tyre Corporation of India	(-) 66.43
Tunghabhadra Steel Products Ltd	(+) 0.07 :
Engineers India Ltd	(+) 123.86 :
Manganese Ore India Ltd	(+) 20.05 :
Sponge Iron India Ltd	(+) 6.64 :
Bharat Opthalmic Glass Ltd	(-) 37.69 :
Instrumentation Ltd, Kota (Mother Unit)	(-) 34.52 :
Hindustan Paper Corpn Ltd	(+) 32.80 :
Hotel Corpn of India Ltd at Centaur Hotel Delhi	(-) 17.73 :

Hotel Corpn of India Ltd at Chefair Mumbai	(+) 0.62 :
ITDC Hotel Samrat, New Delhi @	(-) 2.36 :
ITDC Hotel, Jaipur Ashok	(-) 2.30 :
ITDC Hotel Patliputra Ashok	(-) 0.50 :
ITDC Hotel, Kalinga Ashok	(-) 1.40 :
ITDC Hotel, Jammu Ashok	(-) 0.80 :
Bharat Petroleum Corporation Ltd	(+) 820.12 :
Hindustan Petroleum Corporation Ltd	(+) 1088.01 :
Joint sector hotel properties of ITDC, where Govt is in discussion with state governments	
Hotel Neelchal Ashok, Puri	(-) 0.98
Hotel Lakeview Ashok, Bhopal	(-) 56. 83
Hotel Ranchi Ashok, Ranchi	(-) 71.10
Hotel Brahmaputra Ashok, Guwahati	(-) 0.20
Hotel Pondicherry Ashok, Pondicherry	(-) 0.25
Hotel Donyl Polo Ashok, Itanagar	(+) 0.014
Hotel Punjab Ashok, Anandpur Sahib #	(-) 0.08
Disinvestment process not started again after there was no response to an earlier attempt	
Air-India	(-) 44.13
Indian Airlines	(-) 159.17
Open offer of residual shares in the market	
Maruti Udyog Ltd	(-) 269.40
Recommendation received from the disinvestment commission	
Neyveli Lignite Corpn Ltd	(+) 725.92
Rail India Tech & Economic Services Ltd	(+) 7.47
Project & Equipment Corpn Ltd	(+) 2.58
IRCON International Ltd	(+) 65.60
Central Inland Water Transport Corpn Ltd	(-) 78.26
Cochin Shipyard Ltd	(+) 38.49
Hindustan Shipyard Ltd	(-) 18.58

Including Chefair Delhi # Accumulated losses as on 31-3-2002
@ Lease-cum management control (Loss for the year 1999-2000)

Source : Lok Sabha Question # 205 (Ministry of Disinvestment).

The main objective of disinvestment is to put national resource and assets to optimal use and in particular to unleash the productive potential inherent in PSEs. The policy of disinvestment specifically aims at modernisation and upgradation of PSEs, creation of new assets, generation of employment, and retiring of public debt.

The disinvestment ministry has suggested offloading 23 per cent Govt., stake in HPCL to a strategic partner and 39 per cent in BPCL in the market. The Govt., plans to raise Rs. 12000 crore through stake sales in State firms by March, 2003 but has already admitted it would fail way short of the target after the delay in the sale of HPCL., and BPCL. India has about 232 State companies, almost half of them loss-making, producing everything from condoms to steel with a collective net worth of $33 billion.

The rationale of disinvestment was to take money out of unproductive assets and employ it profitably. Profitability for the nation practically from profitability for an individual. It is more than asset creation. It is also about human resources development, providing healthcare, social sector investment, and infrastructure development. There appears to be no evidence that the proceeds from PSU sales have been, or would be, put into these sectors.

With 60, years of existence, FACT, with around 6000 employees has become a part of the Corporate history of the State and hence the public are finding it hard to digest. Other companies whose fate is on the line include some equally important companies like Hindustan Organic Chemicals, Hindustan Newsprint Ltd., and Cochin Shipyard Ltd.

The Govt., has already secured a commitment from the Dept., of International Development, UK., for assistance in operating Voluntary retirement schemes for employees and workers of the closed units.

A large number of Central PSUs are also earmarked for closure as no private company has shown interest in taking over these companies.

It is essential that the disinvestment process should not result in the creation of monopolies. In the absence of adequate legal safeguards and a strong regulatory machinery, it will be difficult to ensure that consumers are not exploited by monopolies.

For example, the requisite regulatory machinery is absent to prevent exploitation of scarce natural resources for commercial gains. Ultimately, disinvestment will succeed or fail depending on the support the process gets from the public.

Unless, the public understands the issues involved their support for disinvestment will not be forthcoming. It was with this intention that the Disinvestment Commission had recommended the setting up of a Disinvestment Fund, into which all receipts for disinvestment would be spent on earmarked social sector projects such as housing, education and health. The public would then be convinced of the benefits of disinvestment.

So far, the Govt., has not agreed to the creation of Disinvestment Fund on the ground that prudent financial management precludes keeping of funds outside the consolidated Fund of India.

But it has agreed to set up a Road Fund into which receipts from levies on fuel would be spent on development of roads. It is quite clear that unless ugrent and radical measures aimed at reform are taken, most of the PSEs., will be unable to overcome competition. It will be in the Government's interest to remain in business—that are highly profitable and contribute substantially to public interest, and not fitter away its energies in running a host of sundry, unprofitable businesses.

All such enterprises that are not of strategic importance will have to be privatised. And those that do not have to remain in the public sector and that cannot be privatised must be liquidated early.

PSUs should not get any more financial assistance from the Govt., in the form of equity, loans or grants. If they have worth while projects, they should approach financial institutions for assistance.

The time has come when the public sector has to be lean, efficient, and capable of taking on domestic as well as international competition in the wake of globalisation.

However, Considering that a programme such as the public sector disinvestment can succeed only on the basis of consensus or at the least strive towards it, the aggravated posturing in favour of or against a particular method is most unfortunate. It also renders the recent decision to proceed with the programme less noteworthy that what it actually is.

From a practical standpoint the revival of the disinvestment is an achievement. Never mind as some critics say it is not only compromised but also open ended, that is, without a time-frame.

At the core of the ongoing debate over the future of disinvestment is the perceived superiority of private—over the Govt., in ownership and control and of course in running a commerical enterprise. That is why stage-by-stage dilution planned for BPCL is considered inferior to the sale contemplated for HPCL. In fact, many protagonists of reform think disinvestment is an anarchronistic expression; to emphasize the true reform character we should use the word privatisation, according to them.

And, there seems to be no recognition of the fact that no programme esp., one so inherently controversial as the disinvestment will not succeed if it is divested from reality. The reality in India is that words such as privatisation are still anathema to large sections. However, quaint, expressions like disinvestment will help the cause of the programme.

Two other relevant points are also to be mentioned here. On the technical side, the methods—the strategic sale and the public offer route have—there plus and minus points. It seems theoretical to talk of the superiority of one over the other even in the instant cases of HPCL and BPCL., Much will depend naturally on the ways they are put through.

Second, there seems to be no convincing evidence yet in India and surprisingly in countries such as the U.K., that privatisation has delivered on all its promises.

In conclusion, we may add that sources said today consenus is on a modified version of the formula floated by Finance Minister: Jaswant Singh's Advisor Vijay Kelkar who had proposed that HPCL be up for sale only to foreign bidders and BPCL thro' the public issue route. Kelkar had argued that given the presence of Govt-owned IOC and private players like Reliance, this would ensure a level playing field and prevent monoploy.

35

Issues in Monetary and Credit Policy

When we glance through the various monetary policy documents over a decade, it is found that documents look more or less the same following the same patterns of presentation and containing prosaic statements, such as reference to Economic Development, Domestic Sector, External Sector, Policy Measures etc., So much so, we get accustomed to look for that part of the monetary policy in which the person is interested. Although apparently the documents look alike, there has been a paradigm shift in the objectives of the monetary policy and the measures that are adopted to bring about improvement in the financial sector.

For example, Monetary Policy for 1990-91 (April, 12) aimed at "Controlling the growth of liquidity and moderating credit expansion". While in Oct., it is said that "monetary policy must support the cohesive package of measures of macro-economic stabilisation and structural reforms." Similarly, the document relating to April, 1993 reads as follows:

"Apart from continuing with the reform process, monetary policy for 1993-94 must ensure that inflation rate is further reduced while providing stimulus to industrial recovery and growth of agriculture through adequate credit availability."

The Oct., 1994 policy also echoed the same focus while the over-all concern of the monetary policy is to moderate the growth of primary liquidity, banks must ensure that their resources are utilised to meet the requirements of all productive segments—in the economy.

Looking at the recent policy announcements, it is quite clear that these "focussed the structural measures to strengthen the financial system and to improve the functioning of various segments of financial markets."

Moreover, the recent policy emphasises on operation effectiveness, regulator role, prudential norms, credit delivery system and technological development. Thus, it is observed that the traditional objectives of price stability and growth and regulation of the economy seem to have been replaced by the interplay of market forces and the monetary policy aims more on effective functioning of markets, regulatory role, technological development etc., It may be debatable whether such a shift has taken place or not, or these changes also serve the same traditional objectives of the policy.

We may observe from the above that the Monetary Policy document—attempts to deal with so many issues of diverse nature besides the basic issues objectives and instruments of monetary policy. Following liberalisation, many developments are left to market forces and action to be announced only as reaction to volatile markets.

The process of financial reforms which began along with the economic reforms in early 1990, has been carried forward through various credit policy announcements. The recent credit Policy continues the same objective. The new valuation morms of the investment portfolio norms on banks faciliate segregation of investments into those intended for holding till maturity and for trading. As the provisions for depreciation is not required in case of the Govt., securities, it will help the banks to improve their profits.

The Policy provides greater freedom in issuing Commercial papers as these have been delinked from working capital requirements although it may adversely affect the banks. It may increase volumes in capital market and may result in lowering interest rates. The new policy has withdrawn restrictions on transfer of certificate of Deposits in Secondary Market.

The central objective of monetary policy is to achieve a low rate of inflation in the medium; long run. Other objectives, such as real growth of the economy and distribution of the income, are also important.

The best contribution that monetary policy can make towards sustained growth of the economy is by providing price stability. The world over there is a wide consensus that medium-term inflation is a monetary phenomenon and that money supply provides a natural nominal anchor for a monetary policy aiming at safeguarding price stability.

Another difficult area is the basic dictum that a country has a choice between an independent monetary policy and an independent exchange rate. Robert Mundell had clearly enunciated this almost 43 years ago, and this is now part of standard elementary monetary economics.

If a country chooses to have one independent policy it has to give up the freedom to decide the other. this is difficult for the Indian psyche to accept. The populist view is that our macho spirits would never allow a subordination of Indian monetary policy to the dictates of another country and hence our policy preference is to have an independent and flexible monetary policy. But at the same time, our national pride would consider it a failure of policy if we are unable to maintain a nominal fix on an average exchange rate. The public perception is that irrespective of the strengthening or weakening of the US dollar the test of a successful exchange rate policy is expressed in terms of a fixed nominal dollar rupee rate.

In recent years, the RBI has de-emphasised it public commitments to monetary targets, exchange rate indicators, interest rate indicators, and inflation projections/targets. Instead it has talked more generally about multiple indicators and the Monetary conditions Index. This has resulted in less strident criticism of the RBI's policies. Be as it may, there is a need for focussing monetary policy on transparent indicators. This would encourage greater degrees of policy freedom for the RBI, and with it would come greater accountability.

We must recognise that the world over public sector banks are going through painful restructuring and we in India cannot be exempted from this adjustment. The time for debate is over, and the time for action has come. If we do not contain the weak bank contagion it can have serious repercussions on the entire financial system. As Alan Greenspan said: "A financial system is as strong as its weakest link."

It needs to be reiterated that fiscal empowerment by augmenting the volume and scale of the tax and non-tax revenue flows into the budget holds the key to fiscal consolidation in India. Revenue maximisation requires that the tax system be reformed thro' widening the tax base, simplification of tax rules, review of exemptions/incentives, and strict tax compliance along with extensive use of information technolgoy and data warehousing.

Moreover, it is necessary to design a long-term tax policy. This would obviate—the need for a large number to tax changes each year, and would provide stability to the tax system.

In the Indian context, lack of an effective and simple tax regime has been an important factor leading to a decline in the tax/GDP ratio.

As regards indirect taxes, the successful implementation of the Value Added Tax (VAT) at the national level is a major challenge in the drive for improvement in tax revenue.

Poor return on investments in PSEs and statutory corporate entities are areas of concern. The issues of user charges and cost recoveries needs to be addressed in the context of fiscal correction and achieving a reasonable degree of flexibility in public finances. Improvement in fixing and collection of user charges, extension of the same to non-merit goods and progress in cost recoveries is also central to the issue of fiscal empowerment. As such, non-tax revenues, which include user charges and cost recoveries on the services rendered by the Govt., or their entities in areas such as transport, power and irrigation would reflect the cost of services provided.

The PSEs that are making losses need to be restructured so that the profitability of the public enterprises could be a major source of resource generation and support to Govt., finances.

Fiscal consolidation also requires altering the pattern of expenditure. The level of expenditure of the Central Govt., is heavily loaded in favour of obligatory constitutents—interest payments, defence and statutory grants to states-reducing thereby, capital expenditure, which adds to productive capacity in the economy, is being progressively pre-empted by growth in revenue expenditures.

Although explicit subsidies provided by the Central Govt., have declined, there is a wide range of hidden subsidies that need to be contained. Proper targeting of subsidies is needed to reduce leakages. In this regard, the dismantling of the administered price mechanism in the petroleum sector has been a welcome step as it would not only bring transparency to the fiscal operations, but would also improve the productivity, efficiency, and international competitiveness of the domestic petroleum industry.

In this regard, formulating a long-term energy policy, taking into account the future of public sector oil companies, is necessary to exploit the strong forward and backward linkages of the energy sector with other sectors in the economy.

A comprehensive approach to the management of public expenditure would require explicit recognition of macro-economic linkages of Govt., expenditure policies, and ensuring that specified activities are undertaken effectively. In this context, accumulated empirical evidence shows that public sector investment in the infrastructure sector "crowds in" private investment. While the debate around ownership verus efficiency continues, it is necessary to recognise that there is no evidence for automatic reaping of efficiency gains merely from the transfer of ownership from public to private.

On the other hand, there is some evidence suggesting that efficient public ownership in some selected sectors could bring with it external economies of scale and scope which provide a supportive environment for private enterprise esp., when projects are lumpy, involve long gestation lags and where the criticial minimum of infrastructure has to be created.

However, an essential pre-requisite for such positive results to be realised is to make the management of public enterprises autonomous but accountable in terms of economic preformance.

There has been a successful completion of the strategic sale process of some public sector enterprises since last year. The proceeds from disinvestments aggregated to Rs. 5000 crores during 2001-02 which were significantly higher than Rs. 2125 crores raised during the preceding year. The real challenge, however, lies not merely in closing down non-viable public sector enterprises, but in restructuring the potentially viable PSEs and significantly scaling down of Govt., equity stakes in all non-strategic areas.

There are interesting parallels between the monetary policies of India and the U.S., On Oct., 29, 2002, the RBI, through its Mid-Term Review of Monetary and Credit Policy reduced the Bank Rate, the Cash Reserve Ratio (CRR), and the repo rate by 25 basis points each. Although not sensational as the changes in the U.S., the Indian experiment is also record breaking in its own way. The Bank Rate is at its lowest level since Independence. The CRR has been brought down all the way from 11 per cent in Aug., 1998 to the present 4.75 per cent (after the latest reduction). While these fit into the broad objective of a softer interest rate regime, what has been most noteworthy about the review is the admission that the cuts in the benchmark Bank Rate as well as the CRR are unlikely to achieve the two traditional objectives:

(1) A revival of investment demand and
(2) A lowering of interest rates still further.

Are we reaching the limits of monetary policy ? Such a question increasingly posed in several countries including India need not be construed as a condemnation of the policy stance, and its operation. Rather such questions suggest above all no macro-economic policy however refined can single handedly lift the economy out of a particular predicament. Monetary Policy ought to work in tandem with other constituents of economic policy.

India, for instance, the RBI has been consistently emphasising fiscal consolidation as a key prelude for the attainment of the monetary objective of lower interest rates. Also, while stressing the need for financial sector reform to further monetary objectives (including a sustained softer interest rate regime) it admits that some of those are outside the purview of the Central Bank. Expert comments after the steep reduction in the benchmark interest rates in the U.S., have been sceptical of the consequences. For instance, in the US., it was believed that a still cheaper credit regime would sustain the growth in housing sales, which in an ostherwise dull economic scenario has remained a bright spot. Interestingly in India too, the only sector that has gained visibly from the falling interest rates has been the home loan segment.

However, it is unlikely that the extra liquidity that is now being pumped in will boost demand further.

With all the indications of a fiscal turnaround, the Gross Fiscal Deficit during April-July, 2002 shows an increase of around Rs. 1000 crores as compared with the position during the corresponding period last year. There is every likelihood that the deficit will escalate further before: March, 31, 2003, even if the GDP growth this year falls below the projected growth rate of 5.5 per cent. But should this higher level of fiscal deficit cause undue concern, when fiscal policy as such has a vital role in the process of revival of growth. ?

The IMF., is perturbed over the current trends in fiscal deficit in India. It has recently struck a note of warning that if the fiscal deficit cannot be reined in, it would damage the long-term sustainability of even a lower rate of growth.

It has urged the Govt., to push through the stalemated Fiscal Responsibility Legislation. All this cannot alter the fact that vast resources are needed for drought relief, as well as for infrastructure projects, which have remained in the pipeline for years.

The European Central Bank's objective is price stability and that the dangers of undershooting now seem at least as great as those of overshooting. The ECB has made it clear more recently that its response to deviations from the inflations target will be symmetrical, implying that policy rates could indeed decline further depending on the circumstances.

Monetary policy in Japan is also being conducted in a highly unusual environment, namely one of falling prices. While the outcome is by no means certain, most of the ingredients seem to be in place for a continuation of such deflationary pressures. The burden of real debt borne by corporations continues to rise, impeding investment. Unit labour costs are increasing and restructuring will add to unemployment., further depressing confidence and consumer spending. While purchases do not yet appear to have been deferred in expectation of further price declines, as seems to be happening in China, the potential for this cannot be ruled out.

Given global conditions of excess capacity and high or rising unemployment in Europe, Japan and much of the emerging world, supply-side reforms are also urgently required. This might seem paradoxical, since such reforms will eventually further increase productive potential. Yet we should not forget the principal insight of classical economics, namely that changes in relative prices can also contribute materially to the resolution of economic disequilibria. Even with absolute restructuring of the corporate and banking sectors, current excess capacity in many industrial sectors means that investment in those areas will be weak for years to come, with associated multiplier effects on jobs and income.

In these circumstances, it is essential that govt., restrictions and other profit destroying impediments to invest in other sectors, esp., services, be removed. While this applies most clearly in emerging markets, many industrial countries also recognise that they must move in the direction of deregulation. Steps taken in labour markets to increase the likelihood of the jobless being hired act in the same direction, esp., since workers spend and confident workers spend even more. This is perhaps one of the clearest lessons to be learned from the experience of the United States over the last few years.

To sum up: The recent mid-term review of the Monetary Policy emphasises much on strengthening the financial sector. In view of banks facing global competition, it has suggested various measures to strengthen the balance sheets of the banks, improvement in technological upgradation, and improving profitability of the banks. The mid-term review made clear the intention of the monetary authority that it will change the reserve ratios, bank rate and reporates as and when necessary. The policy made clear the emphasis on strengthening the financial sector which will attract long-term investments in the economy.

Though the policy does not suggest any changes in the stance of traditional monetary policy instruments, it may become inevitable keeping in view the inflationary pressures, uncertain forex reserves, falling rupee value, govt., borrowing, internal and external economies etc., The financial stability as highlighted in the mid-term review will bring down the volatility in the foreign exchange market.

The current policy is focussed on attaining best global practices for Indian banks and financial institutions. The increased operational freedom afforded to banks alongwith the stringent prudential and disclosure norms, will pave the way for a healthy, market driven, profit-oriented banking system.

* The latest monetary measures—the lowering of the CRR and the Bank Ratemight have been anticipated. Their justification in the current context can be questioned both from a theoretical and practical standpoint.

* The two visible aspects of the Monetary and Credit Policy (2003-04)

have been the reduction in the Bank Rate and in the Cash reserve ratio (CRR) by an identical 0.25 per cent,

* The Monetary policy's key dilemma is this: It cannot waver from its well-established stance, which is "provision for adequate liquidity to meet the needs of the industrial sector." It might be sooner than is realised but the RBI may have to resolve the inherent contradiction in its interest rate Policy.

(* The Hindu: may 10, 2003).

36

New Economic Policy and Social Justice

The New Economic Policy tends to more towards capitalizm and mixed economy. But really our country is covered by a mixed economic curtain. Thus, Jha believed that capitalism still exists in major forms in India.

Our Planners and Policy markers planned an economic activity to form a socialistic pattern of society. As a result, many radical changes have been carried out. They were nationalisation of financial institutions and major industries etc.,

But our economic system did not gain much. As a result, our planners and policy makers rethought and introduced New Economic Policy. This policy contents: liberalisation, globalisation and structural adjustment. These concepts pave way for privatisation in major areas.

Advocates of economic reforms often argue that there will be net gains to the poor from the higher relative prices of agricultural goods, the removal of restrictions on external trade, and cuts to subsidies on agricultural inputs.

It is argued that relative prices of agricultural goods will benefit the rural sector, where poverty tends to be concentrated in most developing countries, including India. The extent of the gains will depend on a number contingencies. But gains are normally expected.

For a long time, Economic development was taken for granted by many people to be the objective of development. Economic progress definitely is an essential component of development; it is not, however, the only component. For development is not purely an economic phenomenon. It must encompass more than the material and financial side of people's lives. It should be perceived as a multidimensional process involving reorientation of the entire economic and social system.

Besides improving incomes and output there should should also be radical changes in the institutional, social and administrative structures; there should also be changes in popular attitudes, and in many cases even customs and beliefs, and finally, there should be fundamental modifications of the international economic social systems as well.

Development must be conceived of as a multidimensional process involving major changes in the dimensions indicated below:

1. Structures.
2. Popular attitude.
3. National institutions.
4. These changes should go hand-in-hand with acceleration of economic growth;
5. Reduction in inequality; and
6. Eradication of absolute poverty.

Whatever the content of better life, development in all societies must have atleast the following objectives:

(a) Development should mean that the basic life sustaining goods and services like food, shelter, health and protection are made available to all, and distribution of those goods and services are widened to include every citizen in the country.

(b) Development should help raise levels of living thro' higher income, more employment and better education; greater attention should be paid to foster culture and humanistic values which would enhance material wellbeing and generate greater individual and national self-esteem.

(c) Development should provide the where withal to expand the range of economic and social choice to individuals and nations by freeing them from servitude and dependence not only in relation to other people and nations, but also to forces of ignorance and human misery.

These three values of development are lacking very much in developing countries. Actually, there is a low level of living, low self-esteem, and limited freedom. The first refers mainly to economic aspects, and the latter two refer to non-economic aspects of development. The three together portray concisely the nature and the inner meaning of development. These by the process of cumulative causation work towards perpetuaring under-development according to Gunnar Myrdal, "Without improving the level of living within a nation, prospects for development are practically non-exist. Hence, the first priority in moving away from the chronic state of underdevelopment must be by improving people's level of living. Thus economics play a central role in the development process. But the impact of this role would be diminished or even calcified, if determinants of national and personal system and striving to broaden society's freedom to choose are not given priority of attention."

How would be this achieved ? Is there a model of development which would include all elements mentioned above ? There are and should be no ideologies if we want to succeed.

The future development strategy lies in mustering all the energies to design imaginative, but viable alternatives by generating a capacity for greater self-reliance. The alternative consists in creating conditions for the new praxis based on Human Scale Development.

Such a development is focussed and based on the satisfaction of fundamental human needs, on the growing generation of growing levels of self-reliance, and on the construction of organic articulations of people with nature and technology of global processes with local activity, of the personal with the social, of planning with autonomy, and of civil society with the State.

In fact, our planning is not rural based. Our people are becoming poorer and the rich becoming richer. At this juncture, the poor people are unable to get social justice in economy, politics. Our planners and politicians should rethink of providing social justice to the people at all levels. Then only our economy and the nation proudly stand in the realm.

We are deeply committed to social justice. We think we can have stability and progress only if we take a particular economic path—the path of socialism thro' which we give social justice to our people.

The aspect of new economic policies remains in the domain of domestic liberalisation.

If we take globalisation, there are two factors to be borne in mind. First, the needs of the consumer—they are entitled to be best products at the best prices, at the same time it has to be balanced with the domestic industry. To make sure that domestic industry does not get crippled by the globalisation process, and is equipped to face the competition, we have to provide them with a level playing field.

There are a number of measures taken to do so, but there are three measures which are also required in the future to ensure that the level playing field comes so.

One in terms of interest rate available to the industry that is cost of capital, second in labour law reforms, third strengthened infrastructure esp., power sector.

Further, we require competitiveness, in order to move ahead of others and generate wealth which can be used in terms of creating more jobs in an establishment.

Ours is a great democratic institution. A lot of legislative works, debates, concerns on temporary issues are not reflected in the media. Of course, things have to improve. It has to be on the basis of well-set ethics.

Social justice, esp., in a developing country, requires easy, speedy and inexpensive legal remedies, without, in any way, impairing the impartiality of the judicial process.

**

The benefits of economic reforms appear to be a long way off to most of the poor. As per the new norms set by the Planning Commission in 1998, to assess the poverty level, the number of those regarded as poor in fact rose by 100 per cent from 160 millions to 320 millions which is more than one-third of the country's population.

(** Business Line, April, 30, 1998).

The determinants of poverty are not mere income parameters. They include deprivation of basic needs such as food, health, education, and employment.

The evidence on the poverty front shows that rural poverty increased significantly rose from 36.43 per cent in 1990-91 to 43.47 per cent in 1992-93, but declined subsequently to 38.74 per cent in 1993-94. Urban poverty also showed similar fluctuations but much less notable than in the case of rural poverty.

The compulsion to reduce fiscal deficit led to some delcine in the relative role of allocation of social sectors health, education, and poverty alleviation which had an adverse impact on poverty.

In spite of some progress in the field of economic and social development, the picture of economic development appears to be somewhat disheartening and deceptive due to several shortfalls and problems in the economic and social policy over a period of 56 years since our independence.

If we diangose the economic and social maladies over the last 56 years, we are able to find several shortcomings.

Globalisation, liberalisation and opening up of the Indian economy has become an evitable commitment of the process of economic development. The protectionist and License Raj policies cannot work for India.

We cannot live in isolation in this modern world. The basic philosophy behind globalisation and opening up of the Indian economy to invite foreign capital, produce more not only for domestic consumption but also for exports and thus enjoy the fruit of it by all. We have to wait and see what extent this high sounding theory do work in a highly traditional economy like in our country.

In the process of solving problems relating to social justice peoples' participation plays a vital role. The only vehicle which would enable different segments of population to alleviate their grievances will be their participation.

The re-engineering process of solving problems pertaining to social justice should first and foremost concentrate to alter the outdated and redundant rules, regulations etc.,

The problem solving strategy is ideal, esp., in the long-run where systems viewpoint is taken into consideration.

As a result of solving problems pertaining to implementation of policies, there is a great concern for the very purpose of framing such new economic policies. Such an act would certainly result in fulfilling the social fields like social justice in our motherland.

Eventhough globalisation is not an event much less a watershed in the country's continuam in the efforts to move away from insularity to integration with the global economy, it has produced a disruptive impact on the socio-economic life. There is no question that the rich-poor divide has widened with an often 'guestimated' 300 million poor being marginalised with no social security. A burgeoning middle has served not only to stimulate the production of luxury goods but to show in bold relief the contrast between conspicuous consumption and the desperate search for livelihood.

The new technologies ranging from mechanisation of farming to sophisticated information technology and bio-technology have invaded the traditional labour intensive occupations to the visible distress of millions of unskilled labour.

Agricultural employment, esp., for women, has shrunk. Fisheries, the handloom industry and the construction sector have suffered causing despair among the vulnerable sections of the working class. The hope that some trade-off has occurred through export oriented industries providing employment opportunities esp., for women in the garment and leather sectors, for example, is not much of a consolation. The fact is that the long-term neglect of education and skill information for the poor would be difficult to mitigate over the medium term which again brings the issue of social security to the core.

Industrial employment has been stagnating for years and with restructuring gathering momentum in response to the challenge of global competition, redundancies and downsizing have become endemic. Opportunities for self-employment do exist but the economic system is not favourable for the expansion of self-employment.

So what does it all amount to ? The benefits of globalisation have been more or less negated by widespread distress of the poor in rural and urban areas. Nevertheless, globalisation cannot be wished away. As Dr. C.Rangarajan, pointed out in his recent convocation address at the University of Madras, "Opting out globalisation is not a vitable choice. We need to stay and fight."

As for the legitimate fears that the WTO regime would road-roll the domestic agenda, Dr. C.Rangarajan reiterates the need for India "to evolve an appropriate framework to wrest maximum benefits out of international trade and investment. This framework should include:

(a) Making explicit the list of demands that India would like to make on the multinational trade system.

(b) measures that rich countries should be required to undertake to enable developing countries to gain more from international trade and (c) steps that India should take to realise the full potential from globalisation.

Does the New Economic Policy in India predicate 'withering of the State' as an economic entity ? The debate on whether the State is necessarily failure prone has been going on for decades now.

As Dr. C.Rangarajan puts, it, the economic reforms in India do not seek to 'diminish the role of the State', 'but rather to redefine it, Expanding it in some areas and reducing in some others.'

"More market does not mean less government, but only different governments."

So far, reforms is talked of as a generic concept. The initial thrust of the govt., setting the agenda under compulsion from the global funding agencies has yielded to ad hoc policy-making under multiple pressures.

Reversal is quite possible and no time should be lost in planning it.

The challenge of good governance would certainly requires govt., to be reinvented, and non-govt., sector to be reinvigorated with a social motive.

In 'sum' the New Economic Policy in our country has entered social justice that posess new challenges. A millennium that promises to Usher in the Information Age, and with a "Knowledge Society."

India is uniquely poised to benefit from this transition. Though we find many examples of individual excellence, yet, as a country, we have somehow gone astray. We have failed to realise our full potential.

Reforms have reduced some rigidities in the system and supply response has become more flexible. But these have not yet become so flexible as to match the demand released by the supply-side economics.

The new economic policy aims at generating employment through various sponsored schemes such as IRDP., SEPUP etc., But this new policy has failed to attain the targetted level of employment generation.

The time is now ripe to concentrate as structural adjustment in different areas by way of redefining the very concept of growth from a quantitative to a qualitative one that embodies considerations relating to poverty reduction and curtailment of inequalities of income and employment.

The increasing proportion of the world labour force is engaged in activities that are linked to international trade and capital flows. The initiation of the transition to a market economy was an important development. So too, is the increasing participation in the world economy of the most populous developing economy India.

*To identify performance variation and equity in the implementation of the welfare measures across the states in India, the Taxanomic Method is used. to construct the performance index.

It is also used in determining the region or states which serve as Models in fixing the potential targets for each of the component.

(*Dreze and Sen, K.K.: Hunger and Public Action, Oxford clarendon Press).

We can visualise economic growth to take place in may ways. For example, Denison had a study on sources of economic growth for U.S.A., Western Europe. In a more general ways, in the context of Govt., policy, a larger stock of productive assets and human skills can be up.

It should be our policy to utilise available human resources to the utmost. Out stategy for HRD., should be designed to change the quality of life and also to accelerate the pace of development. We must ensure that the less privileged sections of the community get a much better deal.

Social justice needs a problem solving approach, and the process of solving problems needs re-engineering.

The new economic policy has a vision with social justice has been a major cause for a shift. It is high time for us to reorient ourselves towards achieving excellence in the future.

"It is our firm belief that social justice is not only compatible with economic growth, but it is an essential condition for sustained and orderly growth."

(Late: Prime Minister: Smt. Indira Gandhi: March, 17, 1970).

37

Productivity in the Age of Globalisation

The word 'Productivity' has come into fashion today, but the idea itself is old.

Productivity cannot be confined to industry and transport, nor it is enough to include agriculture. Productivity must be built in our basic attitude towards all branches of national endeavour. Essentially, productivity is the most scientific use of our monetary, material, technological and human resources in order to secure the best possible benefits, immediate as well as long-term.

Productivity has two main aspects. The first is the technical aspect, covering techniques of improved organisation, better management, better inventory control, better handling of resources, the avoidance of waste etc.,

The second and more important aspect pertains to psychological and human factors and involves better motivation, better industrial relations, and more imaginative worker education. This aspect has not received due attention. The worker is not a static but an individual who depends to a human approach. Efficiency means making people give of their best and this will be possible if they have a better sense of partnership. What is the purpose of increased production and productivity? Economic growth is not a figure but the indicator of greater socio-economic justice.

On production, Gandhiji wanted manufacture of basic goods first. But the mode of production should not be exploitive. He was not against industrialisation. But he was opposed to industry which replaced human labour, and by which labour was exploited and retrenched. Supreme consideration for him was man, and so Gandhiji welcomed machines and technologies which helped man, and relieved him of the burden by increasing worker's productivity and worked towards his complete control.

Industrialism, as it is, was dependent on two conditions: (1) on foreign markets being open and free competition; (2) on the industry's capacity for exploitation. Such industrialism was built on selfishness and want of consideration for the neighbour. It led to exploitation of one nation by another. Gandhiji could not envisage an India which would exploit other nations.

Industrialism as practised today threw millions of poor manual labour out of jobs. As an alternative to industrialism, he advocated small scale and cottage industries, of which hand-spinning was one, which was to be patronized. Gandhiji would favour the use of most elaborate machinery if it can help India to come over her pauperism; at the same time, large scale industrialisation would necessarily lead to exploitation of villagers thro' problems of marketing and competition. Villages can survive only if exploitation is not there. He wanted villages to be self-contained and manufacturing undertaken even in villages mainly for use.

He did not object to machinery but to the craze for labour saving machinery which threw thousand out of jobs and thus without sustenance.

Lord Kelvin once said that we can know very of little of anything until we measure it. It is worthwhile to identify certain parameters and yardsticks to measure productivity in our public enterprises. This is essential to assess the productivity status within a department, organisation, and facilitate interdepartment/organisations comparisons.

A tentative list of parameters which can be used as yardsticks to measure productivity in order of priorities is given below:

Profits (the bottom line of balance sheet) internal resources, capacity utilisation development of technical/managerial skills, share of public enterprises in industrial production, foreign exchange earnings/ savings, development of ancillary industries/new sources of supplies, management of inventories, labour productivity, labour cost, industrial disputes, rate of absenteeism, accidents, balanced regional development, and model employer.

Productivity is a 'Must' for a high growth rate of economy and for a higher standard of living of the people.

Productivity measures can be classified in several ways. According to one approach, they can be divided into macro and micro level categories. Economists are normally concerned with the first category and engineers with the latter. The economists' general approach has been to develop some kind of mathematical expression for output as a function of input factors by combining observation, economic theory and mathematics. Engineers who mostly operate at the plant level have been mostly concerned with evolving productivity ratios after identifying a set of appropriate output and input indicators depending upon particular work situations.

In the Gandhian system, success would not be measured in terms of ever-rising GNP and standard of living. Success for him would be the absence of poverty and starvation among the masses. This could be measured through full employment of "Bread-Labour." Only Bread-Labour has value and that is derived from the individual needs to maintain healthy body and soul.

Intellectual labour is self-satisfying and according to Gandhiji it has no exchange value; though it has its social utility, and so it has to be rendered freely to the society.

For harmonious growth process, production process should be carried on mainly for oneself just enough to keep the body healthy and the mind trained and educated. Profits have no place in this system and the quantity to be produced would be restricted by individuals needs determined by a socially desirable level which would not hinder individual's total growth.

Each one has to work to earn his own bread by the sweat of his own brow, but then there is a need for various occupations in society such as law, medicine, social work, teaching, and religious services; these are "Intellectual Labour."

Thus the Gandhian production system would guarantee full employment in the society, regardless of cost, since most of the Labour would be self-employed, in such a system, there will be neither underproduction or overproduction, but full employment equilibrium would be achieved.

In the Gandhian approach, there is no market to factors of production, and the trustees bring together agents and factors of production by example and cooperation there can be neither employer and employee relationship, but that of trustees and cooperative; workers; every one will share in the output equally; and there is no place for wage labour and wages. The whole of productive capital would be owned by the community, and capital once employed is maintained without generating incomes. Capital should not ever substitute labour displacing workers; for the function of capital is to enhance productivity without replacing the worker, and diminishing the humaneness of work.

Risk, if any, is taken up by the community as a whole, as all investment decisions are joint community decisions.

*Implied in the above social harmony, which rejects the theory of inevitable conflict between labour and capital, because capitalists were trustees in this system. Social equilibrium is obtained by an optimum combination of material and moral progress through a progressive movement towards a non-violent society founded on economic equality and freedom from deprivation as well as exploitation. This is Gandhian vision of a welfare state which ensures the attainment of a feasible social optimum according to some morally impelling welfare function.

(*Singh, R.S.,Op. Cit.,).

It should be noted that, for India, trade relations with Japan are precious and valuable. Though the content and the value of this trade have been growing, India's share in Japan's trade both in exports and imports is abysmally low. India should strive to at least double this share.

India occupied a very insignificant place in Japan's trade-just around one per cent each in its exports and imports in 1986.

But the Japanese market is too tough to penetrate. In order to penetrate such a market, India's efforts should be to develop those commodities which enter into the Japanese trade, such that they are competitive, both in price and quality. This approach is esp., important in the era of global competitiveness.

In a country such as ours the capital resources would always be scarce. These should be used to produce maximum output in relation to maximum employment, so that consumer goods required by the ordinary people could be produced with comparatively capital-saving and labour intensive methods of technology. Gandhiji accepted that there would be certain areas where capital-intensity would be unavoidable.

He thought of many areas too. Take metallurgy. Surely even in this area there are pockets where, if we insist that capital be priced high, there would be the possibility of replacing capital by labour. We speak of liberalisation all the time. We have been doing that for the last so many years, but we have never spoken about the use of capital, and its price; we have never spoken about steps to ensure that capital becomes costly enough, so that it is not used for purpose for which it should not be used.

We have large number of people available for almost a wage which is not more than their living requirements. Then why should we have the picture of large sections of people getting amounts which include enormous rent; why cannot we have a relative income policy where what is essentially necessary is available from the top to the bottom.

Then the industrialist will not find it necessary to adopt capital intensive technology. He adopts it today because of the very high cost of labour intensity, because he has to pay labour amounts which include enormous rents. The minimum wage of a labourer in Bajaj Auto is Rs. 2500 or Rs. 2700; naturally, the industrialist wants to use more and more of capital intensive technology.

It is a topsy-turvy way of managing our economy; it increases the capital output ratio—with adverse results; instead we should aim at increasing the capital-employment ratio.

Many global models have been developed. These global models hold out a perspective for a global consciousness of resource management, which has to be global in nature. The Indian Renaissance, if we are to have it, in some way has to be based on a global consensus.

The current debate on the future role of the public sector in the Indian economy is influenced by the supply side economy of U.K., and USA., than by a rational investigation into the causes for the failure of the PSU to perform upto original expectations.

The Economic Reforms implemented have been partly influenced by these international trends, esp., the tax-cut and the import liberalisation measures.

What is required is a thorough understanding of the planning of the planning function; how planning is supposed to impose its logic, and its discipline on the market processes; the unorganised sector; informal sector; how it is going to have large interaction with the black economy; and so on.

What is of imperative importance is that planning should not be considered as mere economic planning, but has to move towards greater integration with the existing institutional, organisational, managerial structures which are there. Without such as synthesis the kind of problems that we have perhaps would remain fully distinct as they are.

The real problem in India, as in all developing countries, is how to raise labour productivity gradually all along the spectrum, from the rural areas to the urban areas. That requires planning, planning of resources, investment, and infrastructure which, in the relations of production, is not being done in the best interests of the people.

Normally, our assumption is that economic growth leads to development and, therefore, the nationbuilding process is accelerated. But what we are seeing in northeast as well as northwest India is that because the development process itself has been inegalitarian in various ways, it has thrown up challenges whereby the affluent want a large share of everything, so that those who are left behind have nothing to look forward to.

Second, the whole question of the model and type of development, the goals of development is germane to us, and needs to be seriously examined.

Today, even after more than five decades of our experience with the development planning, elements of Gandhian economics appear to be still holding their logic and relevance, whereby the economic system should produce what consumers would demand with the corresponding purchasing power put into their hands by the production system matching the supply and demand in respect of the quantity and quality of goods and services produced. But the billion dollar question remains whether our planners would be willing to consider these basic elements for the development of a capital short-labour rich economy.

Table 1

Planwise Growth of GDP, Per capita NNP and Population

(First through Sixth Plan)

Plan	GDP					
	Agri., forestry fishing mining etc.	Manu-facturing Construct-tion Elect., Gas Water Supply.	Transport Commun. & Trade	Total GDP	Per Capita NNP	Popula-tion
Ist	3.46*	6.66*	4.68*	4.05*	2.16*	1.85*
IInd	2.94**	5.98*	6.02*	4.04**	1.83^{Ns}	2.00*
IIIrd	0.17^{Ns}	7.48*	6.13*	3.17**	0.64^{Ns}	2.22*
IVth	1.02^{Ns}	2.40	3.17*	2.21**	-0.19^{Ns}	2.32*
Vth	4.48***	7.52*	6.98*	5.84*	3.52**	2.28*
VIth	3.74**	6.48*	5.74*	5.15*	2.50*	2.12*
Overall (1950-87)	2.31*	5.24*	5.32*	3.72*	1.39*	2.27*

GDP & Per Capita NNP were calculated at factor costs at 1970-71 prices

* Singificant at 1 per cent

** Significant at 5 per cent

***Significant at 10 per cent

NS Not Significant

Factors Influencing Competitiveness

If we take govt., public sector management, and public sector worker as three principal 'actors' then each one of them are important determinants of the competitiveness of the PSUs at the collective level as well as on an enterprise level.

In other words, both exogenous factors and endogenous factors have important and equal bearing on the competitiveness of the PSU.,

Exogenous Factors

One of the essential features of the public sector which separates it from the private sector is the presence of "multiple objectives." A private sector unit has a somewhat unified frame for its opeations, (ie.,) to minimise profits for their shareholders. In comparison, the public sector is beset with a number of objectives. For example: model employer, industrialization of backward areas etc.,

The two important policies that adversely affect the competitiveness are: (a) Cost-plus pricing and (b) a phased manufacturing programme. The cost-plus pricing does not provide an environment and encourages minimisation either in capital costs or in terms of variable costs. Similarly, a phased manufacturing programme increases costs by indiscriminate pursuit of import substitution.

Finally, a number of decisions that affect costs require the Govt's approval, and these procedures do not always assist the public sector even they want to pursue that path of cost minimisation.

Endogenous Factors

Many reasons that lead to higher costs are attributable to the factors which are well within the control of the management. In a majority of public sector projects, capital costs get added up due to the management's failure, and these costs become a permanent burden on the public sector.

The analysis presented so far is not something new as it has been documented and commented upon by a number of other studies and observers.

Equally, there are a number of studies and reports which have identified the measures that need to be taken to improve the performance of the public sector.

For instance, Arjun Sen Gupta's Report has given a number of suggestions. Similarly, the Report of the Economic Advisory Committee (EAC) on the public sector, has made a number of suggestions for improving autonomy and accountability of the PSUs; Needless to say, all these need to be implemented without any further delay on the part of Govt., of India.

One of the principal themes of these reports is that Govt., should "distance" from the public sector and there should be an appropriate "balance" between autonomy and accountability of the PSUs., This theme, of course, needs support. However, it is suggested that for this to succeed, it is necessary to have policy reforms. eg., introduce "transparency" vis-a-vis cost implications of meeting multiple objectives, moving towards tariff adjusted pricing for tradeable products, dismantling of the PMP., and improving investment planning and approved procedures governing public sector investments. As the EAC., Report shows even today, the PIB., approvals are not strictly governed by the resource use efficiency eg., DRC., criteria.

Annexure-1

Products with Favourable Domestic Resource Costs (DRC)

PSE	*Product*	*DRC Ratio*
BHEL	210 MW Boiler	1.0
BHEL	Turbogenerator set	1.0
BHEL	Hydroturbine	1.14
HEC	OB Drill	1.3
	Products with Unfavourable DRC	
HEC	Centre Lathe	6.87
HMT	Radial Drills	1.48
MAMC	Crusher 1750	4.8
HEC	Drage line	2.4

Finally, it is suggested that we will have to 'mimic' the discipline of competitive market structure on all the factors, i.e., govt., management and labour that affect the public sector performance.

The important disciplinary features of competitive market structure that we need to 'mimic' are:

1. to encourage efficient and innovative firms to grow and flourish, and
2. to penalise inefficient firms/agents through exist.

To this important and admittedly difficult issue, we will have to seek answers as that alone can guarantee that the public sector not only becomes competitive but also stays competitive.

In 'sum' productivity is not just creating institutional framework. It is a way of life. Every individual should make productivity a mass movement. Every home and hamlet in the country should reflect the concept of productivity.

Steel has always been the backbone of any economy. From an annual production of 30 million tonnes at 1900, a global steel production Soared to 300 million tonnes by 1950 and 842 million in 2000.

The industry is highly capital intensive and more so when a plant is installed in the greenfield. Till the 1980s the industry was not only working under a controlled regime, the major plants were also land-locked. Export was not a priority.

However, with globalisation, newer steel plants at Dolvi and Hazira, like VSP., have come up as port-based plants. In addition, newer plants have the built-in infrastructure for further expansion. Expansion of these plants will definitely lead to lower capital cost as well as economic scale.

On the economic front also, the Indian industry has to go a long way in reaching international standards. Energy consumption is around 4.75 to 5. 0 G.Cal per tonne of liquid steel internationally as compared to 6.50 G.Cal/tls at RINI., and going upto 8-9 G.Cal/tls in some other integrated steel plants of the country. Refractory consumption ranges in Indian industry between 10-16 kg., against 7.5 to 8.5 kg. globally.

India's share in the export market is negligible with only 2.7 mt exported out of the 30 mt production in 2001-02. (i.e) 9 per cent the total production and around 1 per cent of the world's steel trade.

For meeting efficiency as well as product quality, it is necessary that the Indian industry brings greater focus to the export market. India is very favourably placed in this area. It is projected in addition to larger consumption in the country, the major international consumers would be the Asian bloc, esp., the southeast Asian countries.

The domestic industry suffered seriously because of the setback in Russia and increased production in China which led to dumping of steel in the country.

However, in the recent past, with increasing consumption in Russia and China, India should be in a position to capture the markets earlier served by these countries.

Compliance with the WTO., norms is becoming critical internationally. China is also entering this field shortly. Unfortunately, the very purpose of WTO., compliance, which compelled India to lower custom duties progressively, is becoming a hindrance for open trade in steel industry.

Those who were the vocal proponents for WTO., compliance, esp., the US., have themselves become a stumbling block to free trade in steel. Steps like QRs., and duty imposition have created a turmoil world over. Even the European Union is hurt and it is likely to approach the WTO., for redress.

The setback in the American steel industry is an example for the world to learn a number of lessons.

The Indian steel industry does need to look for major changes in the fiscal and labour policies of the Union Govt., The hangover of the controlled regime has to be forgotten and proactive approaches are needed in this area for survival and growth of the industry.

In the wake of global competition, the PSUs., will have to strive hard to achieve maximum productivity by improving their efficiency on all fronts. Efficiency is the capacity to bring proficiency into expression.

In the words of our Late Prime Minister Smt. Indira Gandhi:

"Productivity is an essential part of our urge for self-improvement and achievement of excellence which must be a part of any dynamic society."

38

W T O and India

Globalisation which is a more romantic world indicating the desire to integrate nation-states within the overall framework of the WTO is nothing but a modern vision of the "Theory of comparative Costs Advantage" which was propagated by the classical economists to provide the theoretical foundations of unrestricted flow of goods from Great Britain to other less developed countries at that time, the colonies. It was argued that international specialization benefits both the countries which enter into trade relations. The same argument has been brought forth by the advocates of globalisation now. They want an export-led-pattern of growth to replace the import-substitution-trade policies followed earlier.

The imperialist nations during the 18th and 20th centuries also emphasized—"Capital and technology flows" into the colonial countries. But they could force their will at that time because they were the rulers. However, historical evidence reveals that all these trade, capital and technology flows helped the imperialist nations to drain out resources from the poor colonial nations. Thus, the imperialist nations thrived at the cost of the colonial countries who remained in stagnation and poverty.

India was one of the original contracting parties (CPs) in the GATT., India also joined the WTO at its very inception irrespective of political changes, since 1991 the GOI., has been implementing structural adjustment programmes according to the dictates of the WTO., IMF., and World Bank.

Even though the world today has been globalized through satellites, and Cable T.V., electronic communications via the Internet, the Website, the E-Mail, et al, the totality of the WTO., arrangements, Agreements would be a better expression is unequal, in fact wholly in the interests of the transitional corporations of the developed world, in favour of speculative favour of speculative finance capital looking for quick global gains in developing countries, and indeed, even against fully free trade, the developed countries having mangaed to extract all concessions in of their exports, without conceding any substantial benefit to the developing countries.

The WTO arrangements comprise of a large number of separate Agreements, which form part of the Treaty. Interestingly, while these conditions are all obligatory commitments, the USA., has made them subject to US laws and the decisions of US courts of Law in so far as that country is concerned. The Treaty on "Trade Related Intellectual Property Rights" (TRIPR) is only one of the many Agreements comprising the WTO., arrangements.

The WTO., is but a vehicle of this deep global hegemonic design. The spate of agreements with large international firms in the power, petroleum and telecommunication sectors on terms that are are not determined either in the market place or thro' competitive bidding, represents an unprecedented compromise on national economic interests.

Moreover, we are disturbed by what we consider the increasingly defeatist stand by the Govt., in bilateral and international discussions, and negotiations, manifested for instance, in the extraordinary generous tariff and trade concessions to advanced industrial countries without any reciprocal benefits for ourselves.

The G-7 countries were expecting a firm attitude from India in the GATT negotiations, involving sensitive issues like Intellectual Property Rights, Patent Laws, approach to the problem of subsidies, and import tariff rates.

At every cross-road, we will have to use the dispute settling machinery of the WTO., which will be a time consuming process, with great uncertainty about the future.

The WTO engineered globalisation has detrimental effects on the vulnerable people of India. It adversely affects the poor, the Dalits and the Women. It causes "entitlement failures" and "capability deprivations."

In 1989-90, 276 million Indian people were terribly poor. Their number increased to 406.3 million in 1998. The per capita availability of rice in the country has declined from 80.9 kgs in 1991 to 73.8 kgs in 1999. (Rice Imports: Business Line, Jan 31, 2000).

However, WTO organisation appreciates the position of India in providing leadership to the developing countries and seeks India's help in contributing to the early and positive solution of contentious issues.

Speaking to the Press in Hyderabad (AP): Jan, 8, 2003: on the sidelines of the Partnership Summit 2003, Director General of WTO., Dr. Supachai Panitchpakdi, said "India has the responsibility of playing crucial role in the WTO discussions. Do not underestimate India's capability in intervening and making positive contributions to the ongoing discussions."

"If Cancun meet fails, it will have a strong negative implication on the credibility of the organisation itself. WTO., has been trying to create credibility and predictability in the multilateral trade negotiations. This time it is development agenda and an opportunity is given to developing countries to fully participate", he said.

Elaborating on the significance of Cancun Meet, Panitchpakdi said, "It is to complete a good discussion on what have been left behind from Doha. Now the focus is on all fronts to complete it on time because there will be only one year left after Cancun. Too many unfinished agenda cannot be left and we must wrap up most of negotiations as there are major elections around the world in 2004."

Defending the Green Room decisions and denying that there was any arm twisting from the US., he said, "General Council has been taking all compliants into consideration and we do not restrain from taking action on any country violating multilateral spirit. Meeting of smaller groups are necessary to take decisions and we are taking care to make them inclusive and equitable."

Earlier speaking at the plenary session, Supachai said the failure to meet certain deadlines during last years talks had been disappointing. "We were not able to meet the deadlines related to special and differential treatment for developing countries and access to essential medicines for poor countries lacking capacity to manufacture such drugs. Issues of small economies have to be tackled to help them join WTO.,", he said.

Anti-Dumping Duties: U.S.Violation: Major Victory for India, others in WTO:

In a major trade victory for India and several other countries, the WTO., has held as violation of global trade rules a controversial U.S. law allowing American companies to collect more than $470 million in anti-dumping duties from the US., Govt.

The ruling was given by an Appellate body of the Geneva-based WTO while upholding a finding of a three member Dispute Settlement Panel (DSP) which was challenged by the U.S.

The ruling is the latest in a spate of U.S. defeats at the WTO after India the 15 nation European Union, Australia, Brazil, Canada, Chile, Indonesia, Japan, Mexico, South Korea and Thailand brought the case before the World Trade Body.

"The U.S.continued Dumping and Subsidy Offset Act of 2000 is inconsistent with certain provisions of the WTO agreements on anti-dumping and on subsidies because it is a specific action against dumping or a subsidy", the ruling said.

The high profile case prompted more complaints than any other since the WTO., was founded in 1995, with eleven govts., challenging the so-called Byrd amendment, named after an American Senator who sponsored their law. Six other countries were also parties to the case, and supported their objections.

The three-member WTO panel ruled in Sept., that the US. had unfairly awarded penal duties collected from foreign competitors to American companies including U.S.Steel corp., Hershey Foods Corpn., and Timken Co., which won trade complaints.

The WTO endorsed the views taken by India and other complainants that governments must keep with it the anti-dumping duties slapped on foreign companies and that distributing the funds to companies encourages them to file trade complaints.

"This measure clearly flies in the face of the letter and the spirit of WTO law", said the European Trade Commissioner, Pascal Lamy. "We now expect the U.S. to act quickly in order to repeal" the law.

The appellate body, however, gave some consolation to the U.S., when it overturned the Panel's conclusion that the U.S., may be regarded as not having acted in good faith with respect to its obligations.

To conclude, the WTO and Globalisations have become the realities to be reckoned with. They might bring with them many ills. But, as Basu, Kaushik (2001): India and the Global Economy: Role of culture, Norms and Beliefs (EPW, Oct, 6), observes:

"On balance globalisation will open up more windows of opportunity for India than close. It is beginning to change the nature of management of Indian firms, and will hopefully influence the organisation of government. It is bringing in new ideas of how to organise and how to govern the market. It is changing our beliefs about what is good and what is bad for the economy. These beliefs may be right or wrong, but they will have a bigger impact on the economy than most people realise. There are huge inequities and injustices in the world for us to try to remedy. It is not always clear how we can achieve this and whether this can at all be achieved by a single nation. Therefore, when drafting policy, it is best to recognise the features of the world that we must take as given, and try to do our best subject to those constraints. We could direct some of our effort to change those constraints, but to draft policy assuming that the features of the global economy and the rules of the global game that we do not like are malleable, is to court failure."

39

Global Economics and Sustainable Development

The emergence of the concept of sustainable development is part of a broader process of the problematisation of global survival. This problematisation appeared as a response to the destructive character of growth and development, on the one hand, and the rise of environmental movements in both the North and the South, on the other, resulting in a complex process of internationalization of the environment.

The concept of sustainable development is post social justice formulation. It represents a substitution of environmental for social justice discourse in a milieu in which social justice claims have increasingly lost their standing.

However, the issue of social justice and welfare cannot be relegated to the background. The whole concept of sustainable development implies the delivery of environmental, economic and social benefits. By adopting the concept of sustainable development, two old enemies, growth and the environment are reconciled.

In the last ten years, the world has seen a growth of intergovernmental negotiations to formulate international environmental treaties. This ecological globalisation is the result of ongoing processes of economic globalisation, which not only stitch the world's economies together, but also take national production and consumption levels to a point that threatens the earth's ecological systems.

The world has come closer in understanding each other even as it looks for a common future together as it prepares for the World Summit on Sustainable Development (WSS)—ten years after Rio. This time the meeting must focus on the sharp and growing divide between the rich and the poor in the world.

It must set up the framework for global governance built on the concept of good governace.

The constitution which is being written through the numerous environmental conventions built on the concept of how we will share the world's ecological, and economic space, needs a preamble.

It is vital that world leaders make it clear that their priroity is to focus on the needs of those who are marginalised by the economic globalisation process.

The U.N. World Summit on Sustainable Development will take place in Johannesburg later this year, and places particular importance on the notion of governance at local, national, regional and global levels.

This is reflected both in the text being negotiated by Govts., and in attempts to go beyond inter-governmental agreement and develop "Partnership" involving business, civil society, and Govt., in delivering essential elements of development such as energy, water, and technological assistance.

Human beings need food, shelter, clothing, education, entertainment, cultural and spiritual sustenance, and a host of other material and non-material things.

The process of development is supposed to provide for these, and to ensure that every one has access to them.

However, India's model of development has focussed so heavily on certain material goods that a number of other essential aspects have been ignored. We are today extracting natural resources at a rate far greater than their capacity to regenerate and we are pumping pollutants back into ecosystems at rates far higher than they absorb, and the result is a profoundly unsustainable system.

Nevertheless, India with its large human economic, scientific and knowledge base, has much greater potential than most other developing countries but we are not yet maximising this vast potential.

But far more basic rethinking on development paths, serious policy level changes, and action on the ground, will be needed. Only then can we make this decade of the 21st century a memorable one, for taking the road to sustainability and justice.

How can we ensure that a "Green Revolution Movement" based on genetic and digital technologies is characterised by social and gender inclusiveness ?

Mahatma Gandhiji said long back:

"Recall the face of the poorest and the weakest person you have seen, and ask yourself, if the steps you contemplate are going to be of any use to him."

There is a need to promote awarness of the dictum "Good ecology is good business." The private sector can promote sustainable farming practices thro' contract cultivation, and technical help. It can play a key role in information and skill empowerment and capacity building.

Efforts should be made to ensure the long-term security of food supply and water availability should receive priority in the allocation of public funds.

There has been a constant reduction in the capacity of earth's water systems to sustain the demands made upon it by us currently.

Currently, 166 million people in eighteen countries are suffering from water scarcity, while almost 270 million more in eleven additional countries are considered water stressed. (World bank: Entering the 21st Century World Development Report: 1999-2000: Washington D.C. 2000).

It is believed that by 2025 as much as two-thirds of the world's population will be living with water shortages.

In recent days water is not viewed as a social resource, but an economic resource to be managed by market forces. Govts are stepping back from regulatory responsibilities, giant corporations are acquiring control of water throughout the ownership of dams and water ways, bottled water industry, the development of new technologies, the privatization of municipal and regional water services including sewage and water delivery, the construction of water infrastructure, and water exportation.

Hence, political will of Govt., to frame appropriate and sustainable water policy and equally important indomitable conscience of water users to utilize water judiciously are necessary.

Development is an outcome of efficient institutions rather than the other way around. Focus therefore must be shifted from maximising the quantity of development funding to maximising development outcomes and effectiveness of public service delivery.

What perhaps was most promising in 2002 were projects and joint ventures developed as part of cross cultural innovation initiatives.

Indeed to secure a better quality of life for everyone now and for the future generations—another definition of sustainable development we need more than business as usual.

In recent decades, man's influence on the environment has sharply increased. Since these activities have frequently taken place without consideration for possible ecological consequences their outcome has often produced a deterioration in the environment..

In recent times, human activities have not only greatly intensified influences on the environment, but have also begun to influence large-scale atmospheric processes. This makes possible changes in all components of the global ecological system.

While in many cases contemporary human activities have caused substantial harm to the environment, changes in natural conditions produced by man are not as a rule irreversible, and in such a context it may be said that at the present time there does not exist a global ecological crisis. Nevertheless if present rates of industrial development continue such a crisis may arise in the relatively near future.

Keeping in mind the finding that the stability of the global ecological system is limited, it may be expected that in the absence of ecological planning further technological progress will certainly lead to specific disruptions in that system's stability.

Accordingly, the problem of control over anthropogenic changes in the environment is becoming very relevant. The need for forecasting possible changes in the natural environment and for devising methods of influencing the global ecological system that may prevent its development in undesired directions is evident.

In order to prevent changes in global ecological processes that are unfavourable to man-effective international forms of cooperation are also needed. This property must be preserved from irresponsible activities that may produce harm to the environment within which man exists.

Barry Commoner, Op. Cit. is even more categorical:

"In effect...we now know that modern technology which is privately owned cannot long survive, if it destroys the social goods on which it depends the ecosphere. Hence, an economic system which is fundamentally based on private transactions rather than social ones is no longer appropriate and increasingly ineffective in managing this vital social good. The system is therefore in need of change."

40

Stock Market and Liberalisation

The stock market is essentially one of the instruments for mediation between potential savers and potential investors, behind every financial transaction there should be a real counterpart.

The 1992-1993 Budget, abolishing wealth tax for financial assets, reducing income tax rates for higher incomes, and liberalising the functioning of the economic system was certainly conducive to a rise in share prices from pre-budget levels.

We may have to add that a certain ethical code of behaviour is also a must for the healthy development of the stock market.

In Western countries "Insider Trading" is a penal offence; and Ivan Boesky in the USA, would have gone to jail but for the fact he became an "approver" testifying against others on whom the authorities had suspicions but no concrete evidence." Insider Trading" is to act on the basis of secret inside information.

With the backing of the World Bank Group, many developing countries started giving prominence to stock markets for financing enterprises and allocation of savings. In India too, the process started in the early 1980s. In the wake of increased pace of economic liberalisation initiated in 1991, The Capital issues Control Act, 1947, which till then regulated the issue and pricing of new capital, was done away with and even greater emphasis was placed on the stock market.

As a part of measures to develops the stock market and liberalisation of the external sector, foreign institutional investors were invited to trade directly on the Indian stock exchanges. The main expectations were that the market would help corporates raise resources directly from investors, help attract foreign protfolio capital and facilitate the process of privatization.

A test of a stock market's utility is to mobilise resources for invesment.

In fact that after the fiasco of the mid-1990s, the primary market has been performing poorly. During 2000-01, though the number of issues increased from 93-151, the amounts involved came down to Rs. 6100 crores from Rs. 7800 crores.

While in the previous year, the other sectors claimed about 15 per cent share in resource mobilisation, in 2000-01 their share fell drastically to just about 5 per cent.

In sharp contrast, as per data from other sources, most of the funds raised by corporates domestically were through private placements; 80 per cent as against 70 per cent in the previous year.

Interestingly, out of the total mobilisation, almost 40 per cent from overseas floatations. Also, net inflows to Mutual Fund schemes fell to less than half of what they were in the previous year: Rs. 9128 crores against Rs. 18545 crores. Obviously, the market has been sidestepped by the corporates for their financing needs. The presence of FIIs did not make any difference either.

In key areas such as resource mobilisation, liquidity, regulation of price manipulations, insider trading and foreign portfolio investments, the experience has not been reassuring. We would not be wrong to expect that but for the serious crisis which upset the calculations of the Govt., the scams would not have been exposed at all.

The emergence of private sector mutual funds has added another dimension to the role of FIIs in the Indian stock market. An implication of mutual funds gaining strength on the Indian stock market could be that unlike individual investors, whose monies they manage, mutual funds can create market trends whereas small individual investors can only follow their trends. The situation becomes complicated if the funds gain a vested interest in certain sectors by floating sector specific funds. Since they will have to beat the standard reference market indices to show that they are better at investment, FIIs and mutual funds registered in India thrive on uncertain market conditions and by creating waves. If they too settle for steady returns, obviously there will be little difference between an individual investor, and a fund.

The NASDAQ., President identified that institutions tendency to "roll their funds from one sector to another" as one of the causes for the volatility. Even the UNCTAD., was concerned about the possible distortions that foregin portfolio investments might introduce due to the pressure on them to secure capital gains.

Stock markets are known to appeal to gambling instincts. The volatility has added fuel to this fire as investors are forced to seek quick gains.

The very low delivery ratios in the stock market are a clear reflection of this phenomenon. Progressive de-materialisation and introduction of rolling settlement are unlikely to improve the situation in real terms as unstable markets force investors to be on guard/vigilant all the time.

In the uncertain circumstances investors are likely to play safe because of which it is most likely that trading will get concentrated further among a few top companies.

The volatility due to FIIs, mutual funds and integration with global markets and often does not have any relationship with fundamentals of the Indian economy or the companies concerned. The stock market's role of monitoring, disciplining and supporting good managements has little relevance in such situations.

The Self Regulatory Organisations (SROs) are involved in overseeing in their respective markets. When the questionable data for a stock is discovered, the suitable SRO is asked to supply its data for the same stock and the same period. Market regulators then compare its findings to those of the SRO to determine whether the SRO surveillance system has overlooked anything.

If the regulator determines that an SRO did not provide adequate information, it can direct the SRO to accordingly adjust its surveillance programming. Hence, double check is ensured by this procedure. It is thus high time that SEBI., delegates a significant regulatory authority to privately owned, and operated organisations for overseeing exchanges and stock trading.

It should be mandatory for SROs to formulate rules for trading in their markets and for the business conduct of their members.

Another important issue is the consistent upgrading of computerisation of stock exchanges. Surveillance would be effective and cost effective when the computers maintain a permanent record of the parties responsible for all bids, offers, and transactions.

Looking at the existing status of our stock exchanges other than BSE, NSE, DSE and OTCEI, investors cannot have necessary elements which are a pre-requisite for the confidence in the uprightness of the whole affair. Technological obstacles in developing an automated system still persists in various exchanges.

Further, it is ambiguous that any correlation will be evident in the working of this high profile system in exchanges across the country. The market capitalisation grew ten fold between 1990-91 and 1999-2000. It increased by 221 per cent during 1991-92 and by 107 per cent during 1999-

2000. All India market capitalisation is estimated at Rs. 749, 248 crore at the end of March, 2002.

The market capitalisation ratio, which indicates the size of the market, increased sharply to 57.4 per cent in 1991-92 following spurt in share prices. The ratio increased to 85 per cent by March, 2000. It however, declined to 55 per cent at the end of March, 2001 and to 36 per cent by the end of March, 2002.

The market capitalisation ratio, which indicates the size of the market, increased sharply to 57.4 per cent in 1991-92 following spurt in share prices. The ratio increased to 85 per cent by March 2000. It however, declined to 55 per cent at the end of March, 2001 and to 36 per cent by the end of March, 2002.

The trading volumes on exchanges have been witnessing phenomenal growth during the 1990s. The average daily turn-over grew from about Rs. 150 crore in 1990 to 12000 crore in 2000, peaking at over Rs. 20,000 core. One sided turnover on all stock exchanges exceeded Rs. 10,00,000 crore during 1998-99, Rs. 20,00,000 crore during 1999-2000 and approached Rs. 30,00,000 crore during 2000-2001.

However, the trading volume substantially fell to Rs. 895, 826 crore in 2001-02. The massive sale by foreign institutional investors and the terrorist attack on sept., 11, 2001 seem to have percipitated the fall in volumes.

The Bombay stock Exchange (BSE) which was established in 1875 as "The Native Share and Stockbrokers Association", has evolved over the years into its present status as the premier stock exchange in the country.

The BSE while providing an efficient market also upholds the interests of the investors and ensures redressal of their grievances, whether against the companies or its own memberbrokers. It also strives to educate and enlighten the investors by making available necessary informative inputs.

In fact, with the development by the NSE of a national market in securities thro' the trading terminal throughout the country, the 19 Regional Stock Exchange (RSEs) having assets of Rs. 1000 crore, lost their relevance and some of them are on the verge of closing down their operations.

Like the other bourses, the Madras Stock Exchange (MSE) too has been dwindling volumes and diminishing trades. But at the same time, the Madras Stock Exchange Financial Service Ltd., (MSEFSL), a subsidiary of MSE., has been doing well and making up the losses of the parent organisation, according to P.J.Mathew, Executive Director, MSE. "To face challenges and to make it more competitive, steps are being taken to make MSE a corporate entity", he added.

TURNOVER ON MAJOR STOCK EXCHANGES

Rs. Crore

	1996-97	1997-98	1998-99	1999-00	2000-01	2001-02
NSE	336,782	481,197	519,852	1,143,268	1,770,458	1,562,283
Mumbai	124,284	207,383	311,999	685,028	1,001,619	309,316
Calcutta	105,664	178,778	171,780	357,166	355,035	27,075
Bangalore	4,398	8,636	6,779	11,147	6,033	70
Hyderabad	480	1,860	1,276	1,237	978	41
ICSE	—	—	1	545	233	55
Cochin	1,401	1,783	773	0	287	0
OTCEI	221	125	142	3,588	126	4
Madras	2,315	1,228	370	250	109	24
Bhubaneswar	231	202	77	70	0	0
Coimbatore	2,398	2,136	395	39	0	27
Mangalore	373	308	11	0	0	0

The recent trends suggest that the Indian stock market may weaken its relationship with the domestic economy. Can the developing countries rely on the wisdom of such a stock market, esp., when it starts reacting to external factors, for industrialising their economies is a question that needs to be considered in greater detail. To that extent this phenomenon has been introduced and accentuated by FII operations it gives rise to a doubt whether foreign portfolio investments would serve the objective of local stock market development or the tangible benefits from them would only be confined to getting the Balance of Payment support along with its attendant risks.

Stock markets will have to be developed as a part of domestic corporate financing options. Attracting foreign portfolio investors cannot be a substitute for domestic policy formulation and institutional development. A strong domestic base is a pre-requisite for providing depth and spread to the stock market and to enable it to counter any percipitative action by the FIIs not based on fundamentals.

The only safeguard can be Indian public financial and investment institutions holding large shares and in their capacity for direct intervention. The size of the holdings and internal resources with the public institutions will be an important factor in containing the volatility induced by FIIs.

The heavy emphasis on trading in high-profit and quick-yielding sectors may indicate that for financing infrastructure, and long gestation projects, India may not be able to rely on the stock market. To what extent foreign portfolio investments are beneficial to the Indian economy in general and stock market in particular ?

Should the investors be forcibly made to run to the stock market by lowering interest rates?

The excessive emphasis on the stock markets should be discouraged to the maximum level.

It may be noted from the Press reports that the GOI., is setting up a "Central Listing Authority" which would oversee issues listing at the stock exchanges and monitor use of issue proceeds.

Today, we hardly see any evidence of the corporater raising resources directly from the market on an increasing scale. While the stock market has receded, the financial intermediaries staged a comeback during the second half of the 1990s.

Compared to the days of Liberalisation, now there seem to be a better recognition of the need for financial intermediation, RBI., in its Currency and Finance 2001, observed that:

"On balance, it is desirable to have a diversified and balanced financial system where both financial intermediatires and financial markets play important roles in imparting greater competitiveness and efficiency to the financial system. In the present context of financial liberalisation, stock markets and banks emerge as source of corporate finance and stock market development actually tends to increase the quantity of bank loans through improved debt-equity ratios. Thus, the co-existence of both systems is socially desirable not only because it encourages competition, but also because it reduces transaction costs within the financial system, and helps improve allocation within the economy."

It should not be forgotten that the need for globalisation of capital markets arose from the interests of developed countries themselves. Their banks were losing money in crises in Latin America. They had also to find a secure retired life for their citizens.

The need for foreign capital by developing countries, even if they do not know what to do with it beyond a limit, came in handy for the developed ones. With the emphasis on attracting foreign portfolio investment, the very focus to stock market has been lost.

Stock markets cannot be there for serving the interests of a few. The promoters should be made personally responsible for any omissions and commissions on their part. Access to the market must be related to genuine need for funds rather than to benefits flowing from limited public participation.

Authorities' words should be translated into action. Until then, it may not be wise to push the investors to the stock market by reducing the attractiveness of fixed income investment opportunities.

In the USA, following the de-regulation of the financial system, we had the failure of a large number of savings and loan association in the 1970s, and of a number of banks in the 1980s.

According to an estimate made by the Business Week of New York, the burden on the US taxpayer is likely to be a total of $420 billion.

We, in India, have suddenly decided to deregulate the financial system at its nascent stage.

41

Impact of the Economic Reforms and Banking Industry

A decade of economic reforms had passed by. The Indian economy now witnesses what has come to be called "the second generation reforms" which include more free market, more monetary policy, more foreign capital, more dereservation of small industries. Indeed crucial changes are taking place in the financial sector.

Improvement in financial situation is now-a-days identified as the most crucial component of the economic reform process regardless as to whether they are the first generation, or second generation reforms.

Although the banking sector reforms are still incomplete, there was determination and speed in carry them forward.

The process of deregulation ot the economy in the field of industry, trade and finance began in the 1980s got further impetus when a series of policy changes were announced by the Govt. These changes which are growth oriented in nature will have positive impact on the economy.

The new industrial policy has rationalized the licensing policy to give boost to our industrial production. The policy for the SSI industries has been dovetailed into the overall strategy of liberalisations. The Exim policy has rationalised the quotas to give greater thrust to exports.

More importantly, efforts are being made to deregulate the financial sector in consonance with the changed environment of the real sector.

It is significant to note that these changes are rightly introduced at a time when the economy is passing through critical times. We can no longer remain complacent about the resilience of the Indian economy.

Our inflation rate has gone up alarmingly in recent times despite the good harvests and reasonably good industrial output.

Fiscal deficits have been on the rise. "Balance of payments" situation has worsened compelling India to tap resources from all possible sources

Servicing the large external debt has become a difficult task. The remittances from the Non-Resident Indians has thinned down over the years. Our oil import has been mounting necessitating the country to borrow more and more. Thus in gist, the economy is passing through a criticial period and corrective steps are to be taken to arrest the deteriorating situation.

It is in this context, the GOI., intervened and took a few affirmative steps towards further liberalisation, and deregulation of the economy.

To begin with, Indian rupee was devalued twice, aggregating to about 20 per cent with a view to step up our exports and restrain imports and thereby reduce the balance of payments deficit.

Reasons behind the decline in net financial inflows to the country include the following factors:

(1) The rising investment income inflows which followed the rising private capital inflows.
(2) Despite being liberalised on an extensive scale, capital inflows and esp., FDIs, which provide for long-term investments have not been as elastic as was expected.
(3) With the net financial inflows to the country tapering off and the investment income outflows rising faster than the net financial inflows, the external sector does not seem to be contributing much to the growth and investment potentials of the country.

The current euphoria relating to India's current account, relating to a decade of successful reforms, leaves many matters which are of concern. These cannot be captured by the performance indicators of the Balance of Payments alone. We must look beyond such characterisations and consider the macro economic perspectives in the context of the openness of the economy.

The Industrial Policy announced—incorporated a series of far reaching and radical measures. Practically at one stroke, the new policy abolished licensing for almost all industries irrespective the level of investment excepting a small list of industrial groups.

The threshold limits of assets of MRTP., companies was totally scrapped allowing them to expand.

In order to accelerate the larger inflow of foreign investments the FERA., companies were allowed to retain 51 per cent of foreign equity in thirtyfour select areas.

The convertibility clause enables the financial institution to convert their loans into equity. The liberalised envisages disinvestment of government equity in public sector mutual funds, financial institutions, general public, and employees.

The sick public sector enterprises were brought under the purview of the Board of Industrial and Financial Reconstruction (BIFR). The board-banding facility would be extended to the existing and new industrial units provided they do not demand additional investment in plants and machinery.

It may be recalled that the process of deregulation of the banking sector in certain areas of its operations has already begun in the right earnest.

The future of the financial institutions has been the centre of debate for the last 3 years. It should be clear to all that with the cessation of concessional resources and concessional lending and blurring of short-term and long-term lending the question of continuing with the special status of FIs come to the fore. Narasimham-II had set out that the FIs should either become banks, or NBFCs.

What is emerging is a cafeteria approach under which a FI can either itself become a bank or use the conglomerate approach and set up a banking subsidiary.

The problem of weak banks has been tackled elsewhere and it has to be tackled in India. This is the most crucial issue, and the future course for the Indian financial system is essentially contingent on what is done regarding weak banks. If we fail to take action a pro-bono publico (for the public good) has to speak up.

The current environment in the financial sector is more open and competitive than before. The recent measures taken by the govt., and the RBI., in financial sector are in consonance with the economic liberalisation introduced in the sphere of foreign trade and technology.

The money market is no longer segmented and regulated. Both the commercial banks and financial institutions have diversified from their traditional areas of operation and their business has become more competitive. Greater stress has, therefore, been laid on efficiency, and productivity in banks, and financial institutions.

In view of the opening up of the industrial sector to attract foreign investments, many of the existing units will have to either modernise to withstand competition or else cease to exist. While financing new projects or getting additional credit to these units the banks will have to upgrade the quality of credit appraisal Investment and Merchant Banking Wings of banks, and financial institutions will have to gear up themselves to meet the large volume of work that is likely to come through.

Commerical banks will have to increasingly diversify into various activities like equipment leasings, mutual funds, venture capital, factoring, credit card, housing finance which are going to gain more prominence in the years to come.

Reforms in India's banking sector are largely based on the recommendations of the Narasimham Committee report (RBI: 1991: Report of the Committee on the Financial System)

The rationale of the reforms as contained in this report as well as in writings of various advocates of reforms may be summed up briefly here:

(1) The financial intermediation of banking sector under the "controlled regime" was costly in terms of mobilisation of resources etc., and allocation of resources because of branch banking into rural areas, directed investments compelling banks to hold govt., paper thro' high Case Reserve ratio (CRR) and statutory liquidity ration (SLR), administered rate of interest etc., Thro' this preemption of resources the private sector had been crowded out, compelling it to borrow at higher rates.

(2) Both deposit and lending rates were administered, affecting the operational freedom and profitability of banks.

(3) This "financial repression" has eroded the productivity, efficiency and profitability of the banking system.

(4) Prudential norms in ragard to capitalisation, income recognition etc., had not been followed.

(5) Commercial banks as well as the large number of development financial institutions (DFIs) created to provide long term finance have suffered from administrative, and internal management.

Financial sector reforms have been offered as the best solution to all the aforesaid ills.

India has to open up more vigorously and accelerate the rate of saving. This happened with the announcement of an all-time high package of 2nd generation reform made on the 3rd May, 2001 by the GOI., which interalia includes opening up of defence production, permission to NRI investors to fully repartriate foreign exchange.

However, can we step up with lower rate of interest and halving the corporate dividend tax ?

Contractual saving instruments are really intended to mobilize resources towards long-term investment at relatively lower rates. But given the volatility in the external sector, the degree of freedom of the policy makers to maintain a low interest regime is practically very limited.

There has been a steady reduction in the ratio of interest and prime lending rate (PLR) of the banks on the plea that the rate of inflation has dipped in the recent past, and hence real interest rates must also be lowered. Again the Economic survey of 2001-02 has the following observation on credit flow and industrial growth:

"Allowing the appropirate lags, credit and higher industrial growth are closely related...During 2001-02, the credit offtake did not pick up; the real interest rates remained high with inflation rates falling faster than interest rates."

One of the desired outcomes of the liberalised financial policy should have been its widening and deepening with consequent impact on the rate of savings in the economy. The arrested rate of savings in the economy does not provide any evidence of such an impact of a new financial regime.

On the contrary, a steady and persistent reduction in rates of interest on various types of bank deposits and steep erosion of net asset values of mutual funds is very likely to affect the willingness to save on the part of the general public.

In the ultimate analysis, financial system in India has grown rapidly and its growth has helped the process of growth.

Moreover, the financial system has to gear itself to the needs of industrial expansion if and when it takes place.

There is need to redefine the ends and means of the FSRs in India. Real and financial resources are complementary factors that should ensure the various balances in the economy.

Financial intermediation is important in bringing together savers and investors, lenders and borrowers.

RBI., appears to choose the Laissez Faire" monetarist approach of managing the money supply. This approach also needs a careful re-examination on the part of Govt., of India—While revaluating the economic reforms.

In the changing world of Indian Banking, HRD., will have to manage altogether new challenges for which the old responses will. As Lord Keynes said, it is not difficult to develop new ideas. What is really difficult is to give up old ideas. HRD., in banks as understood today would be inadequate to meet the challenges of change. A total rethinking of HRD., is needed if Indian Banks are to survive in the wake of globalisation.

The main challenge facing the financial sector is, at a mircro-economic level, to be able to cope with this worldwide move towards greater internationalisation new dimensions for credit institution, and a new state of balance for the public finance sector.

In 'Sum', Corporate governance needs to be strengthened.

With rapid technological change, the leaders in innovation would claim the best business. Banks and financial institutions which resist change would, like, dinosaurs, become extinct.

The financial system would need to be guided by three requirements in the process of second generation economic reforms: viz., transparency, rigorous norms, an appropriate incentives. We hope that in the years ahead of us the Indian financial system would face upto these challenges.

"Know the true value of time; snatch, seize, and enjoy every moment of it. No idleness, no laziness, no procrastination, never put off till tomorrow what you can do today,"

(Chester Field)

42

Food Security in India

World Food Day observed on October, 16th globally stressed for "A millennium free from hunger." This theme is of special significance to India that comprises one third on the 830 million people who are chronically hungry world wide today.

India is home for 40 per cent of the World's poor, while her population is about 21 per cent of the total population of the less developed countries.

Our average daily food consumption provides about 2400 K.Cals., per person. However, for the poorest 30 per cent the per capita daily intake is 1599 K. Cals., only, which is very low compared to the minimum norm of 2200 K. Cals. About 60 per cent of India's children suffer from malnutrition.

An alternative estimate by the National Council of Applied Economic Reserach (NCAER) for 1994, based on a four year study of 33 thousand rural households in 13 states, came out with the finding that 16 per cent of th rural population had access to less than Rs. 3 per day and another 18 per cent could scrape together no more than Rs. 5 a day.

The 1995-96 estimate of per capita daily private final consumption expenditure at current prices based on national Accounts of the CSO., of Rs. 19,22 lends a high degree of credence to the NCAER., data on poverty and deprivation.

These indicators may have little to do with levels of food production, imports, food security stocks, etc These factors acquire meaning only in the context of the existing institutional, regional, local, and organisational factors and cannot by themselves be both necessary and sufficient conditions for ensuring micro level food security.

Not only have policies and investments for improving food production not been able to guarantee food security, State interventions of the kind seen so far have yielded meagre results.

The food security challenge that India has been grappling with over the last five decades or so has become increasingly complex over time. In the 1940s and 1950s the challenge of improving food security seemed a daunting, yet relatively straightforward task of increasing food production, and increasing access to food predominantly for rural societies.

Over the last half a century India has changed dramatically and so has the food security challenge. Urbanization and globalisation are becoming pervasive, private sector involvement in agricultural research has been increasing at a very rapid pace, and concerns about the sustainable management of resources have been rising. The food security challenge for India has over time become increasingly complex, and more multidimensional.

Food is the foremost need of the poor and, those below the poverty line spend a very large portion of their earning on food. Families facing chronic food insecurity are caught in a hunger trap.

The inadequacy and uncertainty of their food supply make it difficult for them to take advantage of development opportunities.

(WEP: The Hunger Trap: 1997)

The Report of the State of Food Insecurity in the World: 1999 estimates that in the developing world, 790 million people do not have enough to eat. India alone has more undernourished people around 204 million.

While access of all to adequate quantities of nutritive food is extremely desirable, state failure is reflected in the existence of a subset within this group of 204 million, undernourished people in India, who are unable to have even two square meals a day.

"Jean Dreze" refers to the anomalous situation where we have on the hand the accumulation of 50 million tonnes of foodgrains in the godowns of the FCI., while incurring considerable state expenditure in holding these stocks, and on the other hand we have starvation related deaths.

To help poor households and vulnerable groups meet their food needs, there are a number of food assistance programmes run by the Government, (Table 1).

Table 1

Details of various Food Assistance Programmes

Programme	*Eligibility*	*Commodity*	*Ration size*	*Period*
Public Distribution System	All household	Wheat, rice Sugar	20kgs of household/ month	Through out the year
Drought/Emergency Relief	BPL households	Wheat	5 kgs per per working day	January to May for Drought
Mid day Meal	All Primary school children	Wheat	3 kgs per month	Throught out the school session

Antyodaya	Ultra poor	Wheat/Rice	25 Kgs per month	Through out the year
Annapoorna	Aged people	Wheat	10 kgs per month	Through out the year
Forestry Approximately works #	Tribals residing in forestry areas	Wheat/Rice	2 kgs of cereal, 200 gms of pulse and 100 gm oil	4 months in a year
ICDS	Children of 6 mths to 6 years and pregnant and nursing women	CSB/Indiamix	80 gms/day for children and 160gms/ day for eligible women	Throught out the year (300 days)

*Prices differ for BPL and APL households.

Part payment is in cash.

However, the food distributed thro' this umpteen programmes is too little to take care of food needs of the poor, even though 62 million Metric tonnes of food lies surplus and should be more than sufficient to feed all the hungry in the country.

(Source: N.C. Saxena: Food Assistance And Hunger in India: Presentation at Bhopal: April, 2002)

Since the World Food Conference held in Rome in 1974, several steps have been taken to develop a global Food Security System to insulate humankind from mass starvation due to either widespread crop failure or wide gaps between demand and supply.

These fall into three areas of action as enumerated below:

(a) Identification of famine indicators and establishment of a global famine early warning system.

(b) Creation of an adequate food security reserve and,

(c) Long-term policy changes leading to both more production and more equitable distribution and of resources necessary for this purpose.

"Paul Streeten," the World Bank Development Economist, observes that the principal objective of agricultural policies in many developing countries is to raise the rate of growth of food production. A multi-pronged attack is needed.

"Streeten" lists the following factors on the supply side on which Govt., policies must work, into six "INs" or instruments:

(a) Incentives (or prices)

(b) Inputs

(c) Innovation (or technology)

(d) Information (the diffusion of technologies through extension services)

(e) Infrastructure.

(f) Institutions (Credit, Marketing, land reform)

The six "INs" refer mainly to increasing the supply of food.

Measures are also needed to increase the demand and to improve the impact of food and nutritional status.

Remunerative, productive, satisfying, sustainable livelihoods should be created.

As a result of the liberalisation and globalisation, the food security of the poor has been endangered for a variety of reasons:

Equity in access to food in an economy with a precarious overall demand-supply balance and subject to fluctuating output and prices in the world maket for cereals, and high cost inputs with considerable import content is a major policy imperative for protecting the poor,

Food security to all people, all the time cannot be ensured without ensuring full and adequate security to earn a livelihood in the normal course of their activities. This is how the upper and middle income groups are able to maintain food security. This is indeed a long term task.

That we have a severe resource crunch cannot be made a reasonable ground for postponing the task indefinitely. We must specify the methodology and stages for ensuring food security, as an integral part of livelihood security, focussing on deprived socio-economic groups.

Policies aimed at improving food production and ensuring affordable, regular and adequate transfers of goods by the means of the PDS have not been consistent with the concept of food security as as integral part of livelihood security.

The food security challenge has become more complex today, than it was in the ealier stages.

The problem of food security must be seen within the context of global economic and trade policy.

Food security is not just a problem of increasing production. Improving opportunities for increasing incomes of the poorest of the poor may be as important to their food security as providing them with new productivity enhancing technologies.

From time immemorial, nature cherished with innumerable number of life supporting plants produced on this earth. Some of them are salt tolerant, pest tolerant, temperature tolerant, winter resistent, drought resistance etc.

Due to human interference and selection, the habit of monoculturing of food varieties arose. It replaced the natural diversity in germ plasm. The net result is erosion in genetic quality which in turn resulted in susceptibility to variety of diseases. Famine and poverty arise not because of shortage in nature, but because of manmade disasters.

The role of NABARD, IRDP., FCI are important to uplift the people in agriculture sector by promoting the food security.

As for India, while population growth has not been showing any deceleration, the growth of agricultural production has been showing marginal returns. The cumulative results of both these trends may be disastrous for the future of the economy.

The World Bank in a study on the population growth of India has said:

"If the country succeeds in universalling the two-children family norm, within 2000 AD., the growth of population of a country would stop at 150 crores. In case this is delayed by another ten years, the growth of population would stabilise only at an astronomical level of 300 crores."

Dr. M.S. Swaminathan rightly observed that steps must be taken to consolidate and sustain the growth of agricultural sector to a position of global leadership in the production and marketing of farm commodities.

The agricultural policy has shifted from science to subsidies. No long-term strategy appears to be in sight to insulate our farm families from the flooding of our markets with imported agricultural commodities after the globalisation of our economy, and emergence of the World Trade Agreement.

We have to make agriculture not only an instrument of food security but as the livelihood security of our rural population.

Livelihood and food security elude many, owing to the elite centred and external oriented growth strategy.

The zero elasticity of employment in many progressive regions adds further to growing endemic hunger in India. The much acclaimed success of India in preventing mass starvation deaths is overshadowed by the slow erosion of peoples capabilities.

Under the SAP., food prices have increased faster than the whoesale prices and with the implementation of the WTO.

The new industrial policy of market driven investment with higher import intensity would further slowdown the growth of non-farm employment.

The basic aim of food security must ensure not only that there is enough food but it is also available to all.

The food battle of India is not only of quantity but one of—quality as well.

The solution of global food crisis does not depend on Government, and international agencies but on the efforts of millions of private individuals.

"The destiny of countries depends on the way they feed themselves." (Anthelme Brillant-Savarin, Physiologie du gout)

43

Nehru's Contribution to the Development of Indian Economy

Pandit Jawaharlal Nehru was a multidimensional personality, his contribution too was multifaceted. There is no walk of life in which he did not make an unique and lasting contribution. Whether it was in the cultural field, or in the field of science and technology or in the field of economic development, Nehru left no part of the national life uncovered. His impact on the national life is so all pervading and long losting that even today its impact can be left esp., in the wake of globalisation.

Why Nehru planned ?

In his early political life Nehru developed a deep interest in the promotion of a programme of rapid economic development for the improvement of the financial condition of the masses. The abject poverty of the people moved him, he attributed this to the inequitous and unjust social and economic system and also to the state of the economy. While Nehru conceded that India was an underdeveloped country he found no reason why its vast potential could not be tapped. He wanted the planning process to be used to harness the hidden productive potential of the people. He believed that people shall succeed if they are given the opportunity. Nehru had this optimistic feeling not only for his own country but for the world in general.

With what perspective he planned ?

Nehru was deeply influenced with the Fabianism of England and also the initial success of economic planning in USSR., in putting a backward predominantly agrarian economy on the road to industrialisation and modernisation.

He observed: "Planning consists essentially of balancing; the balancing between industry and agriculture; the balancing between heavy industry and light industry; the balancing between cottage industry and other industry; if one of them goes wrong, then the whole economy is upset."

Nehru was an evolutionary socialist. He was the founder of the system of a mixed economy. Mixed economy is a system in which the public and the private are allowed to co-exist. One exists as complementary to the other. He was convinced that the solution of the problem would require an active state role in economic and social development, and that the spontaneous efforts of industrialists, cultivators, artisans and other producers would need to be organised, co-ordinated, and planned by the State.

While it is true that Nehru was quite impressed by the Russian success achieved through 'Socialism'—he did not subscribe to a rigid or doctrinaire interpretation of the term scientific socialism, instead he chose to adopt Democratic Socialism to cure the economic ills of the country. In other words, he looked at planning as an integrated way of looking at a nation's manifold activities drawn up in a "democratic set up" that is deliberately adopted and enshrined in our constitution.

All these ideas of Nehru took a concrete shape in the form of a resolution and Fundamental Rights and Economic Policy adopted in the Karachi Session of the Congress in 1931. Consequently, under the dynamic Chairmanship of Nehru a National Planning Committee was set up in 1938 as an economic wing of the Indian National Congress. The series of studies prepared by this committee eventually prepared the ground for comprehensive planning which was instituted after our independence.

The Govt. appointed a Planning Commission in 1950 to prepare a blue print of development, taking an overall view of the needs and resources of the country. Commencing with the First Five Year Plan launched in 1951.

The perspective which Nehru visualised right from the days of drafting the Ist FYP., was, in the long run, a self-generating economy, and self-reliant the sum effect of which was aimed at the ushering in of a classless society, organised on a planned basis for the raising of mankind to higher material and cultural value. The concept of the removal of economic, social and regional disparities had gained wide acceptances and had also been applied thro' the process of planning in all parts of the country.

Nehru gave altogher a new dimension and meaning for planning and its purpose. His plan strategy paid wider attention to the significance of social factors in the overall national development. Thus, Nehru's plan strategy incorporated the basic philosophy that the benefits of development should ultimately accrue more and more to the relatively less privileged sections of society. The creation of a milieu in which the small man was enabled to do his best in the interests of the higher standard of living which had first priority in Nehru's scheme of things.

What has been the Achievements ?

A singularly unique achievement of Nehru's planning has been the transformation of India from a decadent, totally backward society teaming with millions of illiterate people into a vibrant forward looking, developing country and set to zoom into the horizons of a fully developed country.

We have a long list of impressive achievements to our credit-thanks to our planners following the foot-steps of Nehruvian thinking. We have the fourth largest scientific manpower in the world; we are in the league of the prestigious space powers of the world by exhibiting our capability in space ventures.

We have achieved all this notwithstanding the serious impediments like unabated growth in population, draining of our precious resources towards defence in view of the unending hostility of our neighbours, increased superpower intervention in our affairs and more than all these the persistent growing poverty of the people.

In the words of Nehru: "Poverty is not a good thing; it is not to be exalted or praised, but an evil thing which must be fought and stamped out.

The Tenth Five Year Plan has raised the growth to 8 per cent per annum and proposes monitorable targets on poverty reduction, primary education, and raising of literacy rate, declines in infant and maternal morality rates, employment growth trends.

State-wise targets will be fixed and monitored and the aim will be to reduce inter-state disparities in economic and social developments.

India's exports of commercal services in 2001 were of the order 20 billion dollars while imports of services were 24 billion dollars. But the development of services in India, esp., the high-value added sectors, essential for gaining a large share in global trade, depends on the development of infrastructure, principally power, with massive investments and greater efficiency of systems operations.

India, has however, made commendable progress in telecommunications with private investments.

If we have been able to achieve success despite all odds, the entire credit goes/will go to the resilence of the system, which has emerged after careful planning, the seeds of which were sown by Late: Pandit Jawaharlal Nehru.

For Nehru planning "was a science of action" He revealed to the world that utter paltriness of the statesman who relied upon force to gain his end. His optimism always kept in mind the large changes that are likely to take place in the alignment of real resources during the process of economic development.

"For us in India, planning is a charter of orderly progress. It provides a framework and space and that binds sectors and regions together and relates each year's effort to the succeeding years, impelling us all constantly to greater cooperative endeavour. By strengthening the economic fabric of the country as a whole and of the different regions, it makes a powerful contribution to our goal of national integration. The plan gives concrete expression to our national purpose. With its implementation, we shall have advanced yet another stage towards our goal of a prosperous, democratic, modern, socialist society."

(Smt. Indira Gandhi: July 18, 1970)

44

Direction and Implementation of Legal Reforms

Law is not a static body of rules but rather a living creature, continually forged and shaped to serve the needs of community that itself is constantly changing. Adaptability, therefore, is truly a condition sine-qua-non of the continued existence of a legal system. Law synthesises change and stability. The relation between law and social change is reciprocal.

As Justice Holmes had said:

The life of law has not been logic; it has been experience; the felt necessities of time...have...good deal more to do...in determining the rules by which man should be governed."

Thomas Jefferson commented that:

"Each generation has a right to determine the law under which it lives, the earth belongs to usufruct to the living."

Law must therefore a "variable constant." Law does not exist in vacuum. It must remain ahead of socio-economic and political needs. The horizons of law are expanding with the growth of modern approaches in a variety of spheres. There are many stimuli for change when the objective is the building of a welfare state. There is hence a constant requirement of the spirit of enquiry and reform, with a view to maintaining integrity between the law and real social needs.

* Judiciary can play a role in ensuring that the social economic reforms go the right way and do not in any way benefit one class of person at the expense of the other. The poor and the disadvantaged should be the prime target of social economic reforms.

* Almost 50 per cent of our population are below the poverty line and these people are without hearth and homes. So it should be the prime duty of the judiciary to ensure that justice reaches such people. Whenever a

judgement is given the Judge should have in mind the ordinary people who is always looking at them, and who expects justice from them. (* Justice P.N. Bhagwati, Supreme Court).

** We, the people of India is how the Constitution begins. That should be the focus and that too on the lowliest and lowest. They should be given be given a sense of belonging, justice and that should be the basis of the changes we should contemplate.

** However, with the new trinity of values, viz., globalization, privatisation and liberalization there has been a total reversal. There is need for legal reforms.

** We need a change in the procedural system, by this we mean we should have free legal services to the people. Without legal services, they cannot come to the court. But we have only made a mess of free legal services project by making a law which does not work. That is because they did not have any people orientation at heart.
(** Justice: V.R. Krishna Lyer, Former Judge, Supreme Court).

***Legal reforms are necessary to speed up the procedural aspects. Overall the system requires serious reforms now. Everybody talks about backlog, nobody talks about proper legal infrastructure. In the last five decades the Courts have not been included in any of our Five Year Plans.

*** We have the problem of a huge population also and as the population grows, number of cases too will increase.

*** The Govt., is one of the biggest litigants. More than 50 per cent cases concern the Govt., so it should come with plans to bring reforms to the system as a whole, providing sufficient and proper infrastructure.

*** Law commission has an important role because it acts on a reference from the Govt., It also undertakes *suo moto* references. Though the Recommendations are not binding on the Govt., it is very difficult to disagree with the Law Commission Reports.

*** The Law Commission may be requested by any Dept., of Govt., to take up a new branch of law making or reform an existing law.

*** We are in a way independent. We recommend those things which are consistent with the provisions of the Constitution, whether acceptable to the Govt., or not.

*** (Justice. M. Jagannadha Rao., Former Judge, Supreme Court: Chairman, Law Commission of India).

** To remove the bottlenecks arising out of the inherent deficiencies in law which results in the law's delays and accelerate th disposal of cases, there is a need to amend the existing statutes and augment the strength of courts to provide them full physical and functional facilities, institute alternative modes of disposal and provide modern information technology to courts.

++ The Law Commission of India made several recommendations in 1996 for speedy disposal of cases; in Jan 2001 another committee under the chairmanship of Mr. Justice V. Mallimath was constitued by the Govt. of India. The amendment of Code of Civil Procedue is also on the parliamentary anvil.

++ Our system is no doubt good on conceiving reform proposals but not on delivering them. The quality of implementation often defeats the very idea of reform.

Position of Vacancies in all the Courts as on 21st November, 2001

Judges in Position:	*Vacancies:*	*Total approved:*	*Strength:*
Supreme Court:	25	1	26
High Court:	465	170	647
Sub-ordinate Courts:	10,705	1500	12205

++ We need to address the problem of arrears in all its verification. We need to redress the disabilities and deficiency of the system.

++ The judiciary, the Legal professsion, the Legislative, the Executive, The Fourth Estate and we, the people of India have to join hands in the quest of justice in the very sanction of the justice system.

++ Reforms are quite indispensable; funds and facilities are essential; Judges and lawyers have to focus their minds on the concerns of the people so that the demon of delay may not destroy the credibility of our justice system.

(Dr. L.M. Singhvi, M.P.)

The judicial reforms will be more effective if it is supplemented by corresponding reforms in administration, development, electrol laws, and education. Of course ! But our basic problem is that we do not have a Mahatma Gandhi in our midst who will be able to give direction to this country, and be able to convince the people of the ideals we should follow.

However, there is ample scope in that we see some business leaders emerging and so too in the academic field we see Dr. Amartya Sen and others. Soon we will have such great leaders.

The level of competence has deteriorated at all levels. The competence of our system depends upon how well we are educated. But now when we talk of globalisation, it is an opportunity for us to look around the world and adopt what is good in it for our systems.

(## F.S. Nariman, M.P. Sr. Advocate, Supreme Court).

In the words of Dr. M.S. Swaminathan: "Having enacted the constitutional Amendment and having proclaimed grassroot level democracy, we have not gone to the next step, except of course the one third representation of women".

In fact, many of the State Acts have regressive laws which give powers to the collectors.

Similarly, some Laws which were framed during the British days are not relevant now. Instead of passing new Legislations we should reform the past Legislations esp., pre-1947 which are outdated, irrevalent, and have been overtaken by events.

The highest priority should be in taking the process of decentralisation.

We must have ground water regulation. A model Act was prepared as early as 1971 circulated among States, even till today there is no concrete step in that direction.

Mere Land Ceiling Act is not enough. We need some "Water Ceiling Acts" also like Israel.

We Need a Comprehensive Legislation for Water itself

These things are not being taken care of by the existing laws. We need to make Legislations to protect environment and atmospheric conditions. The Environment Protection Act and Forest Protection Act are not comprehensive. They must be not merely punitive, but also promotional and offer incentives.

A culture of Legislation which is enabling the people to participate in governance should be evolved.

How do we assess the issue of legal reforms in the light of reforms programme taken up in the financial sector, and the Agenda for the future?

Here, we may quote Mr., N.V. Deshpande, Executive Director & Principal Legal Adviser, RBI., who has opined that:

Legal reforms play a very vital role in the reforms programme taken up in a financial sector. The legal reforms provide support and infrastructure on which the financial sector reforms can stabilise. It is therefore necessary that the issue of legal reforms is not ignored or taken in the lighter vein.

The thrust areas where legal reforms can be a facilitator for functional efficiency of the financial sector, could be identified as that of a credit Information Bureau, and a new Deposit Insurance Institution in place of existing Deposit Insurance and Credit Guarantee Corpn (DICGC) etc.

For a future of banking with internet and e-banking kind of activities are different kinds of laws are needed. The electronic crimes are not regulated by any Penal Code.

The major issue in legal reforms is the tardiness with which the law is made, which results in legal reforms lagging behind the financial sector. The question arises is, therefore, should all legal reforms be carried out only by legislative enactments, or whether an alternative could be thought of which has the effect of law but without the accompanying delay. These reforms could be by way of what is known as Soft Law as against the hard law.

In a legal regime, there are three layers of systems, namely, hard law comprising of legislative designs of substantive law with delegated legislation and case law; Soft Law comprise of guidelines, directions and best practices, and Policy Statements of legal regime enunciated in the policy documents.

The Soft Law could be applied in different areas of supervision thro' the guidelines, directions and best practices Code developed over the period. Best practices may be customary, specific to an organisation, or a Code made by an organisation, to facilitate its employees to function following a due process and to make rule based decisions possible. The best practices Codes as approved by the Regulator ensures the self regulatory system in an organisation, and make a legal compliance of rule based decisions possible in order to make discretionary power of the executive officials not to fall into the trap of any arbitrariness.

Similar strategy can also be worked in the area of recovery where alternative dispute resolution mechanisms can be considered in addition to the forum like Debt Recovery Tribunal (DRT). A forum of institutionalised arbitration on the lines of Banking Ombudsman will be suitable since it will be based on the consent of both the parties and hence is not likely to be challenged by the parties themselves and the awards made in this process would have the force of a decree of law.

The present legal mechanisms for recovery of banks' dues are slow processes and take longer time eventhough the new laws like Debt Recovery Act have been passed.

We can also consider privatisation or outsourcing of certain procedures in DRT., like issue of summons or notices thro' couriers or outsourcing the recovery process to private agents to make recovery on behalf of DRT., or pretrial settlements by the lawyers etc.,

Basically, NPAs., also affects the liquidity position of an institution and for improving which it may be necessary to adopt to newer mechanisms like factoring or forfeiting securitisation and asset reconstruction. These are the methods which will improve the liquidity of an institution having large NPAs.

However, these methods require legal support for successful introduction.

Legal reforms are also needed in the areas which are unregulated today in so far as consumer issues are concerned.

The electronic crimes are not regulated by any Penal Code and the rights and duties of the consumers have not been identified and codified anywhere. As a result, the consumer issues in modern electronic governance need to be covered by legal reforms.

No doubt I.T. Act 2000 deals with some of these aspects but the main subject covered by it, is the digital signature for the purposes of electronic contracts.

Dr. G. Mohan Gopal, Director, National Law School of India University is of the opinion that the legal system cannot be understood in isolation, We must look at the legal system in the larger economic and social context.

The Indian system as we know today, had its origin in the colonial legal system and its purpose was colonial in the sense that to establish, operate and govern a colony, and a subject people whom they ruled without their consent.

Secondly, the legal system was based on conceptual, philosophical, jurisprudential ideas which are Anglo-Saxon in nature.

There is no doubt that in these fiftysix years of our independence, the system has become indegenised in many ways. It has brought in new ideas, institutions, adaptations, which reflect our own experience.

Yet at the core it still remains a very colonial and alien system for us.

We have two challenges about the future of legal education in India. One to invent and indigenous legal system which will serve the common interest of the Indian people today and tomorrow.

Second challenge is to facilitate and foster a legal reform in the country which will lead to an incentive framework and professionalism in the legal profession.

There should be Higher emphasis on merit and performance, greater link between quality, skills and knowledge and reward.

All this will lead to a better legal system which will be able to deliver justice to ordinary people and be more professional, so that demand for skills will improve and the quality of legal education will improve. We need to breed legal institutions which are outside the current limitations.

We need to have collaborations not only with foreign groups but also local groups and need a community based involvement.

In Conclusion we may ad that: Law is a thing which is perpetually moving, which should respond to the temper, to the traditional patterns as well as the modern tendencies and challenges which face us. All these things will have to be taken into account in judging disputes.

What is the kind of life which we wish to lead ? What does law say? Law has end in view, the welfare of all people.

It is not the welfare of the rich or the well-born but the welfare of every citizen of this country. That is what law aims at and tries to fulfil.

So we must make our courts and institutions proper arbitrators of the relations between man and man, between the citizen and the State. If there is to be an end, a goal for our law, that end has been beautifully described in our constitution: Justice, Liberty, Equality, Fraternity. Justice not to be purchased, not to be got by hook or by crook, but impartial justice given to us by people who are wedded to justice and who will interpret the law so that justice may be there.

Justice should not be immanent in every kind of law, otherwise it is not true justice. A kind of law which voices the will of the strong prevailed long long ago. That is not law. Justice must cater to the needs of all the individuals; of the citizens and it must be able to give proper judgement on controversies between citizens and State, the States and the Union Staff. That is the kind of justice which we have to bring about.

We must bring any kind of settlement of peace under the rule of law. All nations must be subjected to this criterion of law. What we try to bring about within our own country, we should try to bring about throughout the world. That is what we are aiming at, and should aim it while making legal reforms.

In a society like ours, law has to serve as a vehicle of social change and as a harbinger of social justice. Even though we have guaranteed freedom of life, liberty, expression and belief under our constitution, we have yet to guarantee freedom to teeming millions from want and ignorance.

It is our responsibility to ensure the basic human rights of the common people. It is in this context of bringing about a socio-economic transformation peacefully by the force of laws that the legal profession has to play an important role.

The National Forum of Forest People and Forest workers has been active for a considerable period of time in charting out the rights and responsibilities of the people towards forests as an alternative to the state ownership of forests. They advocate:

...a complete overhauling of the forest management system through establishment of "Social Ownership" of forests and other natural resources... with legal powers extending to presenting the state if need be.

It is clear that the protection of forests depends heavily as to how fast the property rights on them are shifted from the "State" to the "Society." However, efforts are to be initiated to identify the real shareholders, understand the relationships among them, evolve a platform to ensure dialogues among them in a democratic spirit and subsequently develop a conflict resolution mechanism to concretise the matrix of rights and responsibilities along the different groups of share holders.

The members of the tribal community will obviously have the first say—they being the primary users in most of the forests.

We look at all the things that are happening, the way in which for frivolous reasons, law is being violated and people expect, when there is violation of law, there should not be the assertion of the majesty of law. Anybody who violates the law must be punished. That is the meaning of Civil Disobedience which Gandhiji started. He violated laws but admitted himself to the penal ties which law imposed on him. He never tried to escape from those penalties. That is what we should do. If that happens if our people develop respect for law, and if our courts administer law without ill-will, malice, prejudice or favour, there will be growth in the tendency to respect—when we initiate legal reforms.

"The law is the true embodiment of everything that's excellent. It has no kind of fault or flaw, And I, my Lord, embody the Law."

"W.S. Gilbert

"Let justice be done, though the heavens fall.""

"Lord Mansfield"

45
Epilogue

In the short 20th century (1913 to date), as Hobsbawn describes the post- First War World, we see two rival economic systems emerge, one purporting to be socialist (but with an essentially dirigiste pattern of all decision - making) and the other, supposed to ensure individual freedom but which because of the system of production and production relations- has led, over time, to a worlwide divide between the 'haves' and the 'have-nots' . As a matter of fact, be cause of recent technological developments, as Hans Peter Martin and Harald Schumann of Der Spiegel (1997) have carefully explained, there is now going to be a 20: 80 divide throughout the world now increasingly globalised- only 20 per cent of the available work force being enough to produce all the material needs of mankind, the rest of the population being'redundant' and to be kept- quiescent with the supply of 'titty- tainment', that is, sustenance for life and 'deadly entertainment'. Obviously, the 80 per cent segment has to reject the idea; and that in turn means neither the totally dirigiste nor the totally 'free- market' is acceptable. And- though diferent thinkers have dreamed up diverse alternatives- one ex- treme being going back to Nature- no practical, workable solution, as may be in the interest of and acceptable to mankind, has yet emerged.

Perhaps the tragedy with the last decade of the short 20th century is that the most powerful nations have sought to impose a world system which can only increase inequalities, concentration and monopoly.

We must note that the financial sector reform now being passed by the IMF, the world Bank, the WTO., and the neo-liberal economic thinkers, on the developing countries of the world, is wholly inconsistent with the very ideaof capital controls.

Is there then no hope for mankind ? Perhaps we need an

understanding and apprecition among thebankers and the finance managers of the world and more importantly among the neo- liberal advocates of warped economic theory- of the essential validity of the Wicksellian/Schumpeterian theory; the 'rate of interest' simply cannot exceed the productivity gains arising from new investment; and that savings can get a return only if they are properly invested. Speculation can lead to capital gains for a few; and the capital gains of one person must be at the expense of a capital loss for another.

Just as 'unequal growth' of the world is not sustainable, so also the ongoing unequal development of only a small segment of the Indian population is not tenable. Development has to have an egalitarian basis to be sustainalbe. The present rifts in Indian society, infact the present confusion in the Indian polity arise essentially from the high degree of economic disparities in Indian society. India needs a development strategy which is broadbased, which will esp., benefit the presently deprived segments of the population.

The 'Structural adjustment' that India-indeed, all developing countries-require/s is the transformation of the production system with steadily improving productivity of all workers. That involves the entirety of development strategy; it cannot tbe achieved under a free market system. We need not eschew the market, as was done by the centrally planned economies, over 1948-90; We are back to the concepts of a 'mixed economy' and a 'socialistic pattern of society', much abused as the two concepts are. But, for that we need a fundamental redistribution of resource ownership thro' land reform, thro' the taxation system, thro' the supply of public goods. We need regulation and moderation of market activities. We also need a conscious employment policy, with the Right to Life encompassing the Right to Work.

Where does India go, to day ? If Indians stand together- nearly a billion people no power on earth can deny Indians the right to shape their own destiny. That can, today, take one of only two courses; first, egalitarian growth of all the people of India, and second, a good life for a new compardors of technologically more advanced capitalists from the developed world. The choice is obvious. While the globalisation of the world is, in part, a reality; our own efforts should be to gradually integrate with the world ina manner calculated to benefit all, rather than lead to the accentuation of exploitation of man by- man.

With nearly half the people and close to two-thirds of the women-illiterate -the transformation of the Indian econnomy is no easy task. Even anefficient utilisation of the world market requires production to specification, needs quality control, and depends on an informed consciousness of the economic tasks involved. The success of the East Asian ' tigers' and more recently of China, has been based on a much higher level of literacy and basic education than India has. The persistence of endemic illiteracy in India, even in the younger age groups, is one of the basic failures that shackle the Indian economy and society.

This diagnosis is not concerned primarily with the overall rate of growth of GNP per head, even though it is hard to assume that illiteracy and ill health are not barriers to achieving high economic performance. india has had comparatively higher rates of growth of per capita GNP in the 80s - before the reforms- and can achieve that again and much more in the future. Some sectors of the economy, esp., those that rely on high skills of the kind that India already hs plentifully such as basic computer proficiency- have already been growing fast and can expand a lot faster. But, to have an impact on India's wide-spread poverty, what is needed is an expansion on a much wider basis as has happened in, say, South Korea, China and this would be extremely difficult without a much more inclusive base of basic education.

The central issue is not just the overall growth rate, and the reasons for concern go much beyond the current 'growth frustration', which could well change in the near future. The real need is for participatory growth, which is not the same thing as high achievement in some particular sectors oriented to more specialised and more middle- class skills, nor just the same as a high rate of growth of aggregate GNP per head. For example, in the 60s and 70s, the Brazilian company grew very fast but achieved rather little reduction of poverty, esp., in terms of social backwardness and sectional deprivation. The lack of participatory nature of that growth was extremely important in that outcome. Comparing Brazil's problems of more inclusive growth processes in east Asia tends to bring out the big difference made by participatory growth, and the specific role of widespread basic education in fostering growth of this kind.

There is something quite crucial in this choice. Indeed, India stands in some danger of going Brazil's way, rather than South korea's.

The persistence of extraordinary gender inequalities in India, for instance, is a major obstacle to social progress. There has been no decisive attempt on the part of the Govt., before or after the economic reforms, to challenge these inequalities.

Recent policy developments in India, including those since the reforms have continued the tradition of neglecting the fundamental importance of basic capabilities in economic development, and of he positive role of the state in promoting these capabilities; Judged in that perspecitive, the current reorientation of economic policy is much less of radical departure from the past than it is often considered to be, and perpetuates some of the most debilitating biases of earlier regims. Correcting these biases- not just in political rhetoric but in practical action- calls for a major shift of emphasis in policy- making. There is also an acute need to pay more attention to these issues.

The phrase 'Economics as if people mattered' was first coined over 25 years ago by the British Economist E. F. Schumacher. He was among the earliest people to point out fundamental flaws in modern economics.

It is a fact that many of our ideas of development have become outdated,as even the World Bank and IMF have admitted their approach was wrong many times in the past.

Developing countries has been given loans for 'development' and, as a result find themselves caught in a debt trap—meaning they must take fresh fresh loans just to repay the interest on their old debts. The net resource flows are today from the poor to the rich, not the other way around. The levers of aid, trade and debt are largely weighted against the poor countries.

The Landless, tribal people and marginal farmers, who are losing their lands and livelihood because of various development projects, are not the only people who struggle for an alternative development strategy. In Seattle, thousands condemned the World Bank, IMF., WTO., for the justification of the notion 'Survival of the fittest'.

We need a new approach to globalisation and development. What is the use of a development that displaces people and seems to work against thepoor? What is needed is perhaps a development that keeps people firmly in the picture.

21st century economics must recognise that our common task should be to replace the laissez faire model with some kind of new economics that takes care of everybody, the poor as well as the rich. Local people have to regain control of local resources and gear local economic systems to meeting local needs rather than the needs of the international market.

Until all bariers to the moverment of people in search of work are removed and the world becomes a single market for both capital and labour, we cannot hope for the emergence of a truly global economy.

One of the revealing features of the current situation is that the decline in the economy set in about four years ago, almost the entire period of the current coalition. The GDP., growth was 4.8 per cent in 1997-98. The next year's growth of 6.6 per cent had the advantage of this lower base. In 1999-2000 the growth came down to 6.4 per cent, on the basis of credits from the public service pay increases. By 2000-2001 the growth is back to 5.2 per cent with no prospect of exceeding this level in. Has the growth increased welfare? Food intake was stagnating at a level of about 180 kg/ during 1995-97; since then it is stagnating at a level of about 168 kg/ despite the much higher foodstocks with the Govt., poverty figures are in controversy; there is no improvement if the United nations scales of per day income of $1 or 2 are taken into account.

Organised sector employment growth is now down to just 0.5 per cent per year and excluding the recent space of Volunatry Retirement Schemes (VRS). The educated unemployment rate is going up; females are finding it more dificult to find Jobs. Taking public sector rural employment programmes as the guide the mnumbers are down as the costs are up; agricultural employment would be low when gproduction is stagnating. The farmers' income is down too. While prices of agricultural products have risen by about 4 per cent over the last two three years, input costs went up by 16 per cent. This is a reversal of the trend of prices of agricultural products keeping pace with average rise in input costs between1993-98.

We fail to recognise the fundamental differences between 20th century business corporations and 21st century countries that present complex socio economic problems.

The inherent clash has its impact on the instruments of implementation. The solutions to our emerging problems involve people with diverse interest.

The road ahead is bumpy. The lessons from the slow down of growth in the last four years should guide public policy. India neesds economic expansion to get out of the development country mindset. It needs accelerated capital infusion even labour- intensive and land- intensive production. The precent rate of globalisation is not a disadvantage. the GDP growth rates only in less globalised economies such as India and China have bucked the global trend A recent World Bank research study has noted the gigantic countries like India and China would not need a high level of globalisation for growth. The reasons for the slow-down in the Indian economy are not external but internal, stated our Hon'ble Prime Minister A.B. Vajpayee some time back.

The reforms have not touched on structural change in the federal economic relations.

The government's dependence of the corporate players has not produced a consistent trend in export truth. Foreign partners are taking the first opportunity to dissolve joint ventures in favour of fully owned subsidiaries.

private players are busy in mergers and acquisitions and resorting to a waiting game to public sector assets. Creation of new assets in the economy has been pushed down the priority list in the prevailing policy regime. According to the CMIE., the so-called- "inefficient" public sector is adding more to assets than private industry. Yet a recent CMIE study of 304 projects reveals that 27 per cent found demand as a problem, and 57 per cent did not find govt. clearance as a problem; why there is so much compaint against the Govt., machinery? In such a scenario the Govt's hurry inputting all eggs in one basket has dangerous portents for the future.

A free economy is touted as an economy of choice. Why should the Govt., take a biased view in favour of one player or the other? The Govt., must play the impartial broker and facilitate expansion. This indicates multiple players in the public, private and corporate sectors.

Joint sector or convergence of sectors for economy of scale in terms of global competitiveness may be the correct path. But more than 90 per cent of the GDP is domestic centred. It is time priorities in the vision of the economy are reconsidered. The path of a unidimensional economy will be unsuited in the unfolding global scenario. Domestic saving deserves, in this context, as much incentive as foreign investment. It is a proven fact that the two are mutually supportive. The regime of public and private investment also follows the rule of mutuality. A change in the current policy regime and economic thinking is overdue.

The problem of income growth and shift in the composition of spending classes is a slow process. Corporate sector growth will not address the need. The growth-net has to be widened.

What is needed is productivity and motivating. Labour-intensive growth has to be seen in its roots in micro enterprises. Small scale enterprises are failing since the incentive package is focussed more on the large sector.

Reforms are not addressing the balance between sectors in terms of productivity from scales under Indian conditions.

A time to think "reforms" has arrived. Reforms and declining growth cannot move together. And growth will come by spreading the net wide. People must be part of it. They must have a stake in productivity.

Technology-led growth also requires motivated man-power. It is not merely a question of private, public and the co-operative sectors. Each of them has success and failure in equal measure. The economy must encash success in all of them. The narrowing vision of reforms for development and growth at present must yield place to a broader vision.

The Tenth Plan has targeted an 8 per cent GDP growth. The first year, namely, 2002-03, will deliver a maximum of 5 per cent.

The whole of the 9th Plan delivered an average growth of just 5.2 per cent whereas it was 6.2 during the 8th plan. This is a scenario/that seeks review of the reforms so far. The potential for higher growth exists provided the micro-models of growth potential are explored and the policy and incentive package designed accordingly.

Having been under the academic influence of Neoclassical, Walraisan general equilibrium tradition for long, we are now obsessed with the set of reforms towards marketisation per se. But we need to realise that a market economy relies on a wide array of non-market institutions that perform regulatory, stabilising and legitimising functions that are not inherently generated by the Market (Dani Rodrik : 1999).

These social institutions and values which condition the quality of market performance have become the crux of the—newly emerging subject matter, namely, New Institutional Economics (NIE). This lends the theoretical basis and rationale behind the so-called Second Generation Reforms. But we are yet to introduce this subject area to our students community. Of late about eight economists- Ronald Coase, Richard Posner, Gary Becker, Doughlas North,

Stiglitz, Spence and Williamson from NIE-have been awarded Nobel Prize; but our students are-not exposed to their seminal contributions, which constitute the study of institutional parameters in a non-Walrasian by real world market situation.

According to the NIE, approach, transaction costs are key to the performance of economies. Hence, the need for institutions or rules structuring human interaction in the market in order to curb opportunistic behaviour and reduce the transaction costs.

We are often used to believe in the equity-efficiency trade-off. But there are many instances wherein these two go hand-in-hand. For equity to be sustained, efficiency may be a precondition and vice versa. As one of the radical leftwing economists, Emmanual (1982) once said "If capitalism is hell, there exists a still more frightful hell; that of less developed capitalism".

According to Leon Walras, when the two parties to barter arrive at a deal after initial bargaining, three things happen. First, each party maximises his satisfaction. Second, an equilibrium is established in the quantities of goods to be exchanged. Third, that equilibrium also determines the implicit relative exchange values or prices of the two goods.

Leon Walras' argument was that a competitive market of large number of participants and goods can reach equilibrium thro' bargaining and that when equilibrium is established all participants would maximize satisfaction, and that equilibrium of goods supplied and demanded and the equilibrium relative prices of all goods are simultaneously reached.

The first of these came to be celebrated as the Principle of All Round Advantage thro' Trade (John Hicks). The simultaneous determination equilibrium quantities and prices later came to be enunciated as the duality theorem in welfare economics.

Leon Walras went to say that his attempt was to demonstrate that 'the whole world may be looked upon a vast general market made of diverse special markets'.

The Indian development experience since 1991 has, by means, provided a decisive verdict on Liberalisation and Globalization.

However, addressing the question of an appropriate model of economic growth for India, Dr. C. Rangarajan maintains that accelerated economic growth is a necessary condition for achieving the multi-dimensional socio-economic goals including the fulfilment of basic needs, generation of productive employment opportunities and the harnessing of the creative energies of the people. In the ultimate analysis, efficiency cannot be subordinated to equity nor can equity be expected to emerge out of wasteful use of resources.

As Dr. C. Rangarajan looks at it, "Our development strategy should be anchored in the two imperatives of economic development in the conventional sense of accelerating growth rate of output and social development in the sense of securing for everyone the basic needs". Steadfast pursuit of the two objectives would indeed involve continued improvement in the art of governance.

Future economic prospects are bright. But which country would forge ahead of others will depend on its success in arresting population growth, and putting in right place the right mix of economic policies.

To 'sum' up : the problems that we face today are very critical but they can be sorted out by wisdom and tact and a common understanding in national interest.

The options are limited and the time has come they should be spelt out. The history of the country is our best teacher. We must all rededicate ourselves in the national task of building this great country as per the dreams and vision of those national heroes who made supreme sacrifices so that we may live in a free and—fearless environment.

"A Developed India by 2020, or even Earlier, Is not a Dream. It indeed not even a mere vision in the minds of many Indians. It is a mission we can all take up and succeed"

Dr. A.P.J. Abdu Kalam : President of the Indian Republic.

Bibliography

1. A. Lewis: Theory of Economic Growth: Allin Unwin, London.

2. A. C. Pigou: The Economics of Welfare: 1946.

3. Amartya Sen: Development as Freedom: Oxford University Press, Oxford, 1999.

4. Asian Wall Street Journal: Oct, 21, 1992.

5. Alternative Economic Survey, Rainbow Publishers, Delhi: 1998-2000; 2000-2001 and 2001-2002.

6. Bibek Debroy: India and the GATT: Economic Growth and Social Change, 1994.

7. Beck Ulrich, 2000: What is Globalisation ? U.K. Polity Press.

8. Bongaarts J. 1994: The Impact of Population Policies Comment: Population & Development Review: Vol: 20.

9. Cyril Kanmony. J. "Conservation of Water": Kisan World: Aug., 2001.

10. Development Dialogue, 1981. No. 1.

11. Denis Goulet: The Cruel Choice: A new concept in the theory of Development: Antheneum, NY., 1971.

12. Debrey Ray: Development Economics: Oxford University Press.

13. Duggan P. and Dashner H. (ed) 1994: Introduction in women's Lives in the New Global Economy, Notebooks for study and Research: Amsterdam, No. 22.

14. Economic Review: July-Dec,. 1996.

15. Economic Survey: 1994-95 and 1996. M.O. F., New Delhi.

16. Economic Survey: 1996-97, Govt. of India.

17. Emmanuel A. 1982: Inappropriate or Underdeveloped Technology, John Wilegy, New York.

18. Financial Institutions and Markets: Ker Kohn, Tata Mc.Grand Hill Pub. Co. Ltd..

19. Foreign Trade Review: Oct. 1999.

20. Govt. of India: Ninth Five Year Plan: 1997-2002.

21. Ghosh D.N. Banking Policy of India.

22. Gunnar Myrdal, Asian Drama, Pantheon, N.Y., 1968, Appendix-4

23. H.W. Singer: Education and Economic Development: in Livingstone (ed): Economic Policy for Development, Penguin Books Ltd., Harmandsworth, Middlesex, England.

24. Hollis B. Chenery: This Structuralist Approach to Development Policy: American Economic Review: 1975.

25. In Search of India's Renaissance Vol. 2: CRRID., Chandigarh. Jan. 1992.

26. Industrial Economist: 15-29 Aug., 1997.

27. I.L.O., 1993: Employment, Poverty, and Economic Policies, Geneva.

28. Investments: William F. Sharpe, Gordon J. Alexander, and Jeffry: V. Bailly, Pentice Hall International.

29. Japan's External Trade Organisation. White Paper on International Trade, 1986.

30. Lazonick, WIlliam: Business Organisation, and the Myth of the Market Economy: Cambridge University Press: 1991.

31. Mainstream: Jan., 1992- Dec. 2002.

32. M.J. Manohar Rao: Liberalisation with Stabilisation: Mahalonis Memoral Award: Spl. Lecture: 34th Annual Conference: Indian Econometric Society, Mangalore: March, 27-30, 1998.

33. Management of Credit Risks: Journal of IBA., Jan-March, 1999: Mumbai.

34. M.I. Budy ko: Global Ecology: Progress Publishers, Moscow: 1980.

35. Mc. Kinnon R.I. 1991: The Order of Economic Liberalisation: John Hopkins, University Press, N.Y.,

36. Martin W.F. and Lodge G.C. 1975: Our Society in 1985: Business may not like it: Harvard Business Review.

37. New Delhi: Delhi Science Forum: Alternative Economic Survey: 1996-97.

38. Paul Steeran: Hunger: What can Govts do ? Political Economy Journal of India, Chandigarh Vol. 6, Jan-June, 1997.

39. Paul A. Samuelson and William. D. Nordhaus: 1997: Economics: Mc. Graw Hill Inc. Pub.,

40. Redclift, Michael: Sustainable Development: Exploring Contradictions: Routledge, London, 1987.

41. R.B.I., Report on the Committee on Capital Account Convertibility: Mumbai.

42. Report on Currency and Finance: 1993-94: 1994-95: 1995-96: 1996-97; 1997-98; 1998-99 and 1999-2000. RBI., Mumbai.

43. Rodrick Dani. D: Do Institutions matter ? Quoted in Sarakane and John Starrels, 1999; Second Generation Reforms call for varied approaches to institution building and growth: IMF., Survey, Nov. 22.

44. Sex Education in Schools: The Realities and our Demands: European Network of Women's Rights for Abortion and Contraception (ENWRAC), London, 1992.

45. Third Concept: Jan., 1993-Dec. 2002.

46. The Concept of Poverty. Townsend P. (ed) London, Heinemann, 1970.

47. The State of India's Economy: 1994-95: PIRG., Delhi.

48. Todaro, Michael, P. : Economic Development in the Third World, Longman, 1981.

49. The New Indian Express: Dec., 16, 23, 2002.

50. The New Indian Express: Jan 9, 2003.

51. The Hindu: Aug., Dec., 2002.

52. The Hindu: April 6, 2000.

53.The Times of India: Jan., 16; July 16, 2001.

54.The Hindu Survey of Environment: 2002.

55. The Hindu Survey of Indian Industry: 2003.

56. The Hindu Survey on Indian Agriculture 1997.

57. Theorbecke E. The Role of Agriculture in Economic Development, Ny. 1969.

58. The India's External Debt: A Status Report, June, 1999.

59. U.S. Centre on Transational Corporations: World Investment Report: 1991.

60. Villanueva D. and Mirakher, 1990: Strategies for Financial Reforms: IMF. Staff Papers.

61. Economic and Business: Focus: Vol. 8, 2002.

62. World Development Report: World Bank: 1993.

63. World Bank (1995) World Development Report, 1995. Oxford Unversity. Press. NY.

64. World Development, Vol. 17. No. 5. May, 1998, Spl. Issue on Privatisation.

65. W.A. Lewis: Economic Development with Unlimited supplies of Labour Manchester Schools, May 22, 1954.

66. World Bank: Entering the 21st Century World: Development Report 1999-2000: Washington D.C. 2000.

67. Williamson, J.G. 'Income Growth and Savings' The Philippine Economic Journal, Sept., 1969.

Index

J

K

O

P